A GUIDE TO ST MARK'S GOSPEL

D1461601

TEF Study Guides

This series is sponsored and subsidized by the Theological Education Fund in response to requests from Africa, Asia, the Caribbean, and the Pacific. The books are prepared by and in consultation with theological teachers in those areas. Special attention is given to problems of interpretation and application arising there as well as in the west, and to the particular needs of students using English as a second language.

TEF Study Guide 2

A GUIDE TO ST MARK'S GOSPEL

John Hargreaves

(Formerly Warden, Buwalasi College, Uganda)

WITH A FOREWORD BY

DONALD COGGAN

Archbishop of York

LONDON

S·P·C·K

First published in 1965
by the S.P.C.K.
Holy Trinity Church
Marylebone Road
*London, N.W.*1
Printed by offset in Great Britain by
Hollen Street Press Ltd., Slough
© *John Hargreaves,* 1965

Enlarged and illustrated edition, 1969
published with the help of a subsidy
from the Theological Education Fund
of the World Council of Churches

Reprinted 1972

SBN 281 01866 9

Contents

v

Part Ib. Chapter 6. 1 to Chapter 8. 26
The Ministry outside Galilee

Part II. Chapter 8. 27 to Chapter 10. 52
The Training of the Disciples

Part III. Chapter 11. 1 to Chapter 12. 44
The Events in Jerusalem

Part IV. Chapter 13
Special Teaching

Part V. Chapter 14. 1 to Chapter 16. 8
The Suffering, Death, and Rising of Jesus

CONTENTS

The photographs in this book are repro-
duced by courtesy of the Associated Press
(facing p. 243) and Camera Press Ltd.

Foreword

I warmly welcome this book. Here is methodical, straightforward exposition well set out, its scholarship never obtruded but clearly there in the background.

I see this book as being useful not only for students in Asia and Africa, but also in England and elsewhere, in places where help is needed in understanding the Gospel and relating it to contemporary life and problems of discipleship.

I hope that this is not the last book of this nature to come from Mr Hargreaves' pen. I would like to see the other Gospels similarly treated, and I believe that St Paul's Epistles would come alive to many if they could read and study them under similar guidance.

I hope that clergy and college staffs will widely recommend the use of this book.

Bishopthorpe, York.   DONALD EBOR:

Preface to the First Edition

This book was written with two aims in mind: first, to be a kind of reference book for anyone who is working as student or teacher or preacher, and wants to study both the background to the Gospel and its message for to-day; secondly, to provide notes for all those Christians who find a value in studying a Gospel, verse by verse, as part of their daily prayers.

As regards the first aim, a further word may be useful. The book grew up amongst students and amongst old students on refresher courses while I was engaged in training teachers and ordination candidates. It seemed to me then, as it still seems, that there is apt to be a gap between the Bible as it is studied in college and the Bible as it is used in the pulpit or in the classroom. This gap is partly, but not altogether, a gap between the study of its background and the study of its message. In order to try to bridge this kind of gap, notes used to be produced after each session, on both background and interpretation, out of which this book has grown up. It is hoped that it may in practice be a book which does bridge a gap, and be found of use both in college and after it.

An index has been provided, which contains references both to the background (e.g., through proper names) and to interpretation (through the chief subjects dealt with in these notes).

The reader will notice that there are problems with which this book does not attempt to deal, namely some of the "critical" problems raised by a study of St Mark. On such problems Dr William Neil asks an important question in the introduction to his *One volume Bible commentary* (Hodder & Stoughton). He asks, "Is it not possible . . . to take for granted the general conclusions of Biblical scholars over the past century and to concentrate on the theological teaching of the Bible, what it has to say about the meaning and purpose of life, about God, ourselves, and the world we live in?" I believe that there are very many for whom it is indeed possible, and that this is an approach which has become of special importance.

This does not mean, of course, that these "general conclusions of Biblical scholars" are regarded as unimportant. Indeed this book takes them for granted. But it does mean that critical problems such as the relative reliability of the different manuscripts of this Gospel, and the theory that St Mark was written before the other Gospels, are not dealt with here. Other books have dealt admirably with such matters, for example, Professor A. M. Hunter's *Introducing the New Testament* (S.C.M. Press, 1957). In the college where most of these notes were prepared these questions were dealt with in a special course, separately from the study of the words of the Gospel.

The three books which were found especially helpful when this was being written were: Vincent Taylor, *The Gospel according to St Mark* (Macmillan, 1952); *The Interpreters Bible*, Vol. VII (Abingdon-Cokesbury Press, 1951); Walter Lowrie, *Jesus according to St Mark* (Longmans, 1929). But there have been many other and more recent books to which also I owe a great deal.

Alongside the books referred to, I owe my thanks to friends who have personally helped in the preparation of this book. I owe a special debt of thanks to a group of senior students at Trinity College, Umuahia, Nigeria, who for three hours a week for two years met to study this Gospel. They asked most of the questions which are raised in this book, and contributed fully, out of their experience as Christians, in the search for answers. (The composition of this group was Anglican, Methodist, and Presbyterian, and this led, among other things, to our using the word "minister" to describe an ordained Church leader, a usage which is carried forward into these pages.)

Of the many others whom I would like to thank for advice and encouragement, I must mention the following for their special help: His Grace the Archbishop of York, Dr Coggan, who was one of the first to encourage this project; the Reverend Eric Bishop, formerly Principal, Newman School of Missions, Jerusalem; the Reverend Fred Crabb, Principal of Emmanuel College, Saskatoon, Canada; the Reverend Noel Davey, Director of the S.P.C.K.; Miss Daphne Terry and Miss Joan Petersen, also of the S.P.C.K.; the Community of St Julians, Coolham, England; the Reverend Geoffrey Paul, Principal of Kerala United Theological College, S. India; Miss Vivian Palmer of Co. Kildare, Eire, who typed the whole manuscript;

Miss Clarke Williams, who generously read the proofs; the Reverend Rees Phillips, formerly Warden of St John's Seminary, Lusaka, Zambia; the Reverend Christopher Ssenyonjo and the Reverend Enos Bagona, formerly of Buwalasi College, Uganda; and Miss Marjorie Stewart, of the Community Education Centre, Fiji, South Pacific.

Storrington, 1964.   JOHN HARGREAVES

Suggestions for using this book

In this Guide St Mark's Gospel is studied in sections, a few verses at a time. For each section there is (a) a short *Introduction*, in which the passage and its chief message are summarized and explained, and (b) commentary *Notes* on words and phrases which need more detailed interpretation. The Bible verses themselves are not given in full. It is, therefore, necessary to *read the words of the Gospel passage itself before starting to study each section*. The Guide will serve little purpose unless this is done.

Additional Notes provide a fuller explanation of important themes and subjects, especially those which concern more than one section.

Study Suggestions, as well as illustrations, have been added to this second edition of the Guide in order to help readers who are working alone to study more thoroughly and understand Mark's Gospel more clearly, and also to provide topics for group discussion. They are intended especially:

a. To help students check their knowledge of certain key words;
b. To help them check their grasp of the ideas and points of teaching given;
c. To help them compare such teaching with teaching found in other parts of the Bible; and
d. To help them think out the practical application of the Gospel to everyday life.

These study questions appear all together at the end of the book (pp. 283-314); the chapter and verse references at the beginning of each question show which section of the Guide it refers to.

Three points should be noticed:

1. These Study Suggestions are only *suggestions*. Some readers will not want to use them. Other students or a group of students may want to select and use some of them. Others may want to use them all.

2. The best way to use the questions is: *first* to read the Gospel passage itself, *secondly* to read carefully once or twice the section of this Guide which explains it, and *lastly* to do the work suggested, in writing or group discussion, without looking at the Guide again except when there is an instruction to do so.

3. A *Key* is provided so that readers may check their own work on those questions which can be checked in this way. In most cases the Key does not give the answer to a question; it shows where an answer is to be found, either in the Guide or in the Bible.

Bible Version: The English translation which has been used is C. Kingsley Williams' *New Testament in Plain English* (S.P.C.K. and Longmans). This translation was chosen because it continues to receive high praise from scholars and to be widely acceptable. It is particularly suitable for a study of Mark's Gospel.

It would be an advantage if the reader were to use a copy of Kingsley Williams' translation along with this Guide, but this is not necessary. The most suitable alternative would be the *Revised Standard Version*.

Bibliography: Besides the books mentioned in the Preface to the first edition, students may find the following useful for further reading:

Saint Mark, P. S. Minear (Layman's Bible commentary, SCM Press, London)

The Gospel according to Mark, C. F. D. Moule (Cambridge Bible Commentary on the NEB, CUP, London)

A Note to the Reader
about St Mark and his Gospel

Before we study this Gospel, it will be helpful to consider some questions which people ask about Mark himself; and about the way in which he wrote his Gospel.

1. *Who was Mark?*

Probably he was the same as John Mark, the young Christian worker about whom we read in Acts 12. 25 and 15. 39. He may have been the boy who saw Jesus in the garden of Gethsemane (14. 51); but he had not often been with Jesus. He had, therefore, to obtain most of his information about Jesus from others. A writer called Papias, who lived about a hundred years after Mark was writing, said that Mark received especial information from St Peter, and it is probable that he did.

2. *Why did he write his Gospel?*

There were two main reasons:

1. He himself had believed in Jesus as a result of hearing about Him and by enjoying the fellowship of the Church. He therefore wanted other people to know about Jesus and to believe in Him.

2. He wanted to provide a sort of "handbook of teaching" for evangelists. He wrote for all those preaching about Jesus or who wanted to read a passage aloud during a service of worship. Christians at that time did not worship in special buildings called churches; they often met in each other's houses. So it was for small groups like this that Mark wrote his Gospel. (Writers to-day write "Lives" of great people, e.g., "The Life of Bishop Crowther", but Mark's Gospel was not that kind of book.)

3. *When did he write?*

He wrote about thirty-five years after the resurrection of Jesus, i.e., about A.D. 65.

1

Before he wrote, people had been telling stories about Jesus, about His work, teaching, death, and resurrection. Often they told these stories as part of the regular worship of the Church. Some of the stories and sayings were probably written down, but Mark seems to have been the first person to make a Gospel. He did this not by writing down everything that he heard, but by choosing stories and sayings from the large number that were being told. Then he arranged them in a certain order. This was the first Gospel, and Matthew and Luke used it when they were writing theirs.

In those days a book was not printed on paper, but was written by hand on a rough material called "papyrus". So if more than one person wanted to read the book, the author (or someone else) had to make a copy of it by hand. This is what happened to Mark's Gospel (and to the other Gospels). Some copies were probably made during Mark's life, and it is known that very many were made after his death. These copies are called manuscripts. But because so many different people did this work, the manuscripts were not all the same. We see an example of this in Mark 1. 41: some manuscripts have "He was sorry for him", others have "He was angry". In the case of most of his Gospel we know what he wrote, but there are some verses where we cannot be quite certain.

4. *Who were his first readers?*

1. They were Gentiles in Rome, i.e., people who were not Jews. They did not know Jewish customs or the language in which Jesus spoke (Aramaic). Mark sometimes explained these things to them in his Gospel. (See 5. 41; 7. 3; 12. 42.)

2. Those of them who were Christians were being persecuted when he wrote. In A.D. 64 the Roman Emperor, Nero, had begun a terrible persecution of Christians. This took place partly because the Roman authorities were ignorant about the activities and beliefs of the Christians, partly because they could see that the Christians were serving a king who was above even the Roman Emperor himself. Both St Peter and St Paul were probably killed at this time.

In these two ways, most of us who read his Gospel to-day are like the first readers: we are "Gentiles", and we are likely to be "persecuted" if we follow Jesus closely.

2

5. *What did Mark want to teach?*

Of course, he wanted to teach what Jesus had taught, but from among all the truths that Jesus had taught there were certain ones which Mark believed to be of especial importance for his readers. He draws attention to these in his Gospel. Here are some of them:

1. Jesus was not only the great leader or "Messiah", for whom the Jews had been waiting for so long: He was God's own and only Son. (1. 1, 11; 9. 7.)

2. Jesus was a real human being; He was not God pretending to be man. See notes on 1. 9; 13. 32.

3. The work of Jesus was a fight; He fought on the side of the forces of good against the forces of Satan or evil, and was victorious. Mark chose stories like these to show the victorious fight: the resisting of temptation in the wilderness (1. 12, 13); the overcoming of madness or sickness in a man, and curing him (1. 21–28); the meeting with His enemies and defeating them in discussion (12. 13–17); His being killed and yet rising again.

4. It was by His sufferings that Jesus won His victory, rather than by His teaching. Nearly half Mark's Gospel is the story of Jesus' suffering and death. See 8. 31.

5. The life of Jesus' Church will be like the life of Jesus Himself. So Christians must not be surprised when they suffer, because that is what He did; and just as He rose again, so in the end they will be taken into God's own presence. See Introduction to Chap. 13.

6. It is hard to receive these truths: even the disciples often failed to do so (e.g., 8. 33; 9. 34). A man needs faith in order to see and receive them. Faith is willingness to trust Jesus completely and to be led by Him into deeper understanding. (See Additional Note, p. 91.)

6. *How ought we to read Mark's Gospel to-day?*

As we read, there are certain questions which we should try to answer and this book tries to answer them:

1. "What really took place?"

As we read certain of the events in the life of Jesus, we find that we cannot fully answer this question; but it is always a necessary question to try to answer, because the story about Jesus is about events that actually happened. God really did become man (the man called Jesus), and there really was (and still is) a city called Jerusalem.

2. "What did the words of Jesus mean to those who first heard them?"

When we read a parable which Jesus told, we must do our best to find out what it meant to the Jews who were listening to it. By doing this we shall take the first step in finding out its real meaning.

3. "Why did Mark choose this story and report it?" i.e., What special teaching did he want his readers to learn from it?

If we ask this question, we shall be encouraged to look below the surface of the story and seek for its deeper meaning. See para. 5 above.

4. "What do these words mean for us to-day? i.e., What difference can these words make to our lives?

This may not seem to be an important question if we are reading Mark only in order to pass an examination, but Mark did not write his Gospel for that purpose. He wrote it so that his readers might share the joy which he himself had found when he entrusted himself to Jesus.

We ourselves shall not understand the meaning of the words which Mark wrote, unless we expect it to make a difference to our own lives.

Mark 1. 1–8 : John the Baptizer

See also Matt. 3. 1–12; Luke 3. 1–18; John 1. 6–8, 19–28

INTRODUCTION

Mark's Gospel

Mark was not writing the Life of Jesus, and so he does not begin his story by telling how Jesus was born or how He lived as a young man. His purpose was only to tell his readers: a. about that work of Jesus which resulted in His being killed; b. how He died for all mankind, and was wonderfully raised again.

So he begins his story by describing the person who was preaching about Jesus just before Jesus began His work, John the Baptizer. Chap. 1, vv. 1–13 is about John. The chief part of the Gospel begins at v. 14.

The need for faith and repentance

Two important truths that Mark surely wants us to notice in vv. 1–8 are that: a. Jesus is God; b. men must repent.

John the Preparer

When John began his work, the country of Palestine was in great trouble. The people (the Jews) were forced to pay excessively high taxes by the Romans who ruled over them. Many had already tried to begin a revolution. Everyone was looking for a great national leader. Their Scriptures (the Old Testament) taught them that God would one day send a Messiah, and they hoped that he would come soon and set them free. (See Additional Note, p. 133.) Then John appeared. Some thought that he was the Messiah, but he said, "No, I am not. I am here to prepare the way for the Messiah."

John the Baptizer

He prepared for the Messiah by baptizing (see note on v. 4). This took place in the river Jordan, in the wild desert country in the south

5

of Palestine. He wore the same rough clothes that Elijah had worn, and in many ways spoke and acted like the Old Testament prophets.

NOTES

v. 1.   The good news of Jesus Christ, the Son of God.

1. **Good news:** These words are translated "Gospel" in the A.V. and this word "Gospel" is not always easy to understand, because it is used in different ways: a. a book which we read, e.g., Mark's "Gospel"; b. the message preached *by* Jesus; c. the joyful news which Christians preach *about* Jesus. It is this third meaning which "Gospel" has in this verse.

Our message is joyful because: a. it tells of things that God has done, and especially what Jesus did by living and dying and rising again; b. it tells us how to become free from the power of sin as a result of what He did. If we can tell people how to overcome sin, we have very good good news indeed. It is true that in preaching it is sometimes necessary to give advice and to remind people of rules to keep, but the most important thing is to pass on to them good news like this.

2. **Jesus Christ:** We must note that: a. Jesus was a name often used among Jews; b. "Christ" means the same as "Messiah", i.e., God's Anointed One. (See Additional Note, p. 133.)

By putting the two names together Mark is saying this: The person Jesus was also the Messiah who had been expected so long by the Jews. Most Jews had expected God to send a Messiah to free them from their enemies by force. We now know that Jesus has: a. freed us all, and not Jews only; b. done so by dying, not by fighting; c. Given us something more precious than freedom from foreign government, namely freedom from the power of sin. (See note on 8. 29.)

3. **Son of God:** Mark (writing after Jesus had died and risen again) knew that He was God's own Son, but did those who met him know this? Probably none of them did. a. Most of His friends thought that He was a very good man sent by God; b. Then Peter went a stage further and saw that He was the Messiah (8. 27); c. Then after Pentecost, Christians realized that He was more than the Messiah. they saw that He was God's own and only Son, and Mark wrote his Gospel to say so.

v. 2. It is written in the prophet Isaiah . . .

The words in v. 3 are from Isaiah, but those in v. 2 are in fact from
Malachi 3. 1.

1. Has Mark made a mistake? Some, who attack the religion of
Jesus, say, "The Gospels contain mistakes. Here is one. We cannot
believe or obey what they say." Let us first admit that Mark omits
to say that some of these words came from Malachi. But the important thing to understand is that Christians follow Christ because He
came into our world and died for us and rose again. All the New
Testament says this clearly. So it does not trouble us that Mark
says that both verses come from Isaiah. Mark was indeed led by the
Spirit in his writing, but he was still a man and not divine. But we
do not throw his Gospel away for that reason. What would be said
of us if we·were going a long journey and someone said, "I will
take you in my car", and we said, "No, we cannot trust your car,
because there is some dust on the side of the wheel?"

2. These words teach that the events described had not taken
place by chance. God had made His plans long ago (and Isaiah
and Malachi had understood part of these plans), and then He sent
John at the right time. It is an encouragement to us to know that
God has made plans for us too, and that things that are happening
to us are not happening by chance.

v. 3. A man crying aloud in the wilds, Make ready the way . . .

1. Isaiah said that "one" would come to prepare the way for
"the Lord". Mark said that the "one" was John, and the "Lord"
was Jesus, so that the words of Isaiah had come true.

Did Isaiah know that it would be John the Baptizer who would
come and that it would be Jesus who would be "the Lord"? Probably he did not know *who* would come: he knew that God would
send someone, because he knew that God cares for us.

2. **Make ready . . .** Preparation for God's coming was needed.

a. John was a preparer; his message made some people ready to
receive Jesus' teaching. He was like a labourer who pulls up the
weeds, and then the farmer himself comes and sows the seeds.
There are still people like John to-day. There was an African, "the
Prophet Harris", who prepared many people in the Ivory Coast,
although he himself knew very little about Jesus, and was with them

only a short time. But after ten years' interval, when a minister came, he found the people ready to receive his message.

b. There are many times in our own lives when we can be pre-parers, e.g., we shall receive Jesus into our hearts at Holy Com-munion if we have first examined ourselves and "pulled up the weeds".

c. One day God will come to us as King, at the end of the world: all our work is a preparation for this.

v. 4. Repentance and Baptism . . .

This means, "A Baptism for those who have already repented."

1. **Repentance:** Unless the people repented they would not be ready to receive the teaching of Jesus or to live in the new way that He taught. Many people to-day know that their lives are not what they ought to be: this verse teaches that everyone can have a new kind of life, but that the way to reach it is by repentance.

Repentance is: a. *knowing* that sin is spoiling our life (sometimes we blame other things or other people instead of seeing that we ourselves are the guilty ones); b. *confessing* the sin (see note on v. 5); c. *turning* right round, away from the old ways, and wanting to live in the new way.

2. **Baptism:** This was used by the Jews before John came, in order to admit those who were not Jews into their religion. The new thing that John did was to use it for the Jews themselves. The candidate went into the river and dipped his whole body under the water in the presence of John. It was a sign of being cleaned from old sins, and so being ready for God.

v. 5. Confessing their sins.

Those who were really sorry for their sins confessed them aloud. This is important because: a. it forces us to examine ourselves first to see what is wrong in us; b. if we confess in the presence of others, they can give us help in overcoming our special sins.

They confessed publicly in the presence of John, just as, when John Wesley started his Class Meetings, the members confessed in one another's presence. (See Jas. 5. 16.) This can be a very good plan, but it is not always wise to do it if some of those present do not know how to be silent about the things they have heard. This is one reason why members of some Anglican churches confess their sins aloud to God in the presence of a clergyman who is trained for this work. Confession in the presence of a priest is the rule for all members of the Roman Catholic Church.

In these days some Christians never confess their sins in either of these ways. Is this one reason why the Church is weak?

v. 7. A stronger ... than I ...

John was a humble man: he said he was not good enough to be Jesus' slave (that is what v. 7b means). He was humble, because he compared himself with Jesus. (See John 3. 30.) This is the way in which we become humble. Too often we compare ourselves with other people and find some way in which we are superior (see Luke 18. 11). Even a one-eyed man can become king if he chooses to live in the country of the blind!

v. 8. I have baptized you with water, But he shall baptize you with the Holy Spirit.

1. The difference between Jesus and John was this: John, like the Old Testament prophets, reminded people of God's laws which they were breaking, and sternly warned them of His Judgement which was coming. Jesus, although He also taught people sternly to be ready for the Judgement, spoke much more about the generosity of God. He said that God would always give His Holy Spirit to help us live a new kind of life.

Note: Jesus not only came with a message about the Spirit; but also Himself offered the gift of the Spirit to strengthen us. So we can say that John came with a warning, and Jesus came with a gift. (See also Matt. 11. 11.)

2. We follow Jesus rather than John. Therefore:

a. Christian preachers first of all speak about God's great generosity, i.e., His "grace" and the Gift of the Holy Spirit He is offering us. It is only in the second place that they need to remind people of John's message (the evil results of breaking God's Laws).

b. The most important lesson for all Christians to learn is not how to obey God, but how to receive His gifts humbly and like children (Matt. 5. 6). Many of us are so busy working for God that we forget to accept (e.g., through prayer and the reading of the Bible and Holy Communion) the gifts He offers us. (See Ps. 34. 8.)

3. **He will baptize you:** It is not certain if Jesus Himself did

baptize. Perhaps His disciples did (see John 3. 22; 4. 2), but He certainly told them to use this sign. Afterwards the Church continued the practice in obedience to Him.

Mark 1. 9–11 : The Baptism of Jesus by John

See also Matt. 3. 3–7; Luke 3. 21, 22; John 1. 29–34

INTRODUCTION

Mark's purpose in writing these verses

So far Mark has: a. told us who came before Jesus to make preparations (v. 2); b. reminded us of the reason why Jesus came, i.e., because of the evil in the world (v. 4). Now in v. 9 he says, "At last I tell you of the coming of Jesus Himself, and I shall show you that He was both God and man".

The story

Until He was thirty years old (Luke 3. 23) Jesus lived in Nazareth. It was not a big town, but it was near the main road from the north to Jerusalem. Anyone living there would meet Roman soldiers and Jewish politicians and strangers from other countries, and would hear of important things happening elsewhere. In about the year A.D. 27 (by our reckoning) the news came that John was collecting a group of people who were preparing for the "Coming of God as King". We do not know what was in Jesus' mind, but He certainly felt it right to go and join this group. So He made the eighty-mile journey to find John; it must have taken five or six days.

A Question

Some readers may want to ask, what did our Lord learn at this Baptism? It is, of course, impossible to answer this with certainty, but perhaps He learnt that: a. He was the Messiah; b. He was God's own and only Son; c. He would have to suffer.

In addition He also knew during the Baptism that God was giving

10

Him new power for His work. (The notes on vv. 10, 11 explain these points further.)

But no one can tell us what Jesus knew about Himself before Baptism. (Luke 2. 49 is almost the only information.) So we must say that Jesus either learnt this knowledge for the first time at Baptism, or discovered it at Baptism in a deeper way than before.

NOTES

v. 9. Jesus . . . was baptized by John . . .

1. Why did He ask to be baptized? It was not because He was Himself sinful. He was the only man who ever lived who could say to His enemies, "Which of you can prove me guilty of sin?" (John 8. 46), knowing that He was guiltless. He did ask for Baptism because there was sin in mankind, and He Himself was a man. It was as if He were saying, "I am one of these people. Their troubles are my troubles, and their shame my shame" (2 Cor. 5. 21).

2. He could make Himself one with mankind only because He really was man. He was not pretending to be man. Once the rich Dr Barnardo put on some old clothes and sat like a beggar in the part of London where very poor people lived. He wanted to watch them and find out ways of helping them. But this is exactly what Jesus did not do! He did not "put on the clothes" of a man; He really was man. Dr Barnardo loved those poor people enough to put on those old clothes; how much greater is the love of Jesus who actually became one of the people He wanted to save (Isa. 53. 12).

3. In addition to this Jesus regarded John's baptizing as an opportunity to dedicate Himself to His Father's work on earth.

4. **By John:** Jesus knew that John's message was not perfect (see note on v. 8), but He did not set up a new religion: He used what He found. God does that now. He uses His Church, although it is full of faults. We too shall do God's work well, not by starting a new religion when we see something that is wrong with our congregation, but by joining the body of believers as it is and helping to make it what it should be.

v. 10. Coming up out of the water, he saw the heavens torn open, and the Spirit like a dove coming down . . .

1. **The water:** It is sometimes asked, "Is it necessary to use things

11

which we can see and touch when we are worshipping God?" Jesus very often did. In this case He used water. Ought we not to regard this way of worshipping as a natural and usual way? God has given us, as well as the water of Baptism, the bread and wine of Holy Communion. There are of course times when we shall worship without such things, e.g., in simple prayer meetings. But it seems that God expects us to worship Him with the use of what we can see and can touch.

2. **He saw . . .** We may ask, "Did the sky really open? Did a voice really speak? Did a real dove come down?" (See Introduction 9. 2–8.)

Mark does not say that the heavens opened, but "He saw. . . .". Nor does he say "a dove came down", but "the Spirit like a dove". God could have made a dove come down, but did not do so. Mark is describing what Jesus knew in His heart at this time, i.e., a vision which He had. (Afterwards He must have told Peter and the other disciples about it, and Peter probably told Mark.)

This was not the only vision Jesus had (Luke 10. 18).

3. **He saw the heavens torn open . . .** Perhaps this showed Jesus that God was ready to come at some future time from heaven to earth to rule as King. (He knew that He Himself was to prepare people for that Coming.)

These words teach us that God is not enclosed in a far-off heaven, but is one who has dealings with us men and women. There is no barrier between heaven and earth (Gen. 28. 12).

4. **The Spirit like a dove coming down . . .**

a. Jesus knew by this that God was sending down on Him the strength to do His life's work. Secondly, He knew that He Himself was the Messiah. The Jews taught that the pouring out of God's spirit was a sign that the Messiah had come (Isa. 61. 1).

b. As Jesus received power at this time, so can we also. We look back to the day of our Baptism and say, "God gave me His Spirit then. Am I making use of His gift now?"

v. 11.   Thou art my Son, my beloved, With thee I am well pleased.

1. When He heard these words, Jesus was made certain that: a. He was God's "own and only Son" (that is the meaning of the Greek work translated "beloved"); b. He was the Messiah. (The words,

12

"Thou art my beloved Son", come from Ps. 2. 7, and when the Jews sang this psalm, they thought of the Messiah who would come.)

2. He also learnt from the words, "With thee I am well pleased", that He would have to suffer and die. They come from a part of Isaiah which describes the "Servant" who would save the people by His sufferings (Isa. 42. 1). Now He knew that the Messiah would also be a suffering servant, and that He could not save them except by suffering for them.

3. It has been thought by some people that Jesus was an ordinary man until these words were spoken, and that at this moment He was adopted by God as His Son. The New Testament does not teach this. John 1. 2 says, "He was in the beginning with God", that is, He was always God's own and only Son. He was not adopted at His Baptism.

Mark 1. 12, 13 : The Temptations of Jesus

See also Matt. 4. 1–11; Luke 4. 1–13

INTRODUCTION

The story

After the Baptism Jesus went to a lonely place in order to pray. While He was there, He was attacked by the forces of evil and tempted to do God's work in wrong ways.

This story must have been told by Jesus Himself to His disciples, like the story of what He heard and saw at His Baptism. He knew that it would help them when temptations came to them afterwards.

Mark gives us this story to show that: a. Jesus was really man as well as being God; b. the evil which is at work in the world must be fought.

What we learn from it

We can learn from it three important lessons:

1. It is not wrong to be tempted: indeed the better a man is, the greater his temptations. Temptation is like someone knocking at the

13

door: we commit sin only when we invite it to come in (Heb. 4. 15b).

2. When we are tempted and are not overcome, we become stronger Christians than before, and are more able to resist the next temptation (Jas. 1. 2).

3. Christ can help us to overcome our temptations, because He Himself was tempted and was not defeated. (See notes on 14. 32-42.)

NOTES

v. 12. The Spirit drove him . . . into the wilds.

1. **Drove:** Jesus went into a lonely place, because He knew that God was strongly urging Him to do so. The Greek word for "drove" really means "threw Him out". St Paul had the same feeling when he said, "Necessity is laid upon me" (1 Cor. 9. 16). We too are sometimes driven out by God to do something for Him: let us obey and go!

2. **The wilds:** i.e., the rocky hill-country between Jericho and Jerusalem, where no plants grew, except little thorn-bushes. A man can still walk there for days without meeting another person. Jesus went there in order to escape from other people and to be alone with God. He never ran away from His enemies, but often from His friends. He enjoyed their company, but often gave it up (7. 24; John 10. 40).

v. 13. He was . . . tempted by Satan . . . and the angels waited on him.

1. **He was tempted:** In what way? Mark does not say, but Matthew and Luke do. Jesus had learnt at His Baptism what work God wanted Him to do, and He had dedicated Himself to be the leader of those who would make God their King. But when He considered the way in which He would do this work He had thoughts which troubled Him. Luke says there were three special temptations, because of the power Jesus had: a. to satisfy the needs of people's bodies, e.g., with gifts of food: if He used that power they would follow Him (Luke 4. 3); b. to make them into an army and to lead them to overthrow the Roman rulers: this is what the Jews expected the Messiah to do, and it would be popular (Luke 4. 5–8); c. to do extraordinary miracles; the people would be so astonished that they would follow Him in order to see more (Luke 4. 9–12).

14

In these ways He could soon get a large body of followers. But then He knew that no one can do God's work except in God's ways. He knew that there was no other way of bringing men to love and obey God except by loving them. He must not bribe them with food or political independence or magic; and He knew that if He loved men He would also have to suffer for them. Thus He rejected the easy ways of doing His work and chose the hard way.

Was He really tempted? Some say, "Perhaps He knew in advance that He would be able to overcome the temptations in the end; if so, He was not tempted in the same way as we are." But this is not so. He really was tempted, because He really was man, and not pretending to be a man. He was, like us, free to choose right or wrong. He could have chosen wrong (see Heb. 4. 15).

2. **"Satan"**: Who is Satan? Is he a person? Certainly the Jews regarded Satan as a person and had other names for him: "Devil", "Evil One", "the Adversary". "Demon" means something different. (See note on 1. 23.)

Christians do not all answer this question in the same way. Some, like the Jews, speak of the devil as a person; others speak of the devil rather as a evil force at work in the world. But the important truths on which all agree are: a. There is certainly an evil power which is working in the world. Evil is not simply absence of goodness! We know it is working in our own hearts; it is as active among us as an infectious disease. b. God has given us the power to overcome it.

When we read the word "Satan", these are the truths which we think of first of all.

3. **Angels:** Just as the Jews regarded Satan as a person, they regarded angels as persons. According to the Bible, they are God's messengers sent to human beings to guide them. They also worship God continually (Rev. 7. 11). The important fact in this passage in Mark is that God did send His power to strengthen Jesus in the wilderness; it is also a fact that we to-day can receive that power in our temptations. Whether Jesus saw persons called angels or not could be a subject for debate, but it is less important than these facts.

Mark 1. 14, 15 : The First Preaching in Galilee

See also Matt. 4. 12–17; Luke 4. 14; 15; John 4. 1–3

INTRODUCTION

The Events of Chapter 1. 14–5. 43

1. After the time in the wilderness, Jesus probably began teaching in Judea, which is the country round Jerusalem. (It is John 1. 15–5. 16 which tells us this, not Mark.) It was after this work in Judea that He started on His ministry in Galilee, which is described in this part of Mark's Gospel. (Galilee is a district to the north of Judea and west of the lake of Galilee.) Thus the order of events was probably:

Early in the year A.D. 27: Jesus' Baptism and Temptations;

Later in the same year: His Ministry in Judea;

Towards the end of that year: the imprisonment of John the Baptizer;

Early in the year A.D. 28: the beginning of Jesus' work in Galilee.

2. All through this part of his Gospel (1. 14–5. 43) Mark points out two things especially about Jesus: a. the *authority* with which He taught; b. His *victory* over sin and disease.

vv. 14, 15

These two verses show the things that Jesus was often saying during His ministry in Galilee: a. the Kingdom has already begun to arrive; b. repent; c. put confidence in my message.

Note: In saying this, Jesus was not giving advice; He was saying that God had done something that had never been done before. God had come as King.

NOTES

v. 15. The time has come; The kingdom of God is here; repent and believe. . . .

1. **The time has come:** i.e., the time for God to send His Messiah and for His rule to begin.

Note:

a. *God's patience:* God had made His plans long ago, but waited

16

until it was the right time in His eyes before sending Jesus (see Gal. 4. 4; Eph. 1. 10). Even we can see some ways in which this was "the right time": e.g., the Romans had provided good roads; the Greeks had spread their language among many nations, so that when the message came, it could be distributed widely; and the Jews believed and had taught in many lands that there was only one God, so that in this way, too, the people were ready.

b. *Our readiness:* The word "time" is used often in the New Testament for that moment when God, who has seen certain events taking place in the world, expects us to take action. The greatest "time" was the coming of Jesus. God expected men to accept Him. If they did, they were rescued from sin. If they did not, they were judged guilty, for they had lost the opportunity.

But there are often "times" now, when God says, "Act now" (2 Cor. 6. 2); e.g., occasionally an opportunity comes for Christians to begin working in a new part of a Muslim country; if the opportunity is not taken, it may be a hundred years before there is another one. In the same way, we often have an opportunity to speak to someone to help him; if we do not take it, it may never come again.

2. **The Kingdom of God:** i.e., the Rule of God over mankind. (See Additional Note below.)

3. **Repent and believe:** a. For **repent,** see notes on 1. 4; 14. 12–16. b. **Believe:** means "have faith in" or "have confidence in". If a man has never been in a motor-car, he has to believe a friend, and have faith in him, who tells him that it is safe to travel in this way. In the same way we put confidence in Christ and His message when we become Christians. Like the men getting into the car, we ourselves do not *know* that His way leads to happiness and everlasting life; but we believe Him, and He promises that it does. (See Additional Note, p. 91.)

ADDITIONAL NOTE

THE KINGDOM OF GOD

1. *The Jews' hope of deliverance*

The word "Kingdom" was a word which the Jews at that time were using very often. Their nation was in great trouble They regarded themselves as a race specially chosen by God for His service, yet they were oppressed by the heathen Romans. In this distress and rightful desire for freedom, many of their leaders were giving the people hope by saying, "God will one day deliver us and He will set up a new Kingdom". Then in Galilee Jesus came and said, "A new Kingdom is here!" We can understand with what great interest the people heard these words.

2. What Jesus taught

But when Jesus used the word "Kingdom" He did not mean the same thing as they did. First, most of them thought that their worst evil was the Roman government, and that when the new King came, He would overcome the Romans immediately. Jesus knew of the harshness of the heathen Roman rule, but He also knew that there was a more terrible evil, namely, the sin which was in every man. It was sin that the King would overcome first of all.

Secondly, they thought that the Kingdom would be a place like the old Kingdom of David, with armies and a King's throne. Jesus knew that it was not a place, but the action of God ruling over our hearts.

3. Questions about the Kingdom

We to-day find it hard to understand Jesus' words "Kingdom of God", but those who listened to Him were also perplexed, and no doubt asked Him to explain. These are the kind of questions and answers we might have heard if we had been in Galilee in A.D. 28:

Where can we find the Kingdom of God?
You cannot see it. It is not a place. It is in you (Luke 17. 21).

What is this Kingdom?
It is something that God does. It is God ruling over the hearts of repentant men and women.

Who belongs to it?
Everyone who has made God King of his daily life. This Kingdom is a society of God's subjects.

How can we join it?
By repentance (Mark 1. 15).

Why do you call it Good News?
Because God has now, as King, begun to overcome evil (Matt.
12. 28). Finally, all evil will be destroyed.

Has it come already?
Yes, it has begun to arrive. It is "at hand". It has not yet come
completely (Mark 1. 15).

How can we tell it has come?
I will tell you one way; when you see Me casting out evil spirits by
God's help, you will know that His Kingdom has begun (Luke
11. 20).

Was God not King before this time?
God has always been King. But it is now that He has sent Me to
rescue the world from its evil. He is ruling in a new way.

Will it ever come completely?
Yes, God will be completely victorious over all evil. The "Son of
Man" will come in His glory at that time (Mark 13. 26).

4. *Lessons from Jesus' teaching about the Kingdom*

a. God is King; therefore we have *hope*.
We are sometimes tempted to despair, when we think of all the
evil in the world; but we have hope and joy when we think that God
has already begun the overcoming of evil. We to-day are like
soldiers who are taking part in the last battle of a long war, but,
unlike the soldiers, we know that this is the last battle and also that
it is being a successful battle.
Our preaching, therefore, will be first of all, "Hear what God has
done! Hear how He has begun to overcome all evil!"

b. God is in control of the world, therefore His *laws must be kept*.
Men and nations often behave as though God were not King.
They disobey Him. But because He is King already no one can go
on breaking His rules and escape the evil that will follow. If the
government of my country is in control of its people, I can refuse to
pay my taxes, but before long I must pay or spend some time in
prison. God really is in control of His people to-day.

c. We can *prepare* for the coming of the Kingdom, but we cannot
create it.
Although the Kingdom has begun to arrive, yet it has not come
completely. We can prepare for that day, and are taught by Jesus

B   19

to pray, "Thy Kingdom come". If we pray, we believe that more people will make God King in their lives by obeying Him. In this way the Kingdom is being completed.

But it is God who will bring it. This should make us prayerful but not impatient, active but dependent upon God.

Mark 1. 16–20 : The Call of the Four Disciples

See also Matt. 4. 18–22; Luke 5. 1–11; John 1. 35–42

INTRODUCTION

There are really two stories here. In the first (vv. 16, 17), Jesus comes to Andrew and Simon (who was also called Peter or Cephas); in the second (vv. 18-20), He calls James and John while they are mending nets in a boat near the shore with the other members of their family.

These events took place by the lake of Galilee. This was a lake twelve miles long, not a "sea", although it was sometimes called the Sea of Tiberias. On its shores were large towns where much trading was done, such as Capernaum, where Peter and Andrew lived.

An important truth which these verses proclaim is this: the Christian Church was created by God (through Jesus), not by men.

NOTES

v. 17.   Jesus said to them: Come, follow me, and I will make you go fishing for men.

1. Jesus said: Jesus chose them, they did not choose Him (John 15. 16). We who are followers of Jesus follow Him, because He chose us. In the same way, we love God to-day, because He first loved us (1 John 4. 19). This thought prevents us: a. from being proud; b. from losing hope.

If He calls us, He will continue to take care of us. A man who asks a servant to accompany him on a journey, looks after him.

2. Follow: The Greek words mean, "Come here, behind me".

20

So Jesus leads the way. He does not ask us to endure any sufferings or temptations which He has not first endured Himself (John 10. 4).

3. **Me:** Jesus is the one that they (and we to-day) are told to follow. It is true that we should obey the teaching of the Bible and listen to the leaders of the Church, because they help us to follow Jesus, but we must beware. It is possible to be very regular in reading the Bible and obedient in keeping the Church's rules, and yet to forget Jesus Himself. Jesus, who is alive now, is our guide (Heb. 12. 2).

4. **I will:** i.e., "That will be our work in the future". But first they must learn what Jesus was teaching; afterwards they would bring others. So when Jesus calls a person to-day, He is thinking of what that person will become. (See note on 3. 16.) He had faith in Simon and Andrew, and Acts 2. 41 shows that they did become what He planned they should be.

5. **Go fishing:** A fisherman needs patience and skill. It needed skill to "throw a net" (v. 16). The net was large and round, with pieces of heavy metal sewn to the edges. If it was thrown well the weights sank to the bottom, enclosing the fish. Then it was lifted out by a rope in the middle. So in "fishing for people", we shall need just as much skill (See 2 Cor. 12. 16; Matt. 10. 16).

6. **For men:** Peter and Andrew were called in order that they should call others. (There was another reason—see 3. 13.) They used to catch fish, now they will catch people. They will bring them into the Kingdom, i.e., help them to make God the King of their lives.

This is the work of the Church now. We must not spend so much time in building schools and churches that we have no time to "catch men".

v. 18.   They left their nets and followed him.

1. It seems from these words that they decided very suddenly to go with Him. But perhaps they had already met Him when they were the disciples of John the Baptizer in Judea (John 1. 35). Jesus may have said to them at that time, "Go back to your work now; when I need you I will call you", and so they waited. Then when He did call them, in Galilee, they went. (This was not the only time that He "called" them. Later on (3. 13), He appointed them as members of the Twelve.)

2. They gave up their work of fishing in order to follow Him.

Most Christians are not expected by God to do exactly this. It is true that some are sure that they must do so, like a policeman who recently left his job to become a Methodist minister. But most of us continue in our present work. Yet we also have things that we must leave, e.g., those habits that prevent us from following Him faithfully. It is as hard to do this as it was for Peter to leave his nets.

3. In going with Jesus they took a great risk. Their friends must have laughed at them, and said, "Where will you get your money now?"

4. Why did they go with Him? It was partly because He was such an unusual person, partly because they still hoped that He would begin the revolution against the Romans (Acts 1. 6). We can say that they joined Jesus partly for a wrong reason; and yet He welcomed them. Certainly God does not wait until we are perfect before He calls us and uses us.

v. 20. They left their father Zebedee in the boat, with the hired men . . .

James and John were working with their father, but left him when Jesus called them.

1. Many to-day have to decide whether to obey Christ or their family. Every Muslim who wants to be a Christian has to do this. Jesus knew it was hard to leave one's human father, especially if one was accused of not caring for him (Mark 10. 29; Luke 14. 26).

2. But it is also the duty of Christians to look after their parents, especially when they become old. Zebedee's sons took care that their father still had labourers to help him, when they left him.

3. Why did Jesus not call Zebedee or the labourers? Probably because they were not ready. But we also know that God always does choose certain people (and not others) to do a certain piece of work for Him. That is His method. He is not guilty of "favouritism".

"There is no barrier between heaven and earth" (p. 12). In Christ, God became one with the human race in its need. Jesus cared deeply about the poor and suffering (see Mark 1. 29–45). Yet because of sin there are many barriers between human beings: between the powerful boss and the humble worker, the rich sheikh with his Jaguar and the poor shepherd from the Arabian desert. How can Christians help to break down such barriers?

"Jesus was giving teaching on how to regard all religious regulations" (p. 49).

A regulation of the Hindu religion is that cows are sacred. So they are allowed to wander freely, even among foodstalls and medicine shops in the streets of Calcutta, and Hindus are forbidden to kill their cattle though thousands of people may be starving.

What Church regulations and traditions hinder Christians from doing God's will.

Mark 1. 21–28 : Jesus in the Synagogue at Capernaum

See also Luke 4. 31–37

INTRODUCTION

The story

There are three parts to this story: a. Jesus' teaching (vv. 21–22); b. His healing (vv. 23–26); c. the effect of His work on others (vv. 27–28). Note that this is the first of the miracles described by Mark. (See Additional Note, p. 26.)

These verses are only part of a longer section (vv. 21–45) which tells us of the sort of work that Jesus was doing while He was staying in Capernaum. Not all the events took place on one day. Capernaum was a big town. (It is still possible to-day to see the ruins of a large synagogue there, although the town itself has disappeared.)

By reporting this story, Mark is showing us that: a. Jesus' work on earth was to overcome evil (see note on v. 23); b. Jesus was God Himself (see note on v. 24).

NOTES

v. 21. On the sabbath day he began to teach in the meeting-house.

1. **The sabbath day:** see notes on v. 2. 23–28, and Additional Note, p. 53.

2. **Meeting-house** was a "synagogue". There was only one Temple; it was at Jerusalem. However, there were many synagogues. Most towns and villages had a synagogue, where the Jews met for worship every Sabbath, and it was used for school on the other days.

The service began with prayer, and then someone read a passage from the Hebrew scriptures. Each verse was interpreted into the vernacular (Aramaic). Then the reader preached a sermon, explaining the teaching of the passage he had read. This is what Jesus did when He "taught" (v. 21), having been invited to do so by the ruler or president.

It was Jesus' custom to attend the synagogue. Sometimes He must have thought that the service was badly conducted. Yet He did not sweep it away. With great patience and great love, He, the Son of God, took part.

23

v. 22. The people were astonished at his teaching; for he taught them like one with authority, not like the scribes.

1. **Astonished:** People were very often astonished at Jesus. In v. 22 it was because He taught with "authority"; in v. 27 because He had cured a man without using magic. See 2.12; 5.20,42; 6.2,3,52; 7.37; 9. 15; 10. 23,26,32; 11. 18; 12. 17; 15. 5,44; 16. 5,8.

This shows us what sort of person He was. If we know Jesus, we also are astonished at Him, and above all at His love for us. Some have got so accustomed to the story of Jesus, that they are no longer astonished. Yet "while we were still sinners Christ died for us" (Rom. 5. 8). Ought this not to surprise us all our lives?

2. **With authority:** The people could see that Jesus' teaching was of a new kind. (See also v. 27, "a new teaching".) They said, "He has authority".

a. "Authority" does not here mean "permission". We see its meaning best by noticing two ways in which Jesus was different from the scribes. i. They did not give their own opinions, but passed on what had been taught in the past. But Jesus said "*I* say unto you" (Matt. 5. 21). It was not necessary for Him to find others who agreed with His teaching. ii. They could recite the words of the Old Testament, words such as, "Thou shalt love the Lord". But when Jesus spoke the words, all could see that He *kept* the teaching. They knew we ought to obey God: He obeyed God. They knew the words about God: He knew God.

It was like a class being taught in school about a foreign country. At first they have a teacher who has read books about it. Then comes one who has lived in that foreign land all his life. At once they know "This one speaks with authority: he has been there". So when Jesus spoke of God, they knew, "He has been there".

b. We too can speak "with authority". People listen when they see that we are doing the things we tell them to do; e.g., if we tell others to forgive one another, and if we ourselves are always willing to do so, then we are "speaking with authority".

c. Jesus has authority over us to-day. We accept what He says, because it is He who has said it. We do not need to see if others agree with Him. He Himself is sufficient.

So when He sees evil in us and tells us to get rid of it, we shall obey, as did the unclean spirit, in v. 26.

3. **The scribes:** Their work was to study the Old Testament, especially the first five books, and to find out and learn by heart what the great scribes of the past had said about them. Most of them belonged to the Pharisees.

v. 23. A man with an evil spirit . . .

This is the first of many stories about unclean spirits or "demons".

1. The lessons of the story are clear:

a. Jesus drove it out. That is the important part of the story. He has overcome evil. It is another sign that God's rule has begun (Mark 3. 27).

b. He drove it out because He had a power which other men did not have.

2. But did a spirit really enter the man? Or is that only the old way of saying that the man was ill? There are two answers to that question which Christian people give:

a. Mark (and most people in the world to-day) say, "Yes, evil spirits do exist and enter people. Before a man can be well, the spirit must come out."

b. Others say, "The man himself was sick. No spirit came into him from outside. It is a disease, not a spirit."

It is not necessary for us to decide which is the true answer. Whichever of the two we accept, we are still learning the same lessons from the story, namely that Jesus overcame evil because of the power He had.

3. Do followers of Jesus to-day drive out spirits? Yes, in two ways.

a. When people believe that they are possessed by an evil spirit, a Christian can say to them, "Jesus is stronger than the spirit". Often he can drive it out with God's help. Dr Lowrie, in his book about St Mark, says, "I myself have had experience of driving out evil spirits, which threw young men into convulsions as they went out."

b. God also uses doctors to heal such sickness. If a man asks to be cured of epilepsy, he can sometimes be cured with medicine. But there are many kinds of this disease; some of them are due to a sickness of the mind, not of the body. Doctors cannot yet heal them all. But God is sending His Spirit to help them to know more and more about this disease.

v. 24. What business have you with us. . . . I know who you are—you are the Holy One of God.

1. He meant, "Why do you interfere with us?" Probably the man had been standing quietly in the synagogue. But when Jesus spoke, he became afraid. He knew Jesus had the power to change his life in some way, so he shouted, "You have come to destroy us." ("Us" means "myself and the evil spirit in me".) This teaches two lessons:

a. When the followers of Jesus meet evil things and intend to get rid of them, they are often accused of "interfering", as Jesus was. In one city some Christians saw that a builder was building houses with rotten wood and selling them at high prices. They went to him and said, "You are cheating those who buy these houses". They were told, "This is not your affair". But evil *is* the Christian's affair, just as it was Jesus'.

b. We notice that although the man was ill, yet he was afraid to be healed. He knew that the change would be painful (v. 26). We are often like him. We want to live a better life and yet we fear that it will be painful to give up the old: e.g., it is painful to confess wrong things we have done, but after we have confessed them, we are as happy as the man in this story must have been.

2. **I know who you are:** Did he really know who Jesus was? It is fairly certain that he did not. When he said, "Holy One of God", he probably meant, "You holy man from God", just as the prophets were holy men from God. (He may have meant, "You are the Messiah".) What he did not know was that Jesus was God's own and only Son.

v. 25. Be quiet:

This means, "Hold your tongue". It shows that Jesus spoke to the spirit with great sternness and force. Some of the pictures that have been painted of Jesus do not show this; some make us think He was weak and womanly. Pictures are true only if they show that He was a strong person who was strict on many occasions.

ADDITIONAL NOTE

1. *What is a miracle?*

a. There are three kinds of happenings in the Gospels which we usually call "miracles": i. the cure of sick people by Jesus without the use of medicine; ii. events such as the stilling of the storm (Mark 4. 39) or the feeding of the five thousand people (6. 42); iii. the two great events which concerned Jesus Himself—when He, the Son of God, became man at Christmas, and when He rose from the grave at Easter.

b. We call them miracles, because they seem to us to have happened in ways that are different from the ways of nature. But it is important to remember that we do not fully know what the ways of nature are: e.g., when we say that "water always flows downhill", we have to add that it always happens like that *as far as we know at present*. Only God Himself, who made nature, knows fully what the ways of nature are. So when we read about Jesus stilling the storm or curing a leper, we do not say that God (through Jesus) was "breaking the laws of nature". We say, "This shows that we do not yet know what these laws are".

2. *Why did Jesus do miracles?*

a. He did miracles because it was often the most natural way for Him to do His work; as natural, perhaps, as it is for a mother to bear a child. He had such love for everyone in need that when He saw a sick person, it must have been hard for Him *not* to cure him. But, although it was natural to do such work, it was not easy (Mark 5. 30a).

b. He did *not* do miracles in order to prove to people that He was God. And we to-day do not believe in Him for the reason that He did miracles.

    i. No one would have been persuaded by miracles that He was God. Other men did miracles (Mark 9. 38), but no one treated them as gods.

    ii. Jesus wanted men to repent of their wrong-doing and to love Him and God His Father. He did not want them to regard Him as a magician. Magicians make us surprised or afraid; they do not make us love them or repent.

    iii. He wanted men to follow Him in "faith" and trustfulness, e.g., to take the risk of trusting Him, without having first been persuaded by seeing an extraordinary thing. That is why He refused to provide a "sign", when someone asked Him for one (Mark 8. 11, 12.)

27

3. *Can we be certain that Jesus did miracles?*

a. If God was truly born on the earth as a human being called Jesus (as we believe), then we should expect Him to do things which are unusual or impossible for us to do: e.g., since we believe that the power of God the Creator was in Jesus, then it was natural for Him to control the wind if He wished. So the answer to this question rests on whether we believe that Jesus was God or not. This is not something which we can show to be true in the same way in which we can show that 4 plus 4 is 8. We believe it in faith.

b. But there is no reason to think that the stories in the Gospels are not to be trusted. Not even His enemies denied that He did miracles. Indeed, one of the first events that made them want to kill Him was His cure of a man on the Sabbath (Mark 3. 5, 6). If He had done no miracles, there would have been much less reason to arrest and kill Him.

4. *Is every story of a miracle an accurate description of what happened?*

a. No. It is not possible to say *exactly* what happened at each miracle: e.g., in the story of the healing at Jericho, Matthew (20. 30) says there were two blind men, Mark says there was one, so we cannot be sure which account is correct; both cannot be right. (See also note on Mark 5. 39.)

b. But it would be very unwise to say that, because one part of a story is incorrect, therefore the miracles never occurred at all. We can be sure that Jesus had the power of God in Him, so we are not troubled if we cannot tell exactly what happened in every story.

5. *What do the miracles teach us?*

They teach us little unless we are already believers. They taught the Pharisees nothing, because they had already decided to treat Jesus as an enemy (see Mark 3. 1–6). We must first of all approach Jesus in faith, i.e., first of all take the decision to treat Him as God. If we do that, there are important lessons to be learnt:

a. God's Kingdom has already begun to arrive (Matt. 12. 28). This means that God is already King, and is already overcoming all that is evil.

b. God did not leave the world after creating it. When we read of a miracle, we are reading of God being active in His world. When

28

we overcome any kind of evil to-day, it is God who is active in the world.

c. God is not only active, but loving. Jesus "had mercy". The miracles were the outward sign of the love that God has for all who are in need.

d. God wants men to be healthy both in body and soul. Jesus thought it important both to forgive one man's sins and also to cure him of paralysis (2. 1–12).

Mark 1. 29–31 : The Cure of Peter's Mother-in-Law

See also Matt. 8. 14, 15; Luke 4. 38, 39

INTRODUCTION

This story is about events in a house in Capernaum where Peter and Andrew were living, together with their relations. Peter was able to tell Mark accurately what happened, and Mark has told us.

NOTES

v. 29.   Out of the meeting-house . . . to the house of Simon . . .

Jesus, who did God's work in a public place of worship, continued to do it in a private house. His actions were not more "holy" when He was in a synagogue than when He was in the house. We also .can serve God just as faithfully when we are in our own or someone else's house, as when we are in Church. There is only one rule for all alike.

v. 30.   Simon's mother-in-law was in bed . . . they told him about her . . .

1. **Simon's mother-in-law:** This shows that Peter was married at the time that he was called by Jesus. From 1 Cor. 9. 5 we learn that he and his wife were travelling together in God's service after-wards. Peter was married: Paul was unmarried. God uses both sorts of people.

2. **They told him:** Perhaps they told Him about the woman's fever in order to explain why the food was not cooked, or perhaps they hoped that He would be able to heal her. Whatever their thoughts, it was good to tell Jesus. It is always good to tell Jesus in prayer whatever happens in our lives, especially when someone is ill. (See also v. 32: "That evening they brought to Him all that were sick." This is what we can do in our evening prayers.)

v. 31.   She began to wait on them.

This was a wonderful thing. Even when a severe fever has left us, we usually feel weak for some time. But she was able to get up straight away and cook the meal. Her action teaches us that: a. Jesus heals us in order that we may serve others; b. we show our gratitude by our actions. When John Wesley was a child, he was saved from a burning house. When he was older, he was certain that God had saved him in order that he might serve and save others.

Mark 1. 32–34 : Illnesses Cured in the Evening

See also Matt. 8. 16, 17; Luke 4. 4–41

INTRODUCTION

Many people in Capernaum must have heard about the man cured in the synagogue (vv. 21–28); so they brought their friends who were sick to Jesus. They could not come before the evening because it was the Sabbath, and it was against the law to carry loads until sunset. (The Sabbath ended when the sun had set.)

NOTES

v. 33.   The whole town . . . at the door.

Hundreds of people crowded round the door of Peter's house. What noise and smell there must have been! Those who work in places where there are great crowds, in courts or hospitals, and find it hard to be patient and kind towards each person, may remember that

30

this is how Jesus worked too. He did not have a clean, quiet office with police to keep away the crowds (3. 10).

v. 34. Would not allow the evil spirits to speak. . . .

If the sick man shouted out some name like "Holy One of God" (v. 24), people might think that Jesus was the Messiah. They expected the Messiah to begin a revolution against the Romans, and so Jesus had to prevent people using this title. (We know that He was the Messiah, but he was not the sort of Messiah they expected.)

Mark 1. 35–39 : Jesus Praying Alone

See also Luke 4. 12–44

INTRODUCTION

Mark tells us three times about the prayers of Jesus (6. 46; 14. 35). Each time He prayed at night (or very early in the morning) and alone. Luke tells us more than this about Jesus' prayers (Luke 3. 21; 5. 16; 6. 12; 9. 18; 11. 1; 22. 41, 44.)

NOTES

v. 35. In the early morning, he . . . came to a lonely place: and he was praying there.

1. **Early morning:** Jesus slept with the others in the house at Capernaum. When they woke up early in the morning, they found that He had got up already and had gone out. He had gone to pray then, because it was a time when no visitors would disturb Him.

Jesus did not lay down a law for us about the time for prayer. We pray at any time, but very many Christians find that the house is most quiet and the mind most fresh in the early morning.

2. **A lonely place:** This was not a wilderness, but farmland where no one was working at that time of day. Is it necessary to be alone when we pray? Jesus taught that often it is necessary, although He also taught us to join in prayer with others (Matt. 6. 6). It is difficult

31

to pray alone if you live in a small house with a big family, especially if you are the mother. Some go into a corner of a church, others into a field where there are no houses.

3. **He was praying:** Why did Jesus pray? It was as natural for Jesus to pray, as it is for a bird to return to its nest. He must have prayed very often indeed. But there were probably two special reasons why He did so at this time:

a. He had been giving much help to others: now He needed to receive new strength and peace from God in prayer. Healing the sick was not easy for Him (Mark 5. 30a).

b. He also had to decide whether He could continue His work in Capernaum or not. It is possible that He was tempted to go on doing miracles, in order to collect followers in God's name, instead of teaching His disciples. He spoke to His Father about this, and then knew that He must leave Capernaum.

We too pray for these reasons: i. it is natural for us to talk to our Father; ii. we who are serving others need to receive strength from God, for no one can breathe out, unless he also breathes in; iii. we receive help when we are tempted or find it hard to make plans.

v. 37. They are all looking for you.

Peter and the others woke up and ran out to look for Jesus. They went to rebuke Him and to tell Him that He ought to be in Capernaum, not in a lonely place. "Why do you not go and heal more people?" they said. They made two mistakes:

1. They thought that His chief work was to heal as many as possible.

2. They did not understand that He needed to be alone and to pray. They rebuked because they did not understand. (See note on 8. 32.) When we try to do our work in God's way, especially when we go to pray alone, even our friends will often rebuke us.

v. 38. Let us go on to the towns near by . . . it was for that I came out.

1. **Let us go.** One piece of work had been done. Now the time had come to teach the people of towns in which he had not yet preached. This verse reminds us that life is like a Pilgrim's Progress. We are travelling forward. We should not do the same things in the same

way all the time. God calls us to begin new work at certain times in our lives.

2. **I came out:** Probably this means, "That is why I left Capernaum". (But some readers think it means, "That is why I left heaven and came to earth.")

Mark 1. 40–45 : The Cure of a Leper
See also Matt. 8. 1–4; Luke 5. 12–16

INTRODUCTION

Probably the disease which attacked this man was not exactly the same as the leprosy from which people suffer to-day, but it was very painful and greatly feared. Strict laws were made to keep lepers separate from others (Lev. 13). They had to wear torn clothes and long hair, and could not go into anyone else's house, and they had to shout "Unclean", if they walked along the road. It was very strange for this man to come to Jesus; it was even more wonderful that Jesus cured him. Here is another story showing the power of Jesus to overcome evil.

NOTES

v. 40. A leper came to him and fell on his knees and begged him for help. If you are willing you can heal me, he said.

If you are willing, you can heal me . . . : This means, "I know you have the power to heal me, but are you willing to do so?" He knew that Jesus was powerful, but he did not know that He was loving. (This is the way in which Muslims think about God.) This story thus makes us sure that God is as loving as He is powerful. (See Ecclus. 2. 18.)

v. 41. And he was filled with pity and put out his hand, and touched him, and said to him, I am willing; be healed.

1. **He was filled with pity . . .** It is not certain what Mark wrote

33

in this verse. Probably he wróte "filled with anger", not "with pity". Why was Jesus angry? He was angry when He saw the evil of the disease. He was often angry when He saw *others* oppressed by evil. (See 10. 14; 11. 15–17.) If we were more angry when sick or old people are neglected, we should be more helpful Christians. This is the right kind of anger. (See Ps. 97. 10a; Eph. 4. 26.)

2. **Touched him . . .:** To touch the leper was the most wonderful thing Jesus did on that day, for two reasons:

a. By doing so, Jesus was going against the custom of all good Jews. They thought that if a man touched a leper, that man would become unclean in his soul. Yet Jesus, a Jew, touched him, because He loved him. He was willing to break a custom five hundred years old in order to help him. There are times when we have to go against customs in order to do our duty to our neighbour.

b. The leper knew that Jesus loved him deeply, because Jesus *touched* him. When we love someone greatly, we show it by our actions rather than by our words. The touch of Jesus was an outward and visible sign of His love; we can call it a sacrament.

Two Muslims once came to a hospital in India suffering from sores which made their whole bodies smell horribly. A Christian nurse took great care every day in treating their sores, and sat with them for a time each evening. One of them said, as he was preparing to go home, "In my village we heard your religion; here we have seen it."

v. 42. He was healed.

In the days before Jesus' ministry, if a man got well again after being a leper, it was a law that he should go to the priest (Lev. 14. 2), and the priest said, "Be clean", i.e., "You are now free to meet other people." (See v. 44, "a proof to the people".) But when Jesus said the words, He did not just declare the man to be free; He actually cured him. (See Rom. 8. 3a.) As this paragraph is being written, the news comes that God has given wisdom to chemists and doctors to discover a medicine called "Dapsone". By means of it thousand of lepers are already being cured. So, through the men who discovered it, Jesus is still curing lepers.

v. 43. With stern orders sent him away . . .

Jesus was not angry, but very deeply troubled. He told the man not to say anything at all about his cure. If it became well known, more and more would come expecting to be healed, and Jesus would have no chance to teach. (But v. 45 shows that the man did not obey.)

v. 44. Show yourself to the priest . . .

This shows that Jesus thought it important to keep the Old Testament laws.

It may be asked, "If Jesus kept this law, why do we not keep it?" the answer is that we *should* keep it in the following way:

The Law means, "Love your neighbour. If you have had a disease which is easily spread, do not mix with others until you are sure that you are free of the disease." This law of "loving our neighbour" never changes, although our ways of living have changed: e.g., it is no longer the priest who tells us that we are free of a disease.

v. 45. He began to talk and to spread the story . . .

He was not able to control his tongue and so he made the work of Jesus much harder. The crowds hindered Him. There is a time to talk about Jesus with courage, and a time to keep silent. Sometimes we can serve God better and help people more by keeping silent, e.g., by praying for them rather than by talking to them.

See picture facing page 22.

Mark 2. 1–12 : The Cure of the Paralysed Man

See also Matt. 9. 1–8; Luke 5. 17–26

INTRODUCTION

Chapter 2. 1—3. 6

At the time when Mark was writing, the Church members often asked, "If Jesus was a good man, why was He hated, and why was He crucified?" So Mark collected together in these passages some stories to show why the Pharisees and others hated Jesus. (These stories probably describe events which happened at different times in Jesus' life, not all at the same period.)

This story

The first of these stories is that of the paralysed man (2. 1–12). It tells of two things that Jesus did: a. He cured the man's body (vv. 1–4, 11, 12); b. He forgave his sins (v. 5–10).

It also tells what the scribes thought about Him.

In telling this story, Mark is saying to us, "Since Jesus was Himself God, forgiving sins is just what you would expect Him to do. No one else can do this. As you read this, remember that it is God about Whom you are reading."

NOTES

v. 4. They broke open the roof ...

This roof was flat. A man who made a roof like this first laid long sticks across from one wall to another, and then spread little sticks over them, and then pressed down clay on the top. This clay was baked by the sun, so that it kept out the rain and people could walk on it.

The house was a small one, but had stone steps on the outside. In order to reach the roof, the four men had to push and pull their friend up these steps. Then they began to dig up the baked clay and to break the sticks underneath it.

It is possible that Peter, who told these stories to Mark, remembered what happened so well because it was his own house and he himself had to mend the roof afterwards!

v. 5. When he saw their faith, Jesus said ... your sins are forgiven.

1. **Their faith**: It was *theirs*, not the man's. The man was cured, because his friends had faith. God saves and heals many because of the prayers and actions of others (See 7. 24–30; 9. 14–29; Luke 7. 1–10.)

St Augustine, the great bishop and writer who lived fifteen hundred years ago in North Africa, used to say that it was his mother Monnica's prayers that had rescued him from his bad life. Thousands of children are at this moment being gently led to serve God by those who have been praying for them ever since they were babies, their godparents, sponsors, parents, friends.

A Christian should often ask himself:

36

a. Am I grateful to those whose prayers have helped me in past years? Or do I think that it is only my own efforts and prayers that matter?

b. Who at this minute is needing my prayers? Is there someone who will go wrong if I forget him, and who will go straight if I pray?

2. **Faith:** This story shows the meaning of this word (see Additional Note, p. 91):

a. Faith is in Christ. The men did not think they themselves could cure the man: it was Christ in whom they had confidence. (See note on 10. 52.)

b. Faith is taking a risk. (See note on 1. 18.) These men knew that if they were not successful, their friends would laugh at them. They knew that the owner of the house might be angry when he saw the hole in the roof; and Jesus might be angry when the sticks and clay began to fall on His head. They took these risks. (See also Heb. 11. 8b.)

c. Faith is taking action. They showed that they had real faith by making the stretcher and carrying the man to Jesus.

d. Faith is persistence. First they tried to push the man through the door, but it was impossible. They did not give up, but tried another way. (See also Luke 11. 5–8; 18. 1–5.)

3. **Your sins are forgiven:** Why did Jesus talk about the man's sins, since he was sick in his body?

a. It was not because Jesus believed that *all* bodily sickness is a punishment for sins. The Jews did believe that, but Jesus did not (see John 9.3; Luke 13. 1–5).

b. Jesus knew that *this* man was sick because of a sin he had committed.

How did Jesus know? Perhaps He talked with the man or perhaps it was because He always does know our hearts better than we know them. So when He said to him, "My son", the man must have remembered his sin and been sorry for it. Then, when Jesus had made him sure that God had forgiven it, his body became strong again.

c. Jesus went to the root of the trouble. His Church to-day must do so. Two men in a big town were once talking about a poor and unhappy family who were paying rent to a landlord for an unhealthy old house. One man said, "Make the landlord rebuild the house and they will be happy." The other said, "Yes, I agree. But that is not enough. That family will not be happy until the wife has forgiven her husband for his cruelty to her, and he has told both her and God that he is sorry." The second man wanted to get to the roots of their unhappiness.

d. Doctors are discovering to-day what Jesus knew two thousand years ago: they are finding that very many people are sick in body simply because they feel deeply guilty of sin.

v. 7.   He is blaspheming. Who can forgive sins, who but God only?

This is the first time that anyone made an accusation against Jesus. We note that it was the scribes, i.e., the religious leaders, who made it. (For more about the scribes, see Additional Note, p. 43.) We need to ask three questions:

a. What is forgiveness? It is God saying to a guilty man, "I will treat you as innocent from now on." Paul calls this "justifying" (see Rom. 3. 23, 24). Many of us pretend that we are innocent before God, but we do not have peace of mind. The right way is to admit that we are guilty and to receive God's gift of forgiveness and peace.

b. Who can forgive? The scribes were right in saying that only God can forgive sins against Him. So when Jesus forgave, He was by his actions and words showing that he was God.

c. Can priests forgive? No, it is God who forgives. But ever since the time of Christ, the Church has given authority to certain of its officers to declare the forgiveness of God to those who honestly repent. This was Christ's plan (see John 20. 22, 23; 2 Sam. 12. 13b).

v. 8.   He knew at once in his spirit . . .

He knew what the scribes were whispering. We are reminded of the prayer, "Almighty God, unto whom all hearts be open . . ." Nothing is hidden from God. (See Ps. 139. 1–6; Acts 15. 8.) It is good to remember this, but it should not make us afraid: He is love.

v. 9.   Which is easier . . . ?

This meant, "You think it is easier for me to say, 'You are forgiven', than to heal his body. So if I do what you think is the more difficult task of healing will you believe that I can do what you think is the easier one (of forgiving)?" (Forgiveness, of course, was not

really easier than healing. It cost God the death of His Son to forgive mankind.) They were so puzzled that they could not answer.
They saw the man healed and that showed that Jesus could also do
the "easier" work of forgiving. And yet they knew that only God
could forgive! This would mean that Jesus was God, and they could
not accept such a thought.

v. 10.   The Son of Man has power . . .

Son of Man: does not just mean "a Man". (See Additional Note,
p. 137.) It was a name for a great person Daniel saw in a vision
(Dan. 7. 13). It was a name Jesus often used for Himself:

1. Sometimes He meant chiefly the One who would be judge at
the end of the world, as in Dan. 7. 13 (cf. Mark 8. 28).

2. Usually He meant the One who was going to *suffer* and die for
mankind (8. 31; 10. 45).

3. Here the main thought is the One who acts with all God's
authority, i.e., who is Himself God.

Thus its meaning is very like the meaning of the word "Messiah".
But the Jews did not know this. So His secret (that He was Messiah)
was still hidden from them.

v. 11.   Stand up, take your stretcher . . .

The "stretcher" was a simple mat or bed which could easily be
carried away.

v. 12.   We never saw anything like this.

The crowd had never seen a man cured like that, and they were
astonished and delighted. The scribes, however, were angry and
jealous (v. 7). Jesus (and His Church afterwards) was loved by some
and hated by others. Why should we be surprised if we are both
loved and hated when we follow Christ (Matt. 10. 24, 25)?

Mark 2. 13–14 : The Invitation to Levi

See also Matt. 9. 9; Luke 5. 27, 28

INTRODUCTION

Mark did not write down all the stories he knew about Jesus: he chose out those which were specially useful to Christian leaders. He chose this one because it helped to answer the question, "Who can be admitted into the Church? All men or certain kinds only?" Jesus showed that everyone is welcomed (see also vv. 15–17).

NOTES

v. 13.   By the lake-side . . .

On the shore of the lake of Galilee, near Capernaum.

v. 14.   Levi, the son of Alpheus, sitting at the tax-office; and he said to him, Follow me . . .

1. **Levi:** He may have been the same person as Matthew, or he may have been James the son of Alpheus (3. 18); or he may not have been one of the Twelve at all. The important thing is not his name, but that he was despised by others and chosen by Jesus.

2. **The tax-office:** Levi's work was to collect taxes from the fisher-men of Capernaum and from traders of all kinds and all races who passed through the town. He sat near the lake at a table. Around him were piles of money, and account books, and fish, but few friends.

These were the reasons why the tax-officials were so much disliked:

a. Most of them forced the people, including the very poor, to pay more than the law required, and kept the extra for themselves.

b. The taxes went to Herod Antipas, the ruler of Galilee; he was not a Roman, but was a most cruel man, who would not have been ruling if the Roman army had not supported him.

c. The work forced them to meet Gentile traders, and the Jews regarded the Gentiles as "unclean".

3. **Follow me:** See note on 1. 17. We need to remember three things:

a. Probably Jesus had been working by the lake for many weeks, and Levi had heard Him many times and had already carefully considered going with Him. He was ready when Jesus spoke.

b. It was a very serious matter to leave his work. The four disciples could return to their boats (1. 18), but Levi could never go back to the tax-office. When he got up to follow Jesus, he was following Him for ever. So are we. (See Judges 11. 35: "I cannot go back".)

c. Compare the work Levi used to do with the work he was about to do as a disciple of Jesus. Before, he laid burdens on people; in future, he would show them how to get rid of their burdens (Matt. 11. 28.)

Mark 2. 15–17 : Eating with Tax-Collectors

See also Matt. 9. 10–13; Luke 5. 29–32

INTRODUCTION

If someone asked what the religion of Christians is, and if there was only time to tell him one or two stories from the Gospels, this story might be one of them. It tells how Jesus was invited to Levi's house and freely mixed with: a. those in a very low position in the world; b. those who were living bad lives.

Mark is saying to his readers, "Look! This is how God, because of His love, searches for those who most need Him".

NOTES

v. 15.   Tax-collectors and sinners . . .

This was a group of people, all of whom were regarded as breakers of the Pharisees' rules and very many of whom were living bad lives in God's sight.

1. **Tax-collectors:** These must have been the friends of Levi (see note on 2. 14).

2. **Sinners:** This was the word that the Pharisees used for people who were not Jews ("Gentiles") and all those who were not keeping the rules of religion which they themselves had added to the laws of the Old Testament. Jesus did not agree that if someone broke

41

one of these rules, he was a bad man. So the word does not mean "wicked" people in God's sight. However, it is clear from v. 17 that most of these men were in fact not living good lives.

v. 16. The scribes of the Pharisees saw that he was eating with sinners . . .

1. **The scribes of the Pharisees:** These people were the leaders of the Pharisees. (See notes on 1. 22 and Additional Note, p. 43.)

They spoke against Jesus because they thought that He was acting as though people's sins did not matter. By eating with them, He seemed to be encouraging them to continue in sin.

2. **Eating with sinners:**

a. There are many stories of Jesus eating and drinking with different people (14. 3; John 2. 2; 12. 2; 21. 13, etc.). His enemies called Him a greedy man and a drinker (Matt. 11. 19); they expected a prophet to keep apart from ordinary people. But He enjoyed eating with people like Levi, and that is why they felt at ease with Him.

b. He was able to mix with sinful people without being spoiled Himself—like a lantern which remains alight, even in a storm.

Can we do the same? St Paul in 1 Cor. 15. 33 says that if we think we shall do wrong in the company of certain people, it is better to keep away. But when we ourselves are stronger, we shall want to meet such people and will not be led astray ourselves.

c. Some of the "tax-collectors and sinners" may not have been bad people at all: they were despised and considered unimportant. But they were the special friends of Jesus. Every country has such people to-day: e.g., those of another race or tribe, or the very poor, or lapsed Christians. The Church should be especially friendly to such people.

v. 17. I came to call not the good but sinners.

1. **I came to call:** He not only received those who came, but He actually sought out and called sinners to come and eat with Him in the house where He was staying. By doing this He was showing us something about God that men never knew before. The Old Testament had taught that God would forgive sinners, if they repented. But no one taught that He actually sought out the sinner, except perhaps Hosea 11. 4. (The writer of 1 Chron. 28. 9 even says, "If

you forsake Him, He will cast you off for ever".) Jesus, who was God, went to look for sinners.

Now we see what is meant by God's "grace". (See also Luke 19. 1–10.)

2. **Not the good:** Jesus did not mean that He did not like good people. He meant, "I cannot help anyone who thinks that he is good: such a man is like a sick person who thinks he is quite well and will not listen to the doctor." (See the words, "The strong have not need of a doctor".) That is why Jesus could not help most of the Pharisees. (See also John 9. 41.)

3. **But sinners:** Jesus mixed with them while they were still sinners.

The Pharisees wanted Him to wait until they were good before He ate with them, just as all Jews expected that God would wait until a man was good before He blessed him (Ps. 15. 1–2). But Jesus did not wait. If He had waited until men were good, He would still be waiting now, because everyone has sinned. (See Rom. 5. 8.)

ADDITIONAL NOTE

THE PHARISEES AND THE SCRIBES

1. *The Pharisees*

These were a society of people who tried to keep God's laws strictly. (Most Jews were not Pharisees.) They were not priests, but did work like farming or shopkeeping: many of them were not very well educated. Their chief aim was to keep Jews from imitating the bad habits of heathens. (The word "Pharisee" means "kept separate".) They taught that the best way of doing that was by keeping God's laws very strictly indeed. Very many of them were sincere people. Their errors were:

a. They taught that the many rules which had been added by the scribes when they interpreted the Old Testament laws were as important as those laws themselves. Often they forgot a law of God, such as "Honour your parents", because they were paying so much attention to one of the scribes' rules. (See note on 7. 11.) Jesus taught that God's own laws should be obeyed rather than these. (See notes on 7. 1–13, especially on v. 13.)

b. They condemned all who did not keep these rules as strictly as they did themselves. (See note on 3. 2.) They called such people "sinners" and do not seem to have helped them in their troubles (2. 15).

c. They were too often satisfied with their own success in keeping these rules, and became proud (Luke 18. 11, 12). Jesus called them "hypocrites", because they thought that they were obeying God's laws, when *really* they were failing to honour Him in many ways. (See note on 7. 6.) They hated Jesus, because He pointed out their weaknesses, such as this one, and they joined with the scribes and others in plotting to kill Him (3. 6).

2. *The scribes*

These people were the teachers of the Old Testament laws. That was their daily work for which they were paid. Most of the scribes belonged to the Pharisees, and became their leaders because they were well-educated. Some scribes and some Pharisees held important positions in village synagogues and even in the Sanhedrin, the highest council of the Jewish religion.

In studying the old Testament laws they had to memorize the explanations of them given by scribes of the past. To-day we might call them lawyers, because they did some of their work in the courts, explaining the meaning of these laws. But they also preached and taught in the synagogues. (Law and Religion were not separated, for both were taken out of the Scriptures, and the same person taught both.) Mark (12. 28–34) shows that some of them were good men.

Jesus said (12. 38–40) that most scribes went wrong in their teaching and behaviour. They were guilty of the sins of which the Pharisees were often guilty (see above), but their special weakness was this: their religion was chiefly doing what other scribes had done in the past. They did not listen to what the living God was telling them in the present. (See notes on 1. 22.) So when the Son of God interpreted the Scriptures in a new way, they refused to listen (2. 6; 3. 22; 11. 18).

3. *Ourselves*

Christians are always in danger of becoming like the Pharisees and scribes. We can only avoid it by: a. loving God more than religious rules; b. loving people rather than condemning them; c. being humble enough to be corrected; d. fixing our attention on what the Spirit of the living God is teaching in this present age.

Mark 2. 18–22 : The Old Way and the New Way

See also Matt. 9. 14–17; Luke 5. 33–39

INTRODUCTION

"Since Christ was a Jew, why do Christians not follow the Jewish religion?" This question is often asked and vv. 18–22 help us to answer it.

Jesus taught that the Jews who had come before Him had not understood the will of God rightly, and so He taught a New Way. In these verses we are told two things about those who serve God in this New Way: a. vv. 18–20: they are joyful not mournful; b. vv. 21, 22: if they live in the New Way they cannot live in the Old Way also.

NOTES

v. 18. Disciples of John . . . were keeping a fast . . .

Probably they were fasting because of the death of John the Baptizer. The Jews fasted for many reasons, e.g., to show repentance, but often it was a sign of mourning. It happened that the Pharisees were fasting at the same time as John's disciples.

v. 19. Can wedding-guests fast while the bridegroom is with them?

1. Jesus said, "My disciples cannot fast, because I am with them. This is like a joyful wedding."

Probably He was here comparing Himself to the bridegroom. In the Old Testament, God had often been thought of as the faithful bridegroom, and the people of Israel were called the bride or wife who was often unfaithful to God . . . (See Isa. 54. 1–10; Hos. 9. 1.) Now Jesus and His people are together, like a husband and wife. So it was a time of rejoicing. (Rev. 19. 7–9; Eph. 5. 25; 2 Cor. 11. 2.)

2. Can people tell that we are Christians, because they notice our joy?

The father of a certain family in China died. He had been a good man and was greatly loved by his wife and children. At the funeral they sang hymns of praise to God for having given them so good a father and for His care which would continue to surround their father after death. After the service, two of their friends (who were not Christians) said, "Tell us about your God who can give you joy even at such a time."

3. We rejoice because: a. we know that Christ is present with us (1 Pet. 1. 8). So Holy Communion is a time of joy: we do not mourn His death, but thank Him for it, and we are glad because He is present; b. we are certain that God will overcome all evil (John 16. 22–33).

v. 20.   The bridegroom shall be taken away . . . they will fast on that day.

1. **The bridegroom shall be taken away:** Jesus tells them that He is going to die, but they do not understand (8. 31–33).

2. **They will fast:** This shows that fasting is right for Christians: e.g., by going without food or some other good thing, we can learn how to control our bodies better, and in this way become more useful servants of God. (See Luke 4. 2; 1 Cor. 9. 27.)

There are special times when very many Christians fast, e.g., on Good Friday, and this is an old custom of the Church. But it is only when a man first loves God in his heart and really wishes to become a more useful servant of His that such fasting is good. Then his fast becomes an outward sign of his dedication to the service of God.

But people often fast for the wrong reasons, for instance:

a. Some think that fasting will so please God, because it is a kind of sacrifice, that He will be persuaded to bless us. Such people may fast before going on a journey or taking an examination; but no action of ours can make God love us more than He does already.

b. Others believe that the act of fasting turns us into better Christians, just as taking an aspirin may cure a headache; but this does not happen.

v. 21.   No one sews . . . new cloth on an old cloak . . .

This is the first of the two proverbs which Jesus told to show that His teaching is different from that of other Jews. (The other is in v. 22.)

It means: you do not do any good by patching an old garment with cloth that has not yet been shrunk. As soon as you wash the garment, the new cloth shrinks and tears it. The two cannot go together.

1. In what way was Jesus' teaching different?

Paul says that the old Jewish way was to try to earn God's blessing by keeping His laws; but that Jesus taught us to admit humbly that we cannot perfectly keep His laws, and to accept the free forgiveness that He offers us (Rom. 6. 14 and 7. 6). No one can live in both ways: we choose either the old way or the new.

This is the answer to those who accuse Christians of breaking "God's laws" by eating pig's flesh or working on Saturday. Since Jesus came we are no longer under those laws.

Note: This does not mean that we need no longer read the Old Testament (Matt. 5. 17). But it is an unfinished Book, and we should read it together with the New Testament.

2. We Christians are always in danger of serving God in the old way, e.g.:

a. We may think that keeping a rule is what pleases God most. (See note 2 on v. 27.)

b. We may be tempted to return to old ways. There have been Christians in England for hundreds of years and yet some of them still throw a little salt over their left shoulder when salt is spilt, just as their heathen ancestors used to. It is not easy to put off "the old man" (Eph. 4. 22–24).

c. We may forget that Jesus, through His Holy Spirit, is still showing us new ways of serving Him: e.g., God is leading Christians in many countries to translate the Bible again, even though those countries already have the Bible in their own languages. But when this happens, there are sometimes people who say, "The old words are better, because they are old". It is, of course, true that not everything that is new is good! But at least we must be willing to do God's work in new ways, when the Holy Spirit shows these ways to the Church.

v. 22. Wine-skins

These are bottles for wine made out of the skin of a goat. An old skin gets dry and hard, and if fresh wine is poured into it, it cracks.

Mark 2. 23–28: Picking Corn on the Sabbath

See also Matt. 12. 1–8; Luke 6. 1–5

INTRODUCTION

One Sabbath, the disciples picked a few ears of corn as they were walking with Jesus. Some Pharisees noticed this. They told Jesus, expecting Him to stop them. But in reply He: a. said that the disciples had not done wrong; b. gave teaching concerning both the Sabbath and all religious rules. (See Additional Note. p. 53.)

Note: In America and Africa the word "corn" means maize, but here it means one of the cereal grasses, like wheat or barley, which produce very small "ears" or "heads".

NOTES

v. 24. On the sabbath day what is not lawful.

The disciples were not accused of stealing corn, for according to Deut. 23. 25, strangers were allowed to pick a few ears. Nor were they accused of making a long journey. The Pharisees said they were guilty of "working": picking the ears was called "reaping", which was forbidden by their traditions. But it was not forbidden by the law that God gave.

v. 25. Have you never read what David did . . .?

Jesus seems to have agreed that His disciples had ignored the Sabbath law as it was interpreted by the scribes. But He then said, "Which of these two keeps the day more holy and pleases God more, to keep the scribes' tradition or to help men who are in trouble? Surely to help men in trouble. That is what David did" (1 Sam. 21. 6).

It was impossible for the Pharisees to contradict this, because David was so greatly honoured. But they were not convinced in their hearts. They must have sincerely felt, "If Jesus is teaching men to break the Sabbath, He cannot love God."

v. 26. When Abiathar was high-priest . . .

1 Sam. 21. 1 says that Ahimelech was high-priest at that time. Why does this verse say it was Abiathar?

1. Perhaps in the Old Testament that Jesus used it was stated that it was in Abiathar's time. Not all copies of the Old Testament contained exactly the same words.

2. Or perhaps Mark made a mistake when he was writing. (See note on 1. 2.)

3. Or perhaps someone who was copying Mark made a mistake. Any of these things may have happened, but they do not make any difference to our faith in Jesus. We do not cease to love Him because we find that this verse contains the wrong name! We follow Him because He loved us and gave Himself for us.

v. 27. The sabbath was made for man . . .

Note: "Man" here means all human beings. In this verse Jesus was giving teaching not only to the Jews on how to use the Sabbath, but also to ourselves on how to regard all religious regulations:

1. It was made by God to be of service to man. It existed to give men rest for the body and fellowship with God.

This is how a Christian regards Church regulations and customs: e.g., concerning church-attendance, Bible-reading, almsgiving, fasting, keeping Sunday. We must know how these rules can serve us: e.g., we are right to keep a rule about going to church regularly. But simply keeping this rule is not our goal; we do it in order that we may love and honour God. Loving and honouring God is the goal. (It is easy to forget this. Isa. 1. 14–17 speaks of the sin of attending public worship not in order to honour God, but *instead of* honouring Him and *instead of* dealing honestly with our neighbour.)

2. Sometimes a tradition or regulation has to be ignored in order to please God most fully; e.g., a Christian mother knows that she is "keeping Sunday holy" better by looking after her very sick child than by attending church. Caring for the child pleases God more.

One of the rules of football gives the same guidance: Rule 5(a) says that if a player of "A" team commits a foul, the referee shall stop play and award a free kick to "B" team. But sometimes it would not be to the advantage of "B" team if play was stopped, e.g., if they were just about to score a goal: in this case the referee would not stop play. (Here a lesser rule should be broken in order to keep the greater rule.)

3. These regulations are our servants, but we must not despise

them. Jesus never taught that the Jewish regulations about the Sabbath were unimportant. He only ignored them for very good reasons. We must only act differently from our Church traditions for good reasons, i.e., in order to glorify God more, not through laziness or lack of respect for our Church.

v. 28. The Son of Man is Lord even of the sabbath.

Some think that "Son of Man" here means "mankind". If this is true, the verse means, "Men have the right to use the Sabbath in the way that my disciples used it".

But it is more likely that it means "Messiah", and that Jesus is saying, "I, Jesus, the Messiah, have authority to teach you how to use the Sabbath." He reminds them that David, the great king, was right in using the law about the shewbread in the way he did: now here is a greater King than David, who is using the law about the Sabbath in His own way because of His love for men.

See picture facing p. 23.

Mark 3. 1–6 : A Man Cured on the Sabbath

See also Matt. 12. 9–14; Luke 6. 6–11

INTRODUCTION

This is the last of the five stories collected together by Mark to show why Jesus was hated by the Pharisees. It shows us Jesus engaged in a double struggle against: a. the Pharisees; b. the evil of disease; and being victorious.

The story

Jesus went into the synagogue. As He walked to His seat, before the service began, He saw two things: a man whose hand was paralysed and withered (Luke says that it was the man's right hand, and another account says that he was a builder); and His enemies, the Pharisees, watching to see if He would cure the man. He did cure him, but only after putting a searching question to them.

Jesus' reasons for the healing

The Pharisees' traditions allowed someone to do a work of healing on the Sabbath if the patient was extremely ill. But this man was not: there was time to heal him the next day. Therefore, when Jesus began to cure him, He knew that they would accuse Him of breaking the Fourth Commandment. He healed him publicly for two reasons: a. to let everyone see how wrong was the attitude of the Pharisees, and to try to show this to the Pharisees themselves; b. to teach what the Sabbath was for. (See note on v. 4.)

The Pharisees could find no answer to Jesus' question in v. 4. Instead they began from that time to plan to kill Him (v. 6). (See Additional Note, p. 43.)

NOTES

v. 2.   They watched him . . .

The Pharisees went wrong in three ways:

1. They wanted Jesus to break the Sabbath law. To want some-one else to do wrong is the opposite of love. If we ever hope that someone else will fail in some way so that we may show ourselves to be superior, we are guilty of "malice". (See 1 Cor. 13. 6.)

2. They did not listen to what Jesus said: they had made their minds up before meeting Him. We, too, are judging unfairly if we say, "So-and-so cannot be a good man because he comes from that nation or family or tribe or party."

3. They did not seem to care if the sick man was healed or not. They were religious, but not kind. (A little girl once prayed, "O God, make all the bad people good, and the good people kind".)

v. 4.   Is it lawful to do good on the sabbath or to do harm?

1. Jesus asked this question chiefly in order to show up the wrongness of the Pharisees' teaching about the Sabbath. It meant, "I use the Sabbath for healing ('doing good'); you are using it for plotting to kill me ('doing harm'). Which of these ways of using the Sabbath do you really think pleases God more?" They could not answer this.

2. But the words also show that God is even more pleased with the good that is *done* on the Sabbath (or Sunday), than with the way in which we avoid work, which is forbidden. Most Pharisees did not

understand this, and it is easy for us to forget it. We may say with satisfaction at the end of a Sunday, "I have kept away from the work I do during the week." But God's question will be, "What did you *do*? What lonely or sick people have you comforted for me to-day?"

v. 5a. He looked round at them with anger, pained by their stupidity . . .

1. **With anger:**

a. We have seen in the note on v. 2 what things made Him angry.

b. When is anger good? When someone else is being ill-treated or God is being dishonoured then it is often good to be angry. (See notes on 1. 41; 10. 14; 11. 15.) But too often we are angry because we ourselves have been insulted or are afraid. This is the wrong kind of anger.

c. This shows that Jesus had the same feelings that we have. He was a real man and was angry and pained. Too many people think that Jesus is half-God and half-man. It was Mark who made it plain that Jesus was fully man, a man who groaned and sighed and loved and was angry and sad, as we are (1. 43; 3, 5; 7. 34; 8. 12; 10. 14, 21). It is noticeable that Matthew and Luke do not say as much about this great truth.

Because Jesus was a real man, He shows us what we men and women can become.

2. He was angry at their unkindness; but their stupidity pained Him. They really did think that their planning to kill Jesus pleased God more than the healing of the man. To think this, was a kind of sickness rather than a sin. The A.V. calls this stupidity "hardness of heart", but perhaps "blindness" is a better word.

We too need to pray, "From all blindness of heart, good Lord deliver us." We all have wrong ideas which must pain Jesus.

v. 5b. Hold out your hand . . . and it was made well again.

1. Is it possible to cure a man only by telling him to hold out his hand? How did Jesus heal him? We do not know. (See Additional Note, p. 26.) But we do know that He did it. If He had not done this kind of thing, the Pharisees would not have planned to kill Him.

2. It was Jesus who cured the man, but he was not cured until he had held out his hand. In the same way it is God who makes it possible for us to get rid of bad things such as sickness and sinfulness,

52

but usually He expects us to take our share and to fight against them. Even a baby fed by its mother has to open its mouth, and we are not helpless babies (Phil. 2. 12, 13).

v. 6.   The Pharisees . . . with the Herodians . . .

1. The Herodians were the friends of Herod Antipas, the ruler of Galilee. Herod and his friends were disliked by the Pharisees and other religious leaders of the Jews, partly because they were friendly with the hated Romans, and partly because most of them were heathens, and not Jews.

2. Why did the Pharisees join the Herodians? Because they thought they could help them to kill Jesus. The Herodians also wanted to get rid of anyone who might cause trouble in the country; if there was disturbance the Romans might put someone else in Herod's place.

3. So we see the Pharisees asking for the help of the government (i.e., Herod's friends) in a religious matter. This is nearly always wrong. When a Church asks for help from a government, it is very hard for that Church to make her plans in accordance with God's will: very often she is forced to do what the government says. (See Acts 4. 19.)

What the Church *should* ask from a government is that the laws of the country should be in accordance with the will of God, which has been shown to all men in the Bible.

See picture facing p. 56.

ADDITIONAL NOTE

THE SABBATH

1. *Why the Jews kept the Sabbath*

The Sabbath and Circumcision were the two customs which made the Jews different from all other tribes. Both were therefore regarded as very important. The Fourth Commandment said, "Keep holy the Sabbath day" (i.e., the seventh day). So the Jews attended public worship on that day, and rested. The Old Testament gave two reasons why God gave the Sabbath: a. Ex. 20. 8–11: "Because God rested on that day"; b. Deut. 5. 14, 15: "Because of the needs of those who work for masters."

Thus the Jewish Law was a great blessing. But the religious leaders made two mistakes: a. they paid too much attention to the many rules which the Scribes had made when they interpreted the Fourth Commandment; as a result they forgot that God's purposes when He gave the Commandment were much more important; b. they chiefly taught the many works that should be *avoided*, and almost forgot to teach what should be *done*.

2. *The teaching of Jesus about the Sabbath*

Jesus taught that the Fourth Commandment should be kept, and He Himself worshipped in the synagogue on the Sabbath. He gave new teaching about it: a. what you do is more important than what you avoid doing (see notes on 2. 1–6); b. sometimes it is right to ignore one of the scribes' laws about the Sabbath in order to keep it holy, i.e., in order to please God (see notes on vv. 25, 27).

3. *The Sabbath and Christians*

After Pentecost the Christians continued to keep the Sabbath (the seventh day of the week), because Jesus had not told them not to; but they also kept the first day of the week, because it was on that day that Jesus rose.

Then they began to understand what Jesus meant when He said that no one puts a new piece of cloth on an old garment (2. 18–22). So gradually Christians used the first day for their day of rest and worship, and left the Sabbath free for the Jews.

4. *Sunday*

Christians do not keep Sunday because of the Fourth Commandment: we keep it because of the Resurrection. It is not right to call Sunday the "Sabbath". The law of the Sabbath has gone, just as the laws about sacrifices in the Temple have gone.

The Christian Sunday is not the same as the Jewish Sabbath, but God intends us to use it for receiving the benefits which the Sabbath gave to the Jews: e.g., time to worship, to rest, to serve others, to be taught the truth. Above all, on Sundays we rejoice that Jesus has risen and is alive and present with us.

Note: By keeping the Sabbath, the Jews were offering one day out of seven to God as holy. When Christians keep Sunday, they offer not only that day to God as holy, but the other six days and all the work and recreation of the week as well.

54

Mark 3. 7–12 : The Crowds by the Lake

See also Matt. 12. 15–21; Luke 6. 17–19

INTRODUCTION

After the events in the synagogue, Jesus knew that the Pharisees were determined to kill Him. So He went out of the town to the shore of the lake of Galilee. He was faced with three problems:

1. How could He finish His work before He was killed?
2. How could He teach people since all the time they wanted Him to heal their bodies?
3. How could He prevent them from regarding Him as military leader? (See note on v. 11.)

This is another story in which Mark is saying to us, "See here the Son of God overcoming the evil of disease."

NOTES

v. 7. So Jesus went away . . . and a great crowd from Galilee followed . . .

1. **Went away:** If anyone thinks that He went away because He was afraid, he should read 3. 1–6 and see if Jesus was a coward. He left Capernaum in order to finish His work of teaching before His enemies arrested Him (1. 38). Also, the scribes would not have allowed Him to speak in the synagogue there.

2. **Great crowd.** Just at the time when the Pharisees were planning to kill Him, people were travelling on foot to see Him—from Idumea (200 miles away to the south of Jerusalem) and Perea ("the other side of Jordan"). They came from heathen countries (Tyre and Sidon and Perea), as well as from Jewish areas.

The Pharisees reject Him, the people demand Him! Men are always divided into two groups because of Him (see John 7. 43; 12. 9, 20). We choose either to be with Him or to be against Him.

v. 8. Heard what he was doing . . .

They came because of what He had done, not because of what He had said. Men still want to follow Jesus when they see what He has done for people whom they know. When our friends who are not

55

Christians notice that Jesus has made us happier and more unselfish, then they begin to ask how they too can find Him.

Everyone should know what Jesus has done through His Church: e.g., it was Jesus (through His followers) who built the first hospitals, who first cared for lepers, and who stopped the slave-trade.

v. 9. Have a small boat ready . . .

1. So many people wanted to be healed that Jesus found it hard to get a chance to teach. So someone lent Him a little boat. By going a little way from the shore in it, He could speak without interference.

2. The boat was offered to Jesus and He used it; so to-day we make Him our offerings, e.g., of our money, our strength, our minds, and He uses them (11. 7; 14. 14, 15; 15. 46; John 6. 9).

v. 10. All . . . who pressed upon him . . .

Muslims teach that God is so great that He is far above our troubles. The New Testament teaches that God became a man who was pulled and crushed by the crowds. Only a God who loves would have done such a thing. (See note on 1. 33.)

v. 11. Evil spirits . . . shouted loudly, You are the Son of God.

1. **Evil Spirits:** See note on 1. 23.

2. **Son of God:** When the men possessed with evil spirits said this, they were probably calling Jesus "the Messiah". (See note on 1. 1.) They did not know (as we know) that Jesus really was God's own and only Son.

But Jesus did not want anyone to call Him "Messiah" until He had taught them what sort of Messiah He was. If He did not stop their using this name (v. 12), people would think that He was a leader of a rebellion against the Romans.

"They watched Him, so that they might bring a charge against Him." (Mark 3. 2)

South African students publicly protest (at the risk of being arrested themselves) on behalf of 200 African students who had been suspended from Fort Hare University in East Cape Province.

Jesus came into conflict with the authorities because He publicly protested on behalf of others.

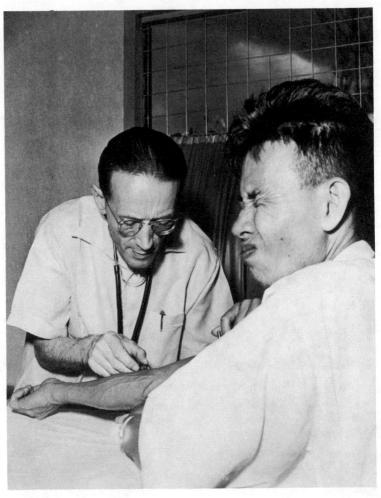

"Why are you so afraid?" (Mark 4. 40)

This patient in Singapore has not yet received his injection from Brother Stanislaus! He is looking like this because he is afraid; he is afraid of the penicillin injection that he needs.

On many occasions fear was the evil from which Jesus offered to set people free.

Mark 3. 13–19a : The Appointment of the Twelve

See also Matt. 10. 1–4, Luke 6. 12–16

INTRODUCTION

Jesus knew that there was only a little time before He would be killed. So He chose a few men to be His companions and workers. The next four chapters show how He trained and taught them. This passage gives the names of those who were chosen.

Mark surely gave us this story to show again that the Christian Church was appointed by Jesus, Son of God.

NOTES

v. 13. He went up the mountain-side, and called to him those that he wanted . . .

1. **Mountain-side:** He went there in order to be away from the crowds. He wanted to think quietly about His work and to plan ways in which others could continue it.

Luke (6. 12) says that He prayed all night. He knew how hard it would be to choose suitable men.

If He could not make wise plans without first asking for God's help, we certainly cannot.

2. **He called:**

a. It was Jesus, the Son of God, who called them, i.e., who founded the body of believers called the Church. This is what makes the Church different from any club or society founded by man.

He invited them: the Twelve did not join together and decide to help Jesus. There were probably a great many who would have gladly gone with Him, but only twelve were chosen (John 15. 16). There are some to-day who believe that they deserve the thanks of Jesus for helping Him in His work. The disciples thought of their work differently: they were very grateful for being chosen.

God could, if He pleased, do His work now without us, but He has invited us to work with Him (Eph. 2. 8–10).

b. It was not a sudden invitation. Several of the men He chose had met Him some months before in Judea (John 1. 35–45). Four had been with Him ever since He found them fishing (1. 6–20).

v. 14a. He appointed twelve . . .

1. Christians do not all agree in their interpretations of these words. All we can say is: a. The "Twelve" were the foundation not only of the ordained ministry, but of the whole Church; what Jesus said to them He says to all Christians; b. most Christians believe that God intends certain people to be "ordained" for special work; c. but we cannot say that this verse speaks of "ordination". The Greek word simply means "appointed" or "made".

2. Who were the Twelve? We are not sure who they were, because Mark and Luke and John do not give exactly the same names. But probably Bartholomew (given by Mark) was the same person as Nathaniel (John 1. 45), and Thaddeus (3. 18) was also called Judas the son of James (Luke 6. 16).

Mark's and Luke's lists of names do not agree, but this does not mean that we cannot trust the Gospels. We can be quite sure that Jesus did found the Church and that He founded it upon men who were like ourselves. These are the important things.

3. Why were there only twelve? It was not by chance that there were twelve, but because there were twelve tribes in Israel. The twelve tribes, who ought to have been the messengers of the Messiah to the world, were rejecting Him; so He laid the foundations of a new Israel by appointing the twelve (Rev. 21. 14). The new Israel is the Christian Church: it is the same Church to which men from *every* nation belong to-day.

4. They were very different from each other. Their trades were different; one had been a tax-collector, four had been fishermen, Simon the Zealot was a member of a society which aimed at the overthrow of the Roman government. They were different also in character. Peter was confident, Thomas was cautious, James and John were violent. They were kept together only because they followed the same Lord.

This is what the Church is like. God has made the members different and surely likes us to remain different. But as soon as we forget to follow Christ, we separate from each other.

v. 14b. To be with him, and to be sent out by him to preach, and to . . . drive out evil spirits.

1. **To be with him:** In order that they should be able to continue His work after He had been killed, they must be with Him. They

were like a carpenter's apprentice: they learnt, by working with Him, to do what He did. People noticed their ways afterwards and said, "These men have been with Jesus" (Acts 4. 13b).

We cannot do His work in the world to-day (such as looking after a family, or working hard and honestly in a factory) unless we also have first "been with Him" in worship and prayer.

2. **To be sent out:** The second reason why Jesus called them was to train them to go out and to continue the work He began. Ever since that day He has been sending out Christians, not only priests and pastors, but everyone. He does His work through us. St Teresa said, "Christ has no body now on earth but yours, no hands but yours, no feet but yours."

3. **To preach:** i.e., to make known by actions as well as by words that God is King.

4. **To drive out evil spirits:** If these words mean curing mad or dumb people, we must confess that Christians have often failed to do it. But the Twelve did it (6. 13) and St Paul (Acts 9. 12). Christian doctors, and others, are now beginning to believe again that this work is God's will for us (see note on 1. 23). But we cannot do it unless first we learn to be "with Him" and in prayer.

v. 16.   To Simon he gave the name Peter. . . .

He gave him the new name "Peter" (which means "rock") to show him that he could with God's help become a rock-like person. And he did so, in spite of failures (Acts 4. 13). (See note on 1. 16.)

v. 17.   Sons of thunder . . .

Probably James and John were called this because they were men of violent nature (9. 38; Luke 9. 54). The Church needs people like this in order to fight against injustice and other evils, but the violence must be controlled. The first Epistle of John shows that John learnt to control this.

v. 18.   Simon the Zealot . . .

He was not from Canaan (as in the A.V.) nor from Cana, but was a member of a society of Jews called the Zealots, who wanted to drive the Romans away by force. Did he continue as a member of this society after he had become one of the Twelve? Mark does not tell us.

v. 19.   Judas Iscariot who betrayed him . . .

1. "Iscariot" means that he came from Kerioth, a village in Judea. All the others came from Galilee. (Possibly they regarded him as a stranger and as a result he was never happy in their company.)

2. Why did Jesus choose Judas? Judas was called for the same reason as the others: because he had the ability to become a faithful leader of the Church. He was free, as we all are; but he made a wrong choice and betrayed Jesus.

Jesus failed in the matter of Judas. Men's sin often spoiled His work (6. 5). But He did not make a mistake when He trusted Judas and gave him the chance of becoming a leader. (See note on 14. 17–21.)

Mark 3. 19b–21 : Jesus' Friends and Relations

INTRODUCTION

In verses 19b to 35 there are three more stories of charges made against Jesus. Not only the scribes, but His own family and friends misunderstood Him.

Mark has given this story to show that only those who had made their own act of faith in Jesus became His followers. Even belonging to His family did not make it easier for a man to believe in Him.

NOTES

v. 21.   His relations came out to seize him; for people were saying, He is out of his mind

1. **His relations:** These people who lived at Nazareth had heard that He had made the Pharisees angry on two Sabbaths and that He was working so hard that He was going without food (v. 20). They thought He must have gone mad. So they began the twenty-eight-mile journey to Capernaum in order to bring Him back to Nazareth and to prevent His travelling any more.

This shows how little they understood what He was trying to do (John 7. 5). The friends of a Christian to-day often try to persuade him to escape from difficult and dangerous tasks. They say, "Take more care of yourself," but he has the strength given by God and will attempt things beyond his own strength.

2. Out of his mind.

a. There are only three ways in which we can speak of Jesus: either i. we, like those friends, regard Him as insane (if so, we do not take any more notice of His teaching); or, ii. we think He was a deceiver (if so, we ought to prevent the spread of His teaching); or iii. He was truly the Son of God. (If so, we shall adore and serve Him with all our heart.)

b. Many Christians who have made great sacrifices or attempted new ways of serving Christ have been called "mad". Paul was called mad (Acts 26. 24). So was St Francis, when he gave away all his money and wore the clothes of a beggar in order to serve the poorest people. So was Dr Albert Schweitzer when he left his university lecturing in Europe and started a hospital which still serves the people of Gabon.

Mark 3. 22–30 : The Sin Against the Holy Spirit

See also Matt. 12. 22–32; Luke 11. 14–23

INTRODUCTION

Some scribes now travelled from Jerusalem to find out ways of stopping the work of Jesus. As some of His own friends were calling Him mad, they made use of this saying and told the people that He was full of an evil spirit. So He boldly invited them to come and see Him.

This is another story which speaks of the power of Jesus to overcome evil. (See note on v. 23.)

NOTES

v. 22.   Possessed by Beelzebub . . .

The scribes were in a difficulty. (See Additional Note, p. 43.) If they said that He was healing people with God's help, they would have to believe in Him and change their ways, but they were not willing to do this. So they said that Jesus did His miracles with the help of evil spirits, i.e., by Beelzebub.

Beelzebub, also called Beelzebul, was the name of a heathen god: it is not certain if it was a name for Satan. But clearly the scribes meant by it "the powers of evil".

Note: Although they criticized Jesus, they freely admitted that He had done miracles. Those who to-day doubt if the miracle-stories are true should notice this.

v. 23. How can Satan drive out Satan?

1. This means, "Use your common sense in talking about right and wrong. A thief cannot steal from himself!" He then gave two short parables or proverbs to explain this: the first (vv. 24–26) about the Divided Kingdom, the second (v. 27) about the Divided House.

2. It is never possible to drive away evil by evil means. Yet parents often try by anger to stop the anger of their children; and one nation accuses another nation of cruelty and tries to drive away that cruelty by war. But war makes everyone more cruel: it never takes cruelty away (see Rom. 12. 21).

3. "Driving away Satan" was the aim of Jesus. His work was a battle against a strong enemy who never slept. This battle is still going on, and those who follow Christ share in it.

v. 25. If a kingdom is divided against itself . . .

Satan, says Jesus, cannot be fighting against himself. If he were, he would have been destroyed long ago.

This saying is used to describe a person who is divided: e.g., one part of him wants to do right and the other part to do wrong (Rom. 7. 19). A congregation can also become divided (Gal. 5. 15). A divided person or congregation is very greatly weakened, but God can give unity to both.

v. 27. No one can enter a strong man's house . . .

This is the second parable. The strong man is Satan, and the one who binds him is Jesus.

62

v. 28. All their sins shall be forgiven the sons of men . . .

Sons of men means all people. There are only two occasions when we cannot receive God's forgiveness: when we are not sorry, and when we refuse to forgive others (1 John 1. 7, 9).

v. 29. Whoever blasphemes against the Holy Spirit, is never forgiven. He is guilty of an everlasting sin.

1. **Against the Holy Spirit**

a. The scribes had seen the good deeds of Jesus, who was filled with the Holy Spirit, but they said they were the deeds of the Devil. So they were in danger of committing sin against the Holy Spirit, the sin of calling evil good and good evil: e.g., Mr A. makes a generous present to the Church, but Mr B. says "He gave it in order that others should praise him." Mr B. is really saying, "The spirit in Mr A. was not the Holy Spirit", and that is denying, blaspheming, or slandering the Spirit.

b. But when Jesus said this, He was not thinking of a single deed or word of blasphemy. Blasphemy against the Spirit is what a man has allowed his whole nature to become: it is one's habit of mind.

It is possible to get this habit gradually. At first a man knows clearly what is good and what is bad. Then he does what is bad and persuades himself that it was good. Then he begins to think that it really was good. Finally he no longer knows the difference between good and evil. This habit is the blasphemy against the Holy Spirit (Isa. 5. 20).

2. **Never forgiven**

a. If anyone has become unable to see the difference between good and evil, he cannot be forgiven. This is not because God does not want to forgive him, but because he has become unable to repent. Repentance is changing from evil ways to good ways; but if evil and good are the same to someone, how can he change?

b. It is possible for the soul of such a man to die, being guilty of everlasting sin. (See Jas 1. 15; 1 John 5. 16; Heb. 6, 6; 10. 26.) But note that Jesus did not say that they had been guilty of everlasting sin. His words mean that they were in danger of committing it.

Note: Some people are afraid that they have sinned against the Holy Ghost, i.e., have committed an everlasting sin. But if they are

63

troubled in conscience in this way, it shows that they are *not* guilty of this sin. It is only those who no longer have a conscience who can be guilty of it.

Mark 3. 31–35 : The True "Family" of Jesus

See also Matt. 12. 46–50; Luke 8. 19–21

INTRODUCTION

The relations who left Nazareth must have reached Capernaum after a day's journey (v. 21). They went to the house where Jesus was, but there were so many people that they had to send a message to Him. But He knew why they had come and so He explained why He could not accompany them (v. 35).

NOTES

v. 31.   His mother and his brothers.

Most probably the "brothers" of Jesus were the sons of Mary and Joseph born after the birth of Jesus. (See note on 6. 3.) If so, Mary was a virgin when Jesus was born, but married afterwards.

Note: Those who believe that Mary was *always* a virgin say that these men were the cousins of Jesus or that they were sons of Joseph by a former wife who died before he married Mary. They remind us that in Palestine (as in many countries of Asia and Africa today) the word "brother" could be used for cousins.

v. 35.   If anyone does the will of God, he is my brother and sister and mother.

1. *Jesus and His family:* of course Jesus does not despise His family. John (19. 26, 27) shows His care for His mother, which has been an example to all Christians. Leaders in the Church to-day know that one of the best ways of serving the Church is by caring for their own families.

2. *The two families:* This verse means that He cared as much for everyone who "did the will of God" as for His own mother. In

this way He did not neglect His own relations but treated them as part of the much bigger family, i.e., the Great Family of those who do God's will.

There are two families to which all Christians belong; the one into which we are born (our "natural" family) and the Great Family of the Church (our "spiritual" family into which we enter at Baptism.) We do not serve our natural family any less when we begin to serve the Great Family.

3. *Which takes first place?* Sometimes, in order to serve the Great Family, it is right to put the natural family into second place. Jesus did this, and many times it must have given pain to His mother and relations and therefore to Himself also. (Luke 2. 35.) Most women who leave their homes to work as missionaries overseas give pain to their mothers. Yet much work in God's Church is done by such people.

4. *The Great Family.* When Jesus called everyone who does God's will His brothers, He made one new Great Family, in which He is the Elder Brother (Heb. 2. 11b). In this family, the Church, we take care of the other members because they really *are* our brothers; they are not just *like* brothers! (Gal. 3. 28). When Christians in one country send help to those in another country (as in Rom. 15. 26), they are showing this by deed.

5. *Who belongs?* It is those who do God's will who belong to this Great Family, not those who are members in name only (Luke 11. 28; Matt. 7. 21–27).

Mark 4. 1–9 : The Parable of the Harvest

See also Matt. 13. 1–9; Luke 8. 4–8

INTRODUCTION

This chapter of parables:

In chaps. 2 and 3 Mark gave us stories of how Jesus was persecuted by His enemies and even rejected by His friends; and those who first read this read it with great interest, because they themselves were being persecuted. Now in chap. 4, vv. 1–35, Mark has collected together a group of parables in which Jesus gave encouragement to all who follow Him.

This parable (vv. 1–9)

a. Jesus was once again surrounded by such crowds that He had to get into a boat and go out a little way from the land. V. 1 says that He "sat down" to teach: this was probably because He wanted to talk as one friend talks to another, not as a lecturer to his pupils. Perhaps there was a piece of land, near the lake, which was being sown by the farmer as He was speaking (v. 3), and which everyone could see.

b. The teaching of this parable is about Jesus' own work, and especially His parables. It shows that although some rejected His teaching and parables, others were accepting them. It teaches that His work will be wonderfully successful in the end. The successful harvest in v. 8 is the important part of the parable. (So we call it the parable of the harvest rather than the parable of the sower.)

c. Mark gives us an explanation of this parable in chap. 4. 13–20. For this reason, notes on certain verses (vv. 4, 5, 7) will be found under that section.

NOTES

v. 2. He taught them . . . in parables.

See Additional Note p. 68.

v. 4. Some seed fell . . . (also v. 5 and v. 7).

Jesus taught great truths by talking about ordinary things that men saw every day. (This is one difference between parables and fables or fairy-tales.) Especially He talked about things that God has made to grow. It was as if He said, "The same God who made these made you also; you can learn about God and yourselves by looking at them." It is a pity to think of Religious Knowledge as separate from Nature Study just because they are separated on school time-tables. Jesus used Nature Study in order to teach Religious Knowledge.

v. 8.   Some fell on good soil . . . and produced a fine crop.

1. **Good soil:** The sower got his good crop only where the soil was good, i.e., nourishing the seeds. So God sows the seed of His good news amongst us, but He never forces anyone to accept it against his will. But when men co-operate with God, evil is overcome.

In a town many years ago, where the drains were very bad, a number of people fell ill with typhoid fever and some died. Many people said, "Why does not God stop this sickness?" The vicar of the town (Charles Kingsley) said, "God will not stop this sickness until the men in the town work with Him and build new drains," and until the owners of the houses did so, he refused to pray publicly for good health.

2. **A fine crop:** This stands for the success of Christ's work. Although much preaching has been rejected, His work and that of His Church will be successful (see Isa. 55. 11; John 4. 35; 1 Cor. 15. 58). There will be a wonderful harvest (as the figures 30, 60, and 100 show), at least in a part of the farm.

We are given courage by the parable. All Christians are tempted to think that, because they often fail, they are losing the battle against evil. The clergy may complain that they have been put among difficult people; parents are troubled about their children's faults; a boy feels that the temptation to be dishonest is never going to be overcome, But all such people can be encouraged by seeing that, in the story, success in one part of the farm is success, though other parts fail. Jesus Himself had no greater success than this.

v. 9.   He that has ears to hear, let him hear.

1. Jesus says: "I did not tell you this story only to interest you. There is teaching inside it and some of you will be able to 'hear' and receive it."

Note: Jesus more often taught that men must "hear" than that they must speak.

2. A man who "hears" Jesus' message is one who receives it in two ways: a. he lets it come into his mind and he *thinks* deeply about it; b. he allows it to change his way of *living*. He is like the good soil (v. 8) which allowed the seed to go deep down inside it and to send out roots in many directions.

As Jesus says, many of us have not yet got "ears to hear", i.e., we listen to the Gospel but do not let it enter us to change us. It is not enough to read the Bible or to listen to a sermon or to memorize a Bible passage in school. Reading, listening, and memorizing are like buying food. The food is of no value to us until we bring it home and eat it. We "hear" when we let Jesus' teaching go deep down inside us (Ps. 95. 7, 8).

ADDITIONAL NOTE

PARABLES

1. *The meaning of "parable"*

The word "parable" is used for sayings like proverbs and also for stories. An example of a proverb is "No one sews new cloth on an old cloak" (2. 21).

2. *Central teaching*

Each parable contains *one* great central piece of teaching. So the first task, after reading a parable, is to ask, "What single lesson does this teach?" The answer usually concerns: a. what God is like; or b. what He wants us to do.

Thus a parable is different from an "allegory". (See Notes on 12. 1–12.) In an allegory there are many parts, and every part teaches a separate lesson. We go wrong if we interpret a parable as if it were an allegory. Mark in 13. 34 gives a little parable, telling of a man who went away and left his servants to look after his house until he came back. Its central teaching is that we must be ready for the coming of Jesus. But it is not an allegory, and it would be quite wrong to say, for instance, that the owner of that house is God. (That might make people think, wrongly, that God goes away from us.)

3. *Why did Jesus use parables?*

a. To teach a lesson clearly, and in such a way that it should be remembered easily.

b. To persuade the hearers to think for themselves what His teaching was. That is why He sometimes put it in the form of a question, e.g., "How can Satan drive out Satan?" (3. 23).

c. To persuade listeners to change their own behaviour (Luke 10. 37).

d. To separate those who had come for instruction from those who had only come to see a miracle. (See notes on 4. 10–12.)

4. *What was in the mind of Jesus?*

The important thing is to try to discover what Jesus Himself wanted to teach the people who were present when He told a parable. We should ask, "To whom was this parable told? What was happening in that country at that time?" This is what we have tried to do in the Introduction to the parable of the harvest (p. 65). If we paid no attention to the events of that time, we might think that that parable taught nothing more than, "Listen carefully to Christian instruction".

Mark 4. 10–12 : Parables Divide People

See also Matt. 13. 10–15; Luke 8. 9, 10

INTRODUCTION

These verses are about the difference between the followers of Jesus and "those outside". His followers (like Christians of to-day) were not better than others, but they followed a better Master, and they were divided from others in this way. One reason why Jesus told His parables was to separate those who sincerely followed Him from those who only came to see Him do a wonderful cure.

NOTES

v. 11. **To you is given the secret of the kingdom of God; but to those outside everything comes in parables . . .**

1. **The secret:** This means the good news that the rule of God over men's hearts has already begun to come.
Note: It is called a secret because only those who have begun to follow Jesus can understand it (John 7. 17); His followers have the task of passing the secret on to others. (See notes on 4. 21–25.)

2. **To those outside . . . in parables:** This does not mean that Jesus

used parables to teach only those outside. He taught His disciples also by parables (Mark 13. 33, 34).

v. 12.   In parables, so that they may look and yet not see . . .

1. Did Jesus intend to hide His meaning from some listeners? It is possible that Mark himself found the parables so hard to understand that he thought Jesus did not mean them to be understood. But vv. 21-22, show that Jesus wanted *everyone* to understand His teaching. He used parables, as other Jewish teachers did, to make things clear.

2. **That they may . . . not see . . . :** These words are from Isa. 6. 9. Isaiah was possibly so distressed at the number of people who were likely to refuse God's teaching, that he thought that God intended them to refuse it. But the New Testament does not say this (see 1 Tim. 2. 4).

God did not intend certain people to reject Jesus. It is true that people sin; God knew long ago that they would do so. But He never forced or wanted them to sin. We are free to choose between right and wrong.

What did Jesus mean when He used Isaiah's words? Perhaps He meant this: "When I tell parables, a few accept the teaching, and many reject it. And the more I teach, the more they reject me. This is what happened to Isaiah (whose words about disbelievers you all know). I intend my parables to be a means by which sincere people are divided from the insincere."

Mark 4. 13-20 : Interpretation of the Parable of the Harvest

See also Matt. 13. 16-23; Luke 8. 11-15

INTRODUCTION

Here Mark gives an account of Jesus explaining the parables of the harvest.

We have already seen, in the Introduction to vv. 1-9, that the most important part of this parable is the success which the farmer had in the end. We have seen that the teaching is: "God's work will succeed!"

In reading vv. 13–20 we notice a strange thing: we see that more attention is given to the soil than to the farmer, i.e., the lesson that people must listen is emphasized more than the lesson that God will be successful. It is not certain why this change from vv. 1–8 has taken place, but it is clear that Jesus' chief message through the parable was "God's work will succeed, although many refuse to listen and accept."

NOTES

v. 15 (and v. 4). Those on the path . . . when they hear, at once Satan comes . . .

1. **On the path:** The path through the farmland is made so hard by people's footsteps that if seeds fall on it, they do not go into the soil. In the same way, Jesus' teaching is never received by those who are "hardened", e.g., a man, especially an ordained minister, may have heard verses from the Bible so often that he is hardly able to receive any of their message; the people of a whole country can grow into a habit so that they forget that it is a bad one: custom has hardened them.

2. **Satan comes:** This happens because the forces of Evil are actively trying to prevent us from following Jesus. (See note on 1. 13.)

v. 16 (and v. 5). On stony ground . . .

"Stony" ground is the soil which is good, but shallow, because of the solid rock which is near the surface. The seed goes in, but cannot send down roots. A man may be like this: he accepts the teaching of Jesus joyfully, but he does not seriously think about it. So he is not prepared for difficulties, for temptations, or for the ridicule of his friends, or for persecution by his enemies. When these come, he loses faith in Jesus.

v. 18 (and v. 7). Among thorns . . .

Thorns (and other tall weeds) prevent a small plant from growing, by taking the nourishment from the ground and keeping the sunlight away. So a man's soul may be so crowded with other things that there is no chance for him to receive the light and nourishment of the Gospel. V. 19 says these things are a. worry; i.e., fearing about what may happen in the future (when we do this we are not trusting Jesus in the present). b. money; e.g., the wish to have power over other people by means of money, c. desires for other things, i.e., for anything at all which makes us forget Jesus.

In the old days Christians often had no recreations, except to attend the services and meetings of the Church. Now, especially in towns, there are many other things to do. We have to decide whether we shall make room for the worship of Jesus or allow these other things to take first place. (See Matt. 6. 24, 33; 13. 45; Phil. 3. 8.)

v. 20.   A good crop:

See note on v. 8. God will not be defeated: take courage!

Mark 4. 21–25 : The Parable of the Lamp

See also Matt. 5. 14–16; 13.12; Luke 8. 16–18

INTRODUCTION

The main lesson here is that those who have "heard" the teaching of Jesus must share it with others. Vv. 21–23 are a short parable; vv. 24, 25 contain two proverbs.

NOTES

v. 21.   Is a lamp . . . put under a bowl . . .?

Unless a little oil-lamp is put high upon a stand, it is not of much use in the house. No one except a madman would carefully light one of these lamps at night, and cover it with a large bowl or hide it under a wooden bed! But this is just what the Jews were doing with the message God had given them through the Prophets. They had kept it to themselves and had not tried to bring other nations to repentance (see Jonah 3. 10—4. 1; Matt. 23. 13).

72

1. God expects us who are Christians to share the Gospel with those who are not. We shall not be content merely to enjoy God's blessings; we shall not make the mistake of thinking that they were given to us as a reward for our goodness (Matt. 10. 8).

2. If we are living the way that Jesus wants, others will notice that this way is different from their own. A group of Christians who live together in fellowship, serving and forgiving one another, become a light that cannot be hidden (Matt. 5. 14–16).

But sometimes we hide our light. The manager of a large factory said recently (concerning one political party in his country), "If a member of that party comes to work here, everyone soon knows what party he belongs to; but sometimes a Church-member comes to work and it is many months before anyone knows that he is a Christian."

v. 22. Nothing is kept secret except to be brought to light.

In v. 11 Jesus said that He had given the disciples a "secret". He called it a "secret" or "mystery", because the "Good News" was at that time only known to those few people who had "ears" that could hear it (v. 9). But this verse shows that the secret must now be made known to everyone who will listen (Eph. 3. 4–6; Col. 1. 26).

v. 24. The measure you give, will be the measure you get . . .

This does not mean that if we are kind to others, they will be kind to us. (No one was ever as kind as Jesus, but men killed Him.) Nor does it mean that if we give money generously to the Church, God is sure to give us success in business.

Its teaching is that it is those who make use of God's gifts who are able to receive more gifts. (See also Matt. 25. 14–30.) If we pass on to others what we understand of the Gospel, we shall begin to understand it better ourselves.

Giving is not losing (Matt. 10. 39b)! An English congregation was in debt and the roof of the vestry was leaking. A new minister was appointed. At this first meeting with the people he asked them to collect £100 and to send it to some very poor churches in India. The people were not at all sure if they could do this as well as paying their own debts, but they agreed, and began to raise the money for India. By the end of eighteen months they had not only collected the £100, but had paid off their own debt and had mended the roof and begun to build another church in the neighbourhood. They had caught the spirit of giving generously and in faith.

v. 25a. Whoever has, shall be given more;

The teaching of these words is like that of v. 24. Those who take the trouble to search out the meaning of Jesus' words will become more able to understand it. Those who use opportunities for doing good are given more opportunities.

The words do *not* teach that a rich man is right to make still more money for himself or that a rich country is right to grab other countries in order to become richer.

v. 25b. Whoever has not, shall lose what he has.

Perhaps Jesus was thinking of His parables when He first said this. Those who did not try to "hear" them might slowly lose the power to "hear" them. This is true of our bodies. If we lie still on a bed for several months and then get up, we find that at first we cannot walk. In the same way, if we never pray or pray very little indeed, we gradually lose the desire to pray. If we pay no attention to our conscience, we slowly lose the power to know what is right and what is wrong.

Mark 4. 26–29 : The Parable of the Seed Growing of Itself

INTRODUCTION

The message of this parable is like the message of the parable of the harvest in vv. 1–9. It is one of encouragement.

1. The farmer's crop grows more through the life that God gives it than by his own work: "He does not know how" (v. 27); "by itself" (v. 28). So the coming of God's complete victory over evil is in God's hands rather than in yours. Work hard for God, but leave the results with Him.

2. The farmer who has sown seed gathers in the harvest in the

end. So God, Who has already begun to overcome evil in the world, will certainly complete His victory one day.

Note: The words, "The Kingdom of God is like this", mean that this is the way in which the Kingdom of God comes.

NOTES

v. 27. Grows up, he does not know how.

Many Jews were impatient with God, and wanted to use violence to make all men obey Him as King. Some of us to-day, also, worry because we do not know how God can ever overcome all evil. That is why Jesus told this story.

Farmers know that when they have sown, and kept the ground free of weeds, there is very little they can do to make the seed grow. The matter is in God's hands. They trust *Him* to give the seeds life (Luke 17. 20).

Many parents know that, when they are troubled about one of their children, it is much better to pray for that child, that God will make him grow up well, than to rebuke him continually.

William Carey was forty years in India before a single man became a Christian as a result of his work. During that time he did not despair. He knew that God would make the seed grow secretly.

We must do our share of the work, but success is in God's hands.

v. 28. The earth bears crops of itself, first a blade, then a head . . .

1. **Of itself:** This does not teach that the earth will produce food without man's work. Nor that the earth has power in itself to produce anything, for all life comes from God, both in plants and in men. The teaching is the same as in v. 27—that God is in control.

2. **First a blade, then a head . . . :** This describes how "corn" (of the sort referred to in 2. 23) develops. The teaching is not that the world is gradually getting better and better, until finally God's rule will appear. It means that God Himself never ceases to work to complete His victory over evil, and is bringing it about step by step.

v. 29. He puts in the reaping-hook because the harvest has come.

At harvest the corn was cut with a sickle, just as grass is cut for thatching. At this time:

1. Useless weeds are separated from good corn. In the same way,

when God's Kingdom comes, and His victory over evil is complete, it will be a time of separation: it will be judgement between those who accepted Jesus and those who rejected Him. Joel 3. 13 (whose words Jesus used in this verse) says this. (See also Matt. 13. 39, 40; Rev. 14. 14–20.)

2. The good corn is put into a barn. This is the end of a long preparation, and a time of rejoicing. The complete victory of God over evil will be a time of very great rejoicing.

Mark 4. 30–32 : The Parable of the Mustard-Seed

See also Matt. 13. 31, 32; Luke 13. 18, 19.

INTRODUCTION

The disciples were disappointed when so many people refused to follow Jesus. They had perhaps hoped that He would overcome all His enemies with armies of angels from heaven. So Jesus told this story to show that, although God's Kingdom was small at the beginning, it would be very great in the end.

NOTES

v. 23.   It . . . grows to be the largest of all plants . . .

1. Jesus spoke about a mustard-seed because the Jews used to say "as small as a mustard-seed", and this seed grows into a plant about 6 ft high.

2. Although He encouraged the disciples with this parable and taught that the little group of followers would one day be a great Church, they must have found it hard to believe, but some had faith and did believe Him. We to-day ought to find it easier to believe than they did; we have seen those Twelve become a Church which is now in every part of the world; we know, for instance, that in Uganda, where a few Africans were baptized in the year 1880, there are now more than a million Church-members.

3. Not all small things become great. It is only a good mustard-seed that becomes a large plant. If we want a great Church in a country, it is better to have one or two men who have really devoted

themselves to God than a large group who are only partly trusting Him. But one man reading this chapter of Mark and allowing it to alter his life, can be used by God to do *great* things.

Mark 4. 33, 34 : Some Words About Parables

See also Matt. 13. 34, 35

NOTES

v. 33. With many parables like these he spoke to them the word, as they could hear it.

1. **Like these:** This shows that Jesus told many more parables than are written down.

2. **As they could hear it:** Jesus used parables because that was the best way in which people could understand His teaching.

a. Christians must be continually looking for the methods by which people can "hear" and understand the message of the Church. The methods that were good in our grandfather's day or in another country may not be the best ones for us to use.

b. In order to speak to people in the way they can understand, we must first know their deepest needs. That is what Jesus did.

v. 34. Without a parable he said nothing to them . . .

This means that most of His teaching was done by parables. It does not mean that He never spoke without using a parable. (See note 3, on 4. 2 for the reasons why Jesus used parables.)

Mark 4. 35–41 : The Storm on the Lake

See also Matt. 8. 23–27; Luke 8. 22–25

INTRODUCTION

At this stage Jesus went on a journey. Mark says that He did four miracles on this journey: this is the first of them. By telling us that

Jesus controlled the wind, Mark is showing that Jesus did what only God can do.

Note: The miracles in previous chapters have been cures of sick people: this miracle was controlling "nature". (See Additional Note, p. 26.)

NOTES

v. 35.   Let us cross over to the other side.

The other side means the east side of the lake. He planned to go there in order to be quiet after the work among crowds, and to rest. (See notes on 1. 35–39.)

v. 37.   A great storm of wind arose . . .

The lake of Galilee has mountains on both sides of it. So when the wind sweeps down from the north, it has no way of escape, and, for a time, it stirs up the water violently. Often this happens without warning. Although the disciples were accustomed to these storms (being fishermen), they knew also how easily boats could be overturned by the huge waves, and the occupants drowned.

v. 38.   He was . . . asleep on the cushion. So they . . . said to him, Master, we are lost. Do you not care?

1. **Asleep:** Jesus was tired. He was Son of God, but at the same time He was a real man and became tired as we do.

2. **The cushion:** This was the leather seat on which the man who steered the boat usually sat. It is interesting that Mark tells us such a small detail as this. It shows that the story was told to him by someone who was present in the boat (Peter): we know that what we are reading is true.

3. **Master:** They used to call Him "Rabbi" (which meant "Teacher" or "Master"), because it was as a teacher that they thought of Him. They did not at this time know that He was God Himself. But we know who He is, and it is better for us to use the name "Lord" for Jesus, rather than "Master" or "Teacher".

4. **We are lost:** They were afraid of being drowned and so they prayed to Him. (See note 1, on v. 40.) It is much better to pray when we are afraid than not to pray at all; but may God save us from being like those who never pray except when they are afraid!

78

5. **Do you not care?** In their fear the disciples actually accused Jesus of a lack of love.

v. 39.   Silence, be quiet. And the wind fell . . .

We ask, "Did the words of Jesus cause the wind to fall?" Some say, "No". They think that Jesus cured sick people, but did not stop the storm. The wind, they say, happened to fall just as He was speaking. But surely we cannot say what Jesus could do or what He could not do. He had in Him the power of God, the same God who created the world and who still gives it its life to-day. Who are we to say that He had power to cure the sick, but not to stop the wind? *Note:* Jesus used exactly the same words, "Be quiet", when driving out a demon in 1. 25 as He used here; in both cases He by His power brought peace.

Jesus did what everyone knew God Himself did, namely, He controlled the wind. When the first Christians read this, they surely thought of Ps. 89. 9; 107. 29. So Jesus *is* God. (But the story does not, of course, *prove* that He is God. It is when we have already and for other reasons believed that He is God, that this story supports our belief.)

v. 40.   Why are you so afraid? Have you no faith yet?

a. Jesus meant, "You would not be afraid if you had trust in God". Here Jesus shows how we can get rid of our fear. Most people are afraid, e.g., of bodily pain, or the hatred of others, or loneliness, or death. Most bad things are caused by fear: most wars are due to fear: many people become sick in body because they are afraid; most of our unhappiness is caused by our fears. But our fears can be overcome if we really believe that God will never neglect us in any circumstances. (See Isa. 26. 3; Deut. 33. 27; Luke 12. 7–12.)

b. This does not mean that if a man trusts God enough, he will never be drowned at sea or killed in an accident. It means that he will not be afraid of being drowned or being killed, because he knows that he will continue to be in God's care, even after death. (See Ps. 23. 4, 6.)

c. Jesus had peace and courage because: i. He knew that if He died, He would still be in God's safe hands; ii. God would not let Him die as long as He had work for Him to do on earth.

2. **No faith:** See note on p. 173 on the "blindness" and lack of

faith in the disciples. Jesus rebuked them. Yet it encourages us to see that He accepted them and patiently made them into trustful and useful servants of God.

v. 41.   They were very much afraid . . .

1. The "fear" spoken of here is different from the fear in v. 40. Here it means "awe" or a feeling of smallness in the presence of something very great and wonderful. They said, "Who can He be?" (See also 6. 50; 9. 6; 10. 32; 16. 8; Luke 5. 8.)

2. If a Christian has *this* kind of fear, he will be able to get rid of the other kind. It was said about John Calvin, "He feared God so much that he feared nothing else at all".

See picture facing p. 57.

Mark 5. 1–20 : The Madman of Gerasa

See also Matt. 8. 28–34; Luke 8. 26–39

INTRODUCTION

The story

It is hard to say exactly what happened, but the events may have been as follows:

Jesus went over to the eastern side of the lake to be quiet, but found there this very violent madman. He said, "Come out, you evil spirit" (v. 8), but the man was not immediately cured. He then said, "What is your name?" and the man said that he was not one person but many (v. 9). By this time those looking after a herd of pigs had left them unattended and had come to see what was happening. Then, in the moment before he was finally cured, the madman made violent actions and shouted wildly, and the pigs were so terrified that they ran down a steep hill and were drowned. But the man was now cured. The news of the death of the pigs reached the town and people asked Jesus to go away. As He was going, He told the man to go back to his own family.

The above may be a true account of what took place, but there are many questions about these events which Mark does not answer, e.g., where did it happen; how did the man know Jesus' name? These, however, are not the important parts of the story.

Why Mark tells us the story

The chief reason why Mark has put this story into his Gospel is that it shows two things: a. Jesus had such power of God in Him that He cured a madman; b. God by the same power is able to-day to set us free from our worst fears and sins and habits. (See note on v. 13.)

NOTES

v. 1. The country of the Gerasenes

1. Jesus came here, the eastern side of the lake, to be quiet and to help His disciples to get away from the crowds (1. 35). But v. 2 says that as soon as they got out of the boat, the madman approached. They did not get even one minute of quietness or rest.

2. Some accounts say "Gadarenes" and others "Gergesenes". We do not know exactly where the event took place. But if one goes to Galilee to-day one can still see on that side of the lake a steep slope near a place called Kersa, and perhaps that was the place.

v. 4. He had often before been fastened with irons . . .

Mark tells us this to show how violent the man was, so that we could see how very great is the power of Jesus who overcame him.

1. In the old days people did not know what to do with mad people, except to put chains on them. Even to-day, after the Holy Spirit has been working amongst us for nineteen hundred years, we sometimes ridicule or treat cruelly those who are sick in mind.

2. They had failed to cure this man by force. Force can restrain people, but we can only help them to become better by loving them. Jesus cured this man by loving him.

v. 6. Fell down before him . . .

He did not worship Jesus, but threw himself down at His feet.

v. 7. What business have you with me, Jesus, Son of God most high?

See notes on 1. 24. (This madman was probably not a Jew since the country on the east of the lake was inhabited by pagans: if they had been Jews, they would not have kept pigs.)

v. 9.   My name is Troops, for there are many of us.

1. **My name:** He thought that if he told his real name to a stranger that person would have power over him. (In the New Testament "name" usually means "power" (John 14. 13). But Jesus had power to cure him without knowing his real name.)

2. **Troops:** The word was really Legion, a body of about 5,000 men in the Roman army. Why did he call himself "Legion"? He may have felt that he had a number of minds, not one mind. Each mind told him to do something different, as if he was a number of soldiers without an officer to direct them. Insane people often do feel that.

This man is a parable of all who are divided in Spirit: part of them wants to do right and part wants to do wrong (Rom. 7. 18, 19). When they let Jesus take control they become "whole" and no longer divided.

v. 10.   The spirits begged him . . .

Some will ask, "Do spirits really exist or is this only a way of saying that the sick man begged Him?" (See note on 1. 23.)

v. 13.   He gave them leave. And the evil spirits went out of the man into the pigs . . .

1. **Gave them leave:** i.e., allowed them to go into the pigs.

a. When Jesus began to cure the man there were no pigs nearby. They appeared suddenly, and were frightened by the man's actions. It was too late now to stop them rushing away into the lake. Perhaps it was in this way that Jesus "allowed it to happen".

b. But surely He did not intentionally destroy the pigs. He was not the sort of person who destroyed other people's property. It is also wrong to say that He, being a Jew, regarded pigs as unclean, and therefore wished to get rid of them. We can see from 7. 19 that Jesus did not think in this way. (But see note on v. 17.)

2. **The evil spirits went out:** These are the important words of the story. It was the power of God in Jesus which cured the man, and we know that God can take away our evil passions and pride and greed, as well as sickness of the mind and body. An old prayer

82

says, "Though we be tied and bound with the chain of our sins, yet let the pitifulness of Thy great mercy loose us". (See Additional Note, p. 26.)

3. **Into the pigs:** The evil which had been in the man sent the pigs rushing to their death. This is a reminder that evil works in and through living beings, and that it is an active enemy. It is not just an "absence of goodness".

v. 17. They begged him to leave . . .

The townsmen were *afraid* of Jesus because of His strange power, and *angry* because of the loss of their pigs, from which they made their money.

1. They were so troubled about the loss of the pigs that they seem to have forgotten about the cure of the madman, but to Jesus a man was more important than an animal or any other sort of property (see Luke 12. 7b).

Some years ago it was found that men who were employed to make and paint pots in one large pottery nearly always suffered from a certain disease. Soon it was proved that the disease was caused by the paint which made these pots especially valuable. The owners of the pottery were good men and said, "Although we make our profits from painting these pots, it is more important to keep the men healthy. We will use no more of this paint until it can be used without harming the men." People matter more than our property or profits.

2. This is only one of many times that people begged Jesus to go away. (See Luke 5. 8.) Men could not bear to have Jesus near them, because He was holy and they were not. Probably we *ought* to feel this more often than we do, for God is indeed holy. If we have never wanted to escape from God, is it perhaps because we have never met God Himself? Have we been worshipping a god which we have created for ourselves: a god that is not very different from ourselves?

v. 19. Go home . . . and tell them all the things that the Lord has done for you . . .

The man was told to do three things. God to-day calls all Christians to do these same things:

1. **Go home:** i.e., to go to his family and friends before going to

others. If we have been helped by Jesus, these are the first people we should tell, so that they can be helped too.

2. **Lord has done:** i.e., to speak about the things that God had done. We sometimes think that people are made better by being told to obey God; but really it is the stories of what God has done (as described in the Bible) and is still doing, that make men love Him and obey Him. One Easter Day a preacher fell ill just before the sermon, and his assistant, having no time to prepare a sermon, just told the story of Luke 24 without adding anything. Someone said afterwards, "That was the best sermon we've had this year."

3. **For you:** to speak of his *own* joy. If we can tell people not only how God has helped others, but how He has changed *us*, they pay special attention.

Note: Usually Jesus said, "Tell no one", (1. 44) but this was pagan, not Jewish, country, and so there was no need to tell the man to keep silent.

v. 20. In Decapolis . . .

This was a group of ten towns, inhabited not by Jews, but by pagans. All of them, except one, were on the east side of the river Jordan.

Mark 5. 21–24 : The Request of Jairus

See also Matt. 8. 18; Luke 8. 40–42

INTRODUCTION

The men of Gerasa had asked Him go to away, and Jesus now returned to the west side of the lake. Here, says Luke, the "people had all been waiting for Him". Note that this story is broken off at v. 25 and is continued at v. 35.

NOTES

v. 22. A leader in one of the meeting-houses, Jairus . . . fell at his feet . . .

1. Jairus was not a priest, but the leader of the council of one of

the synagogues. Thus he was an important man in Capernaum, and belonged to a group which was against Jesus. But he fell at His feet and kept on begging Him for help.

2. What made him go to Jesus? First, his trouble. When people who do not pay much attention to God are in great trouble, they often pray to Him. Then they find that He has all the time been ready to help them. Secondly, his daughter. It was because he loved her that he came to Jesus (v. 23). Many parents have begun coming to Jesus (in prayer) for the reason that they love their children and want to set them a good example. It is only later that they pray because they know the goodness of God and want to praise Him for His own sake.

v. 23. Come and lay your hands on her . . .

See note on 8. 23 about this way of healing.

v. 24. Jesus went with him . . .

1. Jesus had to have great faith in His Father's power in order to go to the house of a girl who was already dying.

2. He had to put on one side His own plans and leave the crowds who were ready to hear Him. (In the same way a woman who had just completed her training to be Matron at a London hospital suddenly gave up the work, because her mother fell ill and she believed that God wanted her to look after her instead.)

3. He was going to help one of the synagogue leaders although they were trying to stop His work (see Rom. 12. 21; 1 Pet. 3. 8, 9).

Mark 5. 25–34 : The Woman with a Flow of Blood

See also Matt. 9. 20–22; Luke 8. 43–48.

INTRODUCTION

As Jesus was walking towards Jairus' house, a sick woman in the crowd touched His clothes. He did not know who had touched Him, but He knew power had gone from Him. She was cured. When He found her, He said she had been cured because of her faith.

Mark has given us this story to show again the power of Jesus over evil. (See note on v. 29.)

NOTES

v. 25. Flow of blood . . .

She had a frequent flow of blood from the womb which gave her great pain and prevented her from mixing with other people.

v. 26. Under many doctors . . . and was made no better.

People to-day often waste money in going to a number of different healers, buying charms from some and modern medicines from others.

In the same way those who are unhappy or are not satisfied with their own behaviour often go to many "saviours" before they reach Christ. St Augustine, the great bishop in North Africa, had belonged to several different religions and Churches before he became a real Christian. Afterwards he wrote: "Lord, Thou hast made us for Thyself, and our hearts are restless till they rest in Thee." (See John 6. 68; Acts 4. 12.)

v. 27. Touched his cloak:

V. 28 may mean that she believed there was power in Jesus' prayer-robe itself. This is possible. But what is certain is that she was showing Jesus that she needed His help when she took hold of His robe.

v. 29. Her disease was cured.

What was it that cured her disease?

1. It was not cured by any power that existed in things; e.g., not by the garment worn by Jesus.

2. She did not cure herself. She was not cured for the single reason that she thought she would be cured.

3. It was the power of God in Jesus that cured her. Jesus had love and power in Him, which were always ready to go out to any-one who was ready to receive them. This woman was ready. (See Additional Note, p. 27.)

There are some who mistakenly think that things connected with

Jesus will save them from the power of sin, e.g., the Bible. Others think that they can save themselves by just thinking that they are becoming better. But Jesus Himself is the one who saves.

v. 30. Knowing at once that power had passed out of him . . . said, Who touched my clothes?

1. **Power:** Jesus was constantly fighting against and overcoming evil because of His power, e.g., at His temptation, in His miracles, on the cross, at the resurrection. Mark 6. 8 shows that He has given this power to His followers.

2. **Passed out of him:** This power was not something outside Himself of which He made use (like a man giving a friend a bucket of water from the river); the power which He spent was part of His own self. He needed to pray, in order to be restored and renewed by His Father.

3. **Who touched my clothes?:** Does this mean that Jesus, Son of God, did not know the answer?

Although He could have found out for Himself who touched Him, He did not want to use His powers to do so. (See also 6. 38; 8. 4.) He asked in order to show the woman that she had been healed by Him, and not by the garment that He wore.

v. 31. You can see the crowd.

The disciples told Jesus that His question in v. 30 was a foolish question. (See Additional Note, p. 173.)

v. 33. Came in fear . . .

. The Jews called anyone who had that kind of sickness "unclean", and she was probably afraid that Jesus would be angry because she touched Him and made *Him* "unclean". She knew He was powerful, but did not yet know He was loving. (See note on 1. 40.)

v. 34. Daughter, your faith has made you well: go in peace and be cured . . .

1. **Daughter:** As in 2. 5, Jesus uses a very friendly word. She knew now that He was loving. He had attended to her as if she was the only person present, in spite of the crowds. So God hears us when we pray, as if we were the only people praying.

87

2. **Your faith:** (See Additional Note, p. 91). She had shown her faith in these ways:

a. she knew she was in need of help;

b. she believed that Jesus would by some means heal her;

c. she did all she could to tell Him of her need. Jesus still makes well those who have faith of this kind.

3. **Has made you well:** These words are sometimes translated "saved" or "made whole". God wants to deliver us from *all* evil, both from sickness, and from sin (Mark 10. 26), so that we shall have life to the full (John 10. 10).

4. **Be cured:** She was already cured. But Jesus sent her away with a blessing, and with a promise that she would remain cured.

Mark 5. 35–43 : The Miracle of Jairus' Daughter

See also Matt. 9. 23–26; Luke 8. 49–56

INTRODUCTION

This is the last of the four miracles done by Jesus during His journey.

While He was curing the woman, Jairus was waiting. Then a message came which Jesus "overheard" (v. 36), saying that his daughter was already dead. But Jesus and he went together, and when He had sent away the crowd, Jesus took the girl by the hand, and she got up. It is a story of Jesus bringing peace and joy in place of noise and fear.

Note: It is not clear from the story whether the girl was dead or only unconscious. (See note on v. 39 and Additional Note, p. 26.)

NOTES

v. 35.   Why do you trouble the Master . . . ?

They did not know that Jesus had come to the earth in order to save, that He was always ready to hear a request. God wants us to go on and on making our requests known to Him (See Phil. 4. 6; Luke 11. 5–10.)

v. 36. Do not be afraid, only believe.

"Believe" means "have faith in God, because He is stronger than the evil things that you fear". These words are encouragement to us, when we see a Christian congregation getting smaller, or evil people apparently living successful lives, or friends lying ill for a long time. Our fears can be taken away. (See note on 4. 40 and Additional Note, p. 91.)

v. 37. Peter and James and John . . .

This is the first time that Jesus took these three alone with Him. Probably they were chosen because their faith in Him was a little firmer than that of the other disciples. (See also 9. 2; 14. 33.)

v. 38. People weeping and mourning loudly.

These "people" were members of her family and friends and perhaps hired mourners.

It is asked, "Did Jesus think that such mourning was wrong?" He stopped the noise partly because it might have prevented the girl from recovering, but probably also because some were wailing for wrong reasons. Consider:

1. Christians, like others, suffer when they are separated by death from someone they love. Jesus Himself wept when Lazarus died.

2. Neighbours are right to come and show their sympathy in a Christian way.

3. But sometimes when people mourn and wail, it is because they forget that God is a God of love; they forget that He will take care both of the one who has died and of those who are left behind.

v. 39. The little girl is not dead, she is asleep.

Was she really dead or only unconscious? Mark probably gave us this story in order to show Jesus' great power: He could cure even a dead person. There are several reasons for thinking that she was dead: a. the noise made by the mourners; b. the words of v. 35; c. The very great astonishment of those present when she got up. Probably Jesus meant by these words that she was dead but not in the way that *they* regarded death. Most Jews believed that when a person died he passed for ever out of all joyful existence and went to a dark place called Sheol. So Jesus' teaching is that death is a sleep from which there will be an awakening (see 1 Thess. 4. 13, 14). This is why the place where Christians were buried was called a "cemetery", which comes from a Greek word meaning a "sleeping-place". (See note on 12. 18-27.)

Note: Some people hold different opinions, such as: a. she was unconscious but not dead; b. her family thought that she really was dead, like the people in 9. 26, 27; c. Jesus was, of course, *able* to raise her from death, but that Mark does not say that He did so.

v. 40. They laughed in his face. Then he put them all outside . . .

1. **Laughed in His face:** People had before this accused Him of being mad (3. 21). In this case, they laughed at Him because He was full of hope when nearly everyone else was in despair. We remember how Christians have often been laughed at for the same reason; e.g., the men who tried to abolish the slave-trade were laughed at, because those who made big profits out of the trade were so many and so powerful. In the same way a teacher who refuses to lose faith in pupils regarded as dull by other teachers will probably be laughed at. (Did Jesus dislike this laughter as much as we do? Certainly He did not fear it as we do.)

2. **Put them all outside:** vv. 25-34 show that Jesus was able to do miracles even in a crowd. But on this occasion (see also 7. 33, 8. 23), He felt that those who were making a noise and who had no faith in Him were a hindrance. How often visitors must be a hindrance to Jesus if they go to see a sick friend and do not really believe that He can make him well. He must want to put them outside and to find a few people who bring with them peace and faith.

v. 41. Talitha kumi . . . Little girl, I tell you, get up.

1. **Talitha kumi:** Most of the Gospel story is in Greek, but these two words are Aramaic which was the vernacular spoken by Jesus Himself. So here (as in 7. 34; 14. 36; 15. 34) we know the actual words He used.

2. **Little girl:** Jesus called her "little girl" or "lamb" (Talitha means lamb). The disciples must have thought it strange that He should leave a crowd to visit a young girl, and speak to her with love as if she were His own daughter. Little girls were usually considered very unimportant; although this one was important to her father. But to Jesus they were as important as anyone else.

90

It was in the name of Jesus that Josephine Butler persuaded the British Parliament to pass a law which protected little girls. She had found girls of only seven years old working for 18 hours a day in coal mines. (This was in 1886.) Others were being sold as prostitutes or forced to do such hard work in factories that they never grew up healthy.

v. 43.   Give her something to eat.

Having done the great work of raising her, Jesus did not forget the lesser matter of giving her some food. In the same way the God who has created all the stars does not forget our lesser matters; e.g., whether we pass our examinations or whether we marry the right person.

ADDITIONAL NOTE

FAITH

1. *The meaning of the word "faith".*

In the Gospel story the word "faith" is used to describe the whole manner in which people with the right kind of outlook behave towards Jesus. Most of those who met him did not have this faith.

What is this faith? A young child who is in a street full of traffic and strange people shows faith by the way in which he behaves towards his mother. Because he has already discovered that she is able to protect him and loves to do so, he holds on to her and entrusts himself to her with complete confidence.

This is how people with faith behaved towards Jesus. We notice:

a. Their reason for faith: They first saw what kind of person He was; they saw what He did, and heard what He said; they saw that He wanted to save them and was able to do so; they saw that He was doing what God had long ago promised to do through his Messiah.

b. Their act of faith: Then they took the decision to entrust their whole selves and lives to Him, to submit to Him, and to hold to Him.

c. The results of their faith: Finally their anxieties began to be taken away (see note on 4. 40), and they entered on a life of obedience to Him.

This shows that "having faith in" and "believing in" are the same. Indeed there is no difference between "having faith in", and "having confidence in", and "trusting", and "committing oneself to", and "believing". All these are translations of the same Greek word *pisteuein*.

2. *Some further notes on "faith"*

a. "Having faith" or "believing" is trusting, and not merely agreeing with someone. People often say to-day that they "believe in freedom" or "believe the Creed", but usually they only mean that they agree with such things.

b. Those who "had faith" had faith in Jesus himself. They trusted a Person, not ideas or sayings. (See notes on 1. 15; 11. 22.) Their confidence was in Jesus and not in themselves. Indeed when they began to trust Him, they saw how weak they were and how much they needed His power. (See note on 9. 24; Gal. 2. 16.)

c. Those who had faith did not think that it was therefore unnecessary to use their minds and intelligence. People sometimes say that faith is "blindly trusting", but faith is not like that at all. People began to trust Jesus by first opening their eyes to see what He was doing, and by using their intelligence to understand what kind of person He was. Thus God gave them reasons for beginning to trust.

d. But although God gave them sufficient reasons for trusting, He did not give them all the reasons. People, such as the disciples, had seen enough to make them trust and follow Jesus, but they were not given reasons by which they could prove that He was the Messiah who would die to save mankind: they could not prove it in the way in which they could prove that the sea was salty. Thus when they left their trade of fishing they were taking a risk. In this way, faith is always taking a risk. (See notes on 2. 5; 8. 29; 10. 52; Heb. 11. 8.)

e. When they entrusted themselves to Jesus, they did not become idle. The people with faith were in fact active and obedient people, e.g., some carried their friends along roads to meet Jesus (1. 32; 2. 4; 6. 56); others were active by persistently calling on Jesus for help. (See notes on 2. 5; 5. 34; 7. 29; 10. 52; 11. 23.)

3. *Our own faith*

Those who showed their faith in Jesus in the ways we have noticed above show us how to entrust ourselves to God to-day. We note especially:

a. We, like them, must first open our eyes to see the things He has done, i.e., the things which create faith. Perhaps we have been given even more reason to believe in Him than they were given: we know not only that God kept His promises by sending His Messiah, but also that He raised Him from the grave and has, since then, made ordinary people into saintly members of His Church.

b. When we have in this way seen that God is completely to be trusted, we show faith by committing ourselves to Him for ever, and to his Son Jesus. This is what becoming a Christian means.

c. From this time on we are bound to Him, and begin to grow in obedience and trustfulness, but faith comes first.

See picture facing p. 104.

Mark 6. 1–6 : Jesus Rejected at Nazareth

See also Matt. 13. 53–58; Luke 4. 16–30

INTRODUCTION

Jesus travelled twenty-eight miles with His disciples from Capernaum to the town where His home had been. There the people refused to receive Him. They had known Him as a boy and could not believe that He had come with a special message from God (John 1. 10). Luke (4. 16–30) gives us more information about this visit.

This is the first of a large group of stories contained in chapters 6. 1 to 8. 26. Most of these stories show Jesus working away from the lake of Galilee and outside the districts ruled over by Herod.

Here Mark gives us another story showing what people did who lacked faith.

NOTES

v. 3. Is not this the carpenter, the son of Mary, and the brother of James . . . And they felt shocked.

1. **The carpenter:** The Greek word which is here translated "carpenter" can also mean smith or mason. Whichever of these was Jesus' trade, it was manual work.

When God came into the world, He became a real human person. He did the kind of work which is done by most of the people of the world, namely work with His hands. Some people to-day think that a man who works with his hands must be less wise and less holy than one whose work is in an office or a classroom. (This wrong idea came to us from the Greeks, probably because they had slaves to work for them.) But the Jews did not think in that way, nor should Christians.

2. **The brother of James:** This verse tells us that Jesus had both brothers and sisters. For a note on the "brothers of Jesus" see 3. 31. Of these names, James is the only one about whom we know much, but the "brothers" are mentioned in 1 Cor. 9. 5. James seems to have begun to believe in Jesus after the Resurrection (1 Cor. 15. 7). Later he was head of the Church in Jerusalem (Acts 15. 13).

3. **They felt shocked:** At first they were astonished (v. 2) and they fixed their eyes on Him (Luke 4. 20). But very soon they began to take offence and to be "shocked" and angry at Him. Why was this? Probably because:

a. They were jealous of Him; they felt annoyed that one who had grown up with them should seem to have something which they had not got;

b. He was already known to them; they expected that God would send His messages by someone new or unusual.

This is why we Christians often fail to receive the messages God sends through the Bible or members of our own family or a teacher who lives in our town. We wrongly expect Him to use new or extraordinary ways (2 Kings 5. 10, 11).

v. 5. He could do no miracle there . . .

1. Not even Jesus, Son of God, could heal or save people who were unwilling to trust Him at all. (From 4. 2–9 we learn this.) A doctor to-day who treats us cannot cure us unless we take our share and agree to drink the medicine he gives.

2. So to-day not even God forces us to repent or to be healed. It is necessary for us to *want* to get rid of sin or sickness, and to believe (if only a little) that He can do it for us. If He forces us, He would be treating us like babies; He does not do that.

Of course God has in Himself power to do anything, but He has

94

chosen to put a limit to His power. He has done this because He wants us to be *free*, i.e., free to accept or refuse Him.

3. So the words do not mean that Jesus was weak or powerless. Perhaps Matthew thought that we might interpret them in that way, for when he wrote his Gospel (after Mark) he put "He *did not* do many miracles" instead of "*could not*".

v. 6. He was astonished . . .

The people were often surprised at Jesus: here it is He who was astonished at them because: a. they chose to be sick in body and soul rather than to be healed and saved; b. they could not trust Him.

This shows that Jesus *expected* that men would trust Him, just as He trusted His Father in Heaven. (It was partly because Jesus *expected* people to trust Him that so many did.)

Mark 6. 7–13 : The Sending Out of the Twelve

See also Matt. 9. 35–10. 15; Luke 9. 1–6

INTRODUCTION

The Purpose of the Journey

Jesus had for some time been training the Twelve so that they could do His work after He had gone. But this is the first time that He had sent them out alone.

However, the chief object of the journey was not to train the disciples, but to warn the people of Galilee that the Kingdom of God had begun to arrive. This was also the object of sending out the Seventy (Luke 10. 1–16). Mark 3. 6 shows that there was very little time before He was arrested.

In 6. 30 we are told of their return from this journey.

The Instructions He gave

These instructions are for us to-day as well as for the Apostles. They are also for all Christians and not only for ordained ministers.

1. To preach (v. 12). We see the message they were to give in

95

Matt. 10. 7. It was like Jesus' own preaching in 1. 14, 15: "Repent while there is time." To-day we must say this, for the End may be very near. (See Introduction to chap. 13, and 1 Pet. 4. 7.)

2. To heal (v. 13). Taking care of people's bodily needs must go along with preaching to them.

3. To travel quickly (vv. 8, 9). There was no time to waste. They were not to carry loads, and not to spend time looking for a comfortable lodging, but to stay with the first people who were willing to accept them. To-day also there may be so little time in which the Christian Churches can do their work that they must be careful not to waste time on things that are unimportant (1 Sam. 21. 8b). (One congregation held meetings for two months to decide whether to paint the walls of their priest's house. There is no time for this sort of thing.)

4. To trust God to put it into the hearts of people to provide them with food and lodging (vv. 8–10). They should not be worried about carrying supplies.

We need to trust God and pray to Him more in our Church work, and to spend less time on the *things* that we use in His service, the buildings, the books, etc.

NOTES

v. 8a.   He called the Twelve to him, and began to send them out two by two . . .

1. *Began to send them:* The message of Mark 1–5 is "He called them"; that of chaps. 6–end is "He sent them". (Notice the words "began to", which show that this was only the first of many such occasions.) So Christians of all nations are "missionaries" if they serve others and pass on the story of what God has done for us. "Missionary" comes from a Latin word which means "one who is sent". It is a pity to use it only for those who leave their own country to work in another one.

Note: When we are "sent" by Christ: a. we do what *He* has planned for us rather than what we plan; b. we go with His power and speak in His name; we do not just offer our own opinion (Matt. 10. 40; John 20. 21).

2. **Two by two:** Christian workers whenever possible ought to work in this way (Acts 13. 2; 16. 25). In times of success one can

save the other from pride, and in times of failure he can save him from despair (Eccles. 4. 9, 10). In addition, God's gift of the Holy Spirit is promised to us when we are in company (Matt. 18. 20; Acts 2. 1, 2).

v. 8b. He forbad them to take anything for the journey except a staff . . .

1. They were allowed to take a staff and sandals and one shirt with them, but not to take food or money or a spare shirt or a bag for collecting money. (This is the bag which is called a "scrip" or "wallet".) Thus they would be able to go quickly from place to place.

2. "Does Jesus expect us also to obey commands like these to-day?"

a. He does not ask us to keep exactly the same rules as He made for them then, e.g., it was possible for them to travel wearing only one shirt because it was May, and in Palestine that is not a cold time of the year, but Christians who did this in the north of Canada would die of cold. Jesus did not lay down rules for us.

b. What He did was to give us His Holy Spirit, with whose help we can have the same goal as He and His disciples had on that journey.

c. But sometimes people believe that Jesus is calling them to follow exactly a command like this one. St Francis of Assisi, at the age of twenty seven, heard the words, "Take no gold . . . nor bag nor two shirts", being read from Matt. 10. 9, 10. From that time he wore only the garment, tied with rope, which Franciscans still wear to-day. But even St Francis did not say that we should all do the same.

3. Do these words show that clergy and ministers of to-day ought not to be paid for their work?

a. No, the disciples were told to let others provide their food: so the clergy cannot be called un-Christian if they accept payment with which to provide for their needs (Matt. 10. 10; 1 Cor. 9. 14; 1 Tim. 5. 18).

b. But these words do not show that the clergy must always accept full payment from the Church; Paul made tents (Acts 18. 3) while working for the Church in Corinth, and some of the clergy to-day are earning part of their salary doing other work.

v. 11.   Shake off the dust . . . as a warning to them.

1. The disciples must not waste time complaining when people refused to receive them. Their duty was to *attempt* work for God: the *result* was in His hands.

2. Shaking off the dust was not a way of cursing: it was a sign of the division that existed between those who did repent and those who would not. (See notes on 4. 10–12 and 6. 5.) This division exists, and we Christians must not be ashamed of being different from those who do not follow Christ. But we must not regard ourselves as superior, nor must we be glad when others refuse to obey God, as Jonah was (Jonah 3. 10—4. 4).

v. 13.   Put oil on many sick persons . . .

Oil was often used in dressing wounds (Luke 10. 34), but here they used it in curing people of their diseases. For hundreds of years the Church used this as a way in which sick people could receive God's healing power (Jas. 5. 15). They called it "Holy Unction". Later it was used only as a sacrament when people were dying ("Extreme Unction"). To-day Holy Unction is again being used for healing.

Mark 6. 14–16 : Herod's Fear

See also Matt. 14. 1, 2; Luke 9. 7–9

INTRODUCTION

While the disciples were sent out on their journey, many people were hearing about Jesus for the first time, and probably news of His powers reached Herod from several parts of Galilee. The news made him very much afraid: he thought that perhaps Jesus was John the Baptizer, who had risen and returned to life. From this time, it is probable that Herod, in his fear, wanted to arrest or kill Jesus. We see that, shortly after this, Jesus had to work outside the districts of Galilee and Perea (over which Herod ruled), and perhaps Jesus, seeing what had happened to John, knew that He too would soon have to die.

Note: There are three rulers in the New Testament called Herod:
1. Herod the Great, who killed the little children of Bethlehem (Matt.
2. 16); 2. Herod Antipas, son of Herod the Great, who is referred to
here; 3. Herod Agrippa, grandson of Herod the Great (Acts 12. 1).

NOTES

v. 14.   People were saying . . .

Some agreed with Herod that Jesus was John the Baptizer risen
from the dead, perhaps because He was so courageous. Others said
He was Elijah, because Malachi 4. 5 says that Elijah would return
to earth in order to announce the coming of God's Kingdom. Others
said He was "one of the old prophets" because He taught in the way
in which the old prophets used to teach, i.e., by parables.

They all said "He is like someone we know". They did not see
that He was different from anyone who had gone before: this is
what Peter saw in 8. 28, 29. Jesus was Messiah, and He was God.

v. 16.   It is John whom I beheaded; he has risen from the dead.

Did Herod and others believe that the spirit of John had returned
and now lived in Jesus? Perhaps they did and perhaps Herod was
especially afraid of this spirit because he had killed John violently.
(Some Jews who had been influenced by the Greeks did believe that
a person's spirit could return in that way. See note on 9. 13.)
However, Herod may just have meant, "Here is another trouble-
maker, like John."

Mark 6. 17–29 : The Murder of John

See also Matt. 14. 3–12; Luke 3. 19, 20

INTRODUCTION

The story

About six months before the sending out of the Twelve, Herod had
arrested John (1. 14), partly because he was afraid that John might
lead a rebellion against him, partly because John accused him of

committing adultery with Herodias. John was shut up in a hot, dark prison called Machaerus in wild country on the east of the Dead Sea. He remained there until he was murdered, as this story tells.

Is Mark accurate?

Mark calls Herod "King" in v. 14, although he was only the ruler or "tetrarch" of Galilee and Perea, and the Romans had forbidden him to use the title of King. In v. 17 he calls Herodias the wife of Philip, but really she was the wife of another brother of Herod (whose daughter married Philip). This shows that the information given to Mark on these matters was not accurate in every detail. But in all important details Mark's story agrees with other records about Herod.

NOTES

v. 18. John said to Herod, It is not lawful . . .

1. John loved God so much that He attacked those who broke God's laws.

Herod's first wife was the daughter of the King of Arabia. But he divorced her as soon as he met Herodias, whom he married, although she was still the wife of his brother. John had the courage to attack Herod. See Matt. 11. 7–11a for Jesus' own words about John. As a result John was imprisoned. Although some friends were allowed to see him, he was lonely and without news about Jesus. Perhaps he was tempted to doubt whether Jesus really was the Messiah (Matt. 11. 2, 3). Finally, he was murdered.

St Thomas More had the same courage. In 1527 Henry VIII of England, who was married to Katharine of Aragon, decided to marry someone else. He knew that this was wrong, but he made Parliament pass a bill to state that it was right, and that all who were asked to do so must publicly declare that it was right. Thomas More was an important man, and was told to make this declaration. He hesitated for a long time; he knew that he would be killed if he disobeyed. Finally he made up his mind, and, thanking God that his "battle had been won", he publicly refused to make the declaration, and was executed.

2. It is the duty of all Christian leaders and people to "speak the truth, boldly rebuke vice, and patiently suffer for the truth's sake"

(Collect for St John the Baptist's Day). This is, of course, different
from rebuking someone who has offended or injured us personally,
and is much more difficult.

v. 19.   Herodias . . . wished to kill him . . .

Why? It was surely because she knew in her heart that John was
right, and that she was wrong to have married Herod. When we act
with violence, it is often because we know that we have done wrong.

v. 20.   Herod was afraid of John . . . he was very uneasy in mind . . .

1. *Herod's character*
   a. He had done wrong in marrying Herodias and arresting John.
He was known to be as cruel as a fox (Luke 13. 32). He liked to
listen to John (v. 20), but did not do what he said. One act of sin
led to another and greater one. He would never have murdered
John unless he had first left his own wife. No sin is "only a little
sin".
   On this occasion: i. he encouraged a nineteen-year old girl to
dance alone in a room full of drunken men (v. 22); ii. he boastfully
offered her half his "kingdom", although he was not a king (v. 23);
iii. he kept a terrible promise (and so killed John) because of pride
and fear of his visitors; iv. he was "very sorry indeed" (v. 28), but
he did not turn towards a new way of living.
   b. But no one is completely evil: we note that he was able to see
the goodness of John, and respected him, and he tried to protect
John against Herodias (v. 20). (We always respect those who have the
courage to correct us.)
   2. **Was very uneasy:** This is probably what Mark wrote. "He did
many things" (A.V.) is not likely to be correct.
   Herod was like Felix in Acts 24. 25. It shows that his conscience
was troubling him, and there is always hope for someone when that
happens. (See note on 3. 29.) Also, he was uneasy because he was
pulled in two directions: he was pulled by John to do right, by
Herodias to do wrong.

v. 24.   She . . . said to her mother, What am I to ask for?

The girl was old enough to know that she was doing a terrible thing.
(She did not merely ask for John's head, but said, "now at once", to

prevent Herod from changing his mind.) She herself was guilty of murder.

But it was her mother who led her into it, and who therefore was doubly guilty. (Probably she had planned it with her daughter before the feast.) Parents and teachers and all grown-ups can easily lead younger people into doing wrong: sometimes intentionally, like Herodias; more often, without thinking.

v. 26. He would not break his word to her.

Usually it is right to keep a promise, but on this occasion it was wrong to do so, because the promise was a foolish one, and it had been made through fear and pride.

Mark 6. 30–34 : The Return of the Disciples

See also Matt. 14. 13, 14; Luke 9. 10, 11; John 6. 1–3

INTRODUCTION

There are three parts to this short story: a. the Twelve returned from their journey and made a report to Jesus; b. Jesus took them away to be quiet; c. the people followed and Jesus taught them.

What seems to have happened is this: after Jesus had heard their news, He and they took a boat from a place near Capernaum, planning to go over to the east side of the lake. But there was a strong wind against them, and they travelled so slowly that some of the people who went on foot reached the place before them. They probably landed at the north of the lake, about seven miles from Capernaum.

NOTES

v. 30. The Apostles . . . told him all that they had done . . .

1. **The Apostles:** Usually Mark uses the words "the Twelve" or "the disciples". But the word "Apostle" is used here because they had been healing and preaching as representatives of Jesus Himself. (The Greek word from which "Apostle" comes means "sent forth".)

One reason why God's Church is called "Apostolic" (as in the

Nicene Creed) is that it is a body of people who are always being sent forth: a. to relieve the suffering of others; b. to tell them of the great things God has done through Jesus. Another reason why it is called "Apostolic" is, of course, that it is entrusted with the faith handed down by the Apostles.

2. **Told him all:** Their work was not complete until they had talked it over with Jesus who had begun it. We remember the prayer that speaks of "All our works, begun, continued *and ended* in Thee". This is just how every day should end for us. We return to Jesus who sent us out in the morning to tell Him what we have done and what we have left undone.

v. 31. Come away to some lonely place by yourselves apart and rest a little . . .

See note on 1. 35 which is like this verse.

1. **Come:** i.e., "Come with me". It was in His company that they would find rest after their hard work; and so do we.

2. **Lonely place:** It was necessary to get away from the crowds "coming and going" to a quiet place. (It was not "desert": there were farms nearby.) He was helping them to find peace, which they needed as much as a hungry man needs food; he was not encouraging them to be lazy. From time to time all Christian workers need to find a quiet place of "retreat" away from others, in order to have peace in the company of Jesus.

3. **Yourselves:** The A.V. says "Come ye yourselves" which may be the right translation. It would remind the Apostles that usually they helped others, but now it was time for them *themselves* to be taught and given peace of mind. Preachers become dried up in mind and spirit who do not allow themselves to be renewed (see Rom. 12. 2; 1 Cor. 9. 27 b; Eph. 4. 23).

4. **Rest:** Rest for the body and refreshment for the mind and spirit were both needed. It is not a sign that we are holy if we neglect to look after our bodies, nor when we work so hard that there is no time to pray or read books. This is why a part of each day (and also one day in each week) needs to be set aside for quiet.

v. 34. He was moved with pity for them, because they were like sheep . . .

1. a. **Pity:** Jesus had planned to be quiet and to give an op-

103

portunity for prayer to His disciples, but the crowds spoilt this plan and came shouting around Him. Instead of being angry, Jesus had pity on them. Luke (9. 11) says, "He welcomed them." When people disturb us as we are saying our prayers or studying, or just as we are beginning some work for God, may He deliver us from selfishness, and give us the pity that Jesus had.

b. What is pity? Jesus put Himself into the place of the hungry people, and knew what their feelings were. We need this kind of pity if we are going to serve other people as He did. People of one nation show pity when they put themselves into the place of a suffering nation and send them help. An employer shows pity by knowing in himself the fears and hopes of those he employs, and treating them justly.

c. Jesus had pity for a whole crowd. It is hard for us to imitate Him in this. There are to-day many millions of people in the world who are without homes of their own. We are tempted to say, "I am sorry for them, but there are so many of them that there is nothing I can do." But if we really have pity, we shall find that there *is* something we can do. We can send even a little money to help to provide, at any rate, a few of them with clothes. We shall not neglect to show pity in a small way just because we cannot show it in a great way.

2. **Like sheep:** There were two ways in which these people of Galilee were like sheep without a shepherd:

a. they did not get help from the leaders of their religion; this is why Jesus said they were like sheep;

b. they longed for freedom from the Roman Government, but they had no one to lead them. (Some hoped that Jesus would lead a rebellion.)

The words come from Ezek. 34. 2–6; 1 Kings 22. 17; Num. 27. 17. They are a good description of millions of people to-day who want to follow someone, but do not know whom to trust.

"We show faith by committing ourselves to God" (p 93).

The Norwegian scholar Thor Heyerdahl believed that the earliest inhabitants of Polynesia had come from South America. To prove that the voyage was possible without modern ships, he and five others built the raft *Kon-Tiki* and made the 4,300-mile journey across the Pacific from Peru to one of the Tuamotu islands. Their friends said they were "mad" to risk their lives, but Heyerdahl had studied history and was convinced they would arrive safely.

"He saw a large crowd. His disciples said, 'Send them away' . . . But He answered, 'Give them something to eat' " (Mark 6. 34–37).

In 1965 there were 3,300 million people in the world, all needing food. By 1980 there will be 4,000 million. Believing in God means believing that feeding that number is not impossible for God. It also means that He will do it through the willingness of human beings to use their knowledge of science for this purpose.

Mark 6. 35–44 : The Feeding of the Five Thousand

See also Matt. 14. 15–21; Luke 9. 12–17; John 6. 4–13

INTRODUCTION

What did Jesus do?

At this meal for a crowd of people in the open air, Jesus did *two* things: a. He increased the amount of food in a wonderful way; b. He taught them by these actions about the Coming of the Kingdom of God. This event, therefore, was both a Miracle of Feeding and also an Acted Parable.

A Miracle of Feeding

1. The disciples put the food into Jesus' hands, and He said a prayer and gave it back to them to distribute. They came back to Him over and over again, and He always had more to give them. That was a miracle. Jesus was thus acting with the power of His Father, God, who is the Creator. He did that evening what God did "in the beginning" and still does for us every year, when He makes a small amount of seed become enough food for a large number of people.

2. How did Jesus do it? Mark does not tell us; what he tells us is *who* did it, namely the Son of God in His love. It is, of course, not wrong to ask, *how*. But we must remember that, if we cannot answer the question, that does not show that the event never occurred. (See Additional Note, p. 26.)

An Acted Parable

1. When Jesus gave the people supper, He was actually *doing* the parable of Luke 14. 16–24. He was showing them by means of the feeding that He was the Messiah, who had been spoken of in Isaiah. So the meal was a way of saying to them, "The Kingdom of God has already begun to arrive, and you will be able to share in its joys: indeed you can *already* receive new life for your soul which members of the Kingdom have." Thus this supper was like the Lord's Supper on the night before His death, and all services of Holy Communion. We notice the same words are used in v. 41 as in chap. 14. 22; and according to John, Jesus gave His teaching about Holy

105

Communion immediately after this feeding miracle (see John 6. 33–35, 53–56).

2. We are thus reminded that Holy Communion is: a. a time of looking forward to the coming of the perfect Kingdom of God; b. a time when we can ourselves receive the Bread of Life into our souls; for the same Lord feeds us who fed the five thousand with bread and fish, and who fed the disciples at the Last Supper.

NOTES

v. 36. Send them away.

We, too, like the disciples, often try to escape the work of helping others.

v. 37. Give them something to eat yourselves. They said . . . Are we to go and buy ten pounds' worth of bread . . . ?

1. **Give them something to eat:** This is a command to look after others who are hungry or starving or sick. It shows that the Church has a duty not only to preach and to look after men's souls, but also to supply the needs of their bodies (Jas. 2. 14–17). Those of us who have enough to eat must take every chance to help those who are in want. As these words are being written, two-thirds of all the people of the world are living in continual and severe hunger.

2. **Yourselves:** This word is important. We, as they did, so often expect people's needs to be supplied by others, by the government or those whom we call "They" or "the Authorities": if they do not do it, we forget that it is our own duty. Here Jesus makes it clear that it is *our* job.

3. **Are we to go?** The disciples cared about the hungry people much less than Jesus did, and rebuked Him because He told them to feed so many. They rebuked Him often, e.g., in 4. 38; 5. 31. *We* are silently rebuking Him whenever we think it is impossible to do what He has told us to do, e.g., to love those who have injured us. (See Additional Note, p. 173.)

Note: "ten pounds' worth" is translated as "two hundred penny-worth" in the A.V.

v. 40. They sat down in groups . . .

The Greek word which is here translated "groups" really means "flower-beds" and must have been used because the people sitting in order on the green grass (see v. 39) in their brightly-coloured clothes looked like flowers in a garden. It is words like these that show that the story comes from someone who was there and that we can trust it as a true story.

v. 41 a. He took the five loaves . . . and looking up to heaven, he gave thanks . . .

1. **He took:** It was because the simple food was willingly offered to Jesus and taken by Him, that it became of such great value. (If they had kept it and tried to distribute it among the people, it would only have been enough for two or three.) This is what happens when a man of to-day willingly offers himself to Jesus: his life becomes of far greater value to God and to the world. We have only a little to offer, but it becomes enough when it is given into His hands.

2. **Loaves:** These were round, flat, baked cakes. John says they were of barley, which was the food of poor people. John also says it was a small boy and not the disciples who gave the food.

3. **Looking up to heaven:** He did not do this because He thought that God lived in the sky, but as a symbol or sign of worshipping His Father God. No one on earth, not even Jesus, could do without symbols and signs when talking to God or about God, e.g., we say that Jesus "ascended into heaven", not because He flew into the sky, but simply to say that He left the earth to be with His Father.

4. **Gave thanks:** i.e., He "said grace". We know the Jewish "grace" that He probably used. "Thanks be to Thee, O Lord our God, King of the World, who bringeth forth food from the earth." (Thus they were words of prayer, not magical words.)

v. 41b. He . . . broke the loaves, and gave them to the disciples . . .

This shows that this meal was of the same kind as the Lord's Supper and the Holy Communion. The Holy Communion is called "Breaking of Bread" in Acts 2. 42–46; 20. 7, 11; 27. 35; 1 Cor. 10. 16; 11. 24, and in every church since the days of the Apostles the minister at Holy Communion has "broken the bread" as part of the Service.

Jesus broke it in order to show that what He gave should be shared, and we remember this as we accept His gifts. (See notes on 4. 21; 14. 22.)

vv. 42, 43. And they all ate and were satisfied; and they took up the broken pieces, twelve baskets full, besides the fish.

What He gives is more than enough.

See picture facing p. 105.

Mark 6. 45-52 : The Crossing of the Lake

See also Matt. 14. 22-33; John 6. 15-21

INTRODUCTION

The Story

After the feeding of the crowd there was a great danger that they might take Jesus and try to force Him to become their leader in a rebellion against the Romans. (See John 6. 15.) Even the disciples might have wanted to do this, and so Jesus "compelled" them to go away by boat (v. 45). Probably He then assured the people that He would not desert them and said farewell to them. Then He said His prayers. Much later He went to the help of the disciples when they were in trouble on the lake.

Questions we want to ask

Did Jesus, being truly man, really walk on the water? If so, how did He? Was it necessary for Him to do such a miracle? Why did He wish to "pass them by"? (v. 48.)

If anyone were to say that he could not become a Christian until he knew the answer to all these questions, he would never become one. There is much that we shall never know about Jesus' life, but when we make a decision to follow Him, it is because of what we *do* know; we trust Him to give us as much knowledge as we actually need in order to live our lives as Christians.

The teaching of the story

Here we learn that we can trust God; we believe that He has the power to look after us in times of difficulty, even though we cannot see Him. (See note on v. 50; Matt. 28. 20 b.) This must have greatly encouraged the persecuted Christians for whom Mark wrote his Gospel.

NOTES

v. 45.   Cross over . . . to Bethsaida . . .

They must have planned to go to Bethsaida (which is on the north shore of the lake and near the place of the "Feeding"), but, owing to a very strong wind, they had been driven across to Gennesaret, as is stated in v. 53.

v. 46.   He went up the mountain-side to pray.

1. How *difficult* it was for Him to get a chance to pray! He had to send people away.

2. How much He seems to have *needed* to pray. He was faced with so many problems: the Pharisees and Herod both wanted to arrest Him; the people wanted to make Him the leader of a rebellion. It is possible that He Himself was still tempted to save them in that way. (See note on 1. 13.) He must have prayed for several hours, since He did not go to the help of the disciples until three or four o'clock in the morning, as v. 48 says.

v. 48.   Walking on the water.

We cannot understand how Jesus did this, but it would be very foolish to say that when God became man, He *could not* do such a thing. We know that Jesus controlled the wind on the Lake. (See notes on 4. 39 and Additional Note, p. 26.)

Note: There are some who think that Jesus could have walked on the water, but that He did not do so. They say that when the disciples saw Jesus He was in the shallow water near the shore, and that in the moonlight of the very early morning they could not see clearly and thought He was walking on deep water. (But this does not tell us why the disciples were "beside themselves with astonishment" (v. 52). They would soon have found out their mistake.)

v. 50.   Courage, it is I; do not be afraid.

This verse (like 4. 40) teaches that we *can* get rid of our fears. Here the disciples were not afraid of the storm, but of the person they saw. They thought it was a spirit come to harm them.

Jesus said, "It is I". Many of us are afraid in our hearts that the spirit which controls the world is an unfriendly one, a sort of Fate which is against us, but a. God says, "It is I, the God of love" who

E

controls the world; b. God is present, not absent. (See v. 48. "He went unto them".)

The disciples did not fully understand this at the time. But they believed it after God had raised up Jesus, and people were surprised at their courage (Acts 4. 13).

It is these two beliefs which make any Christian who is being persecuted able to stand firm. (The Greek word in v. 48 which is translated "distressed" or "struggling" really means "tortured".) And anyone who is in pain or trouble, or afraid of failure or afraid of death finds his load of fear made lighter (or taken away altogether) when he accepts these beliefs. (See also Isa. 43. 2.)

v. 52.   They had not understood about the loaves; their minds were stupid.

1. **The loaves:** This is a note added by Mark to explain why the disciples were surprised when Jesus walked on the water. They were surprised because they had not understood the power of Jesus, even when He fed a whole crowd from a few loaves. At this time they still had not discovered that Jesus was truly God, and that He had all the power of God in Him.

2. **Stupid:** The New English Bible says, "their minds were closed", i.e., were not yet open to receive the truth about Jesus. (See Additional Note, p. 173.)

Mark 6. 53–56 : Healings at Gennesaret

See also Matt. 14. 34–36

INTRODUCTION

These verses are like 3. 7–12.

Note:

1. How quickly the good news travelled round the neighbourhood when Jesus arrived in a village (v. 55);

2. How great faith they had in His power (v. 56);

3. How eager people were to bring to Jesus those of their friends who were in need (vv. 55, 56);

110

4. How Jesus was still prevented from teaching His disciples or from finding a quiet place for prayer.

NOTES

v. 53. They came to land at Gennesaret . . .

Gennesaret was a plain, on the west side of the lake, south of Capernaum. Probably they were driven there by the storm.

v. 56. Touch the border of his cloak . . .

This "border" was the fringe or tassel which all Jews wore. (See notes on 5. 27, 30.)

Mark 7. 1–13 : Teaching about Tradition

See also Matt. 15. 1–9

INTRODUCTION

The Story

Some Pharisees and scribes had been sent by the authorities in Jerusalem to find out what Jesus was saying and doing. They saw with distress that He allowed His disciples to break one of the "unwritten laws" or traditions and they asked Him why. Instead of answering them, He boldly accused *them* of forgetting God's own commandments! (See note on v. 11.) After this, they must have been more than ever determined to arrest Him.

Those who keep man's traditions but forget God's Laws

The Jews knew what God's Laws were, because they were written down in the Old Testament, especially in the first five books of it. (These commands were called "The Law" or "Torah".) But for hundreds of years, the scribes had been trying to explain the meaning of the Law, and their teaching about it was remembered and handed down to others. This unwritten teaching or "tradition" became like another set of laws in addition to the written Law. Many Jews

111

thought it was as important to keep these traditions as to keep the Law itself. Some even paid so much attention to the traditions that they forgot God's Law. In these verses Jesus shows how wrong this is. Two examples are given of such traditions: a. hand-washing (vv. 1–8); b. the vow of Corban (vv. 9–12).

Traditions of Christians

The Christian Churches also have their "traditions" or customs: e.g., about kneeling in church, or how much we should contribute to Church funds or how often we should attend Holy Communion. These rules help us to do our duty, although they were not given to us directly by Jesus Himself. In keeping these rules we must not imagine that we have kept the *whole* law of God, which is to love Him and our neighbours. (See notes on v. 8, which sums up this section.)

NOTES

v. 1. The Pharisees and some of the scribes . . .

See Additional Note, p. 43.

v. 2. His disciples ate their food with "unholy", that is unwashed, hands.

1. Washing hands before a meal is an example of a tradition which many Jews kept very strictly, while forgetting the much more important laws of God. ("All the Jews" in v. 3 means "most Jews".) Such Jews washed their hands as a sign that they were God's chosen people, not because they had studied hygiene and wanted their hands to be clean before eating. They would have explained it like this: "We may easily have been touched by a Gentile (i.e., anyone who is not a Jew) on our way back from the market, and to wash our hands is a sign that we are keeping ourselves separate from others and are not copying the religion of heathens. After touching a Gentile, we are unclean in God's sight until we have washed."

2. There was much good in this rule since it encouraged habits of cleanliness, but Jesus had two things to teach about it:

a. Don't think that, when you have washed your hands, your hearts are clean in God's sight (vv. 14–23 are on this subject).

b. Don't become so interested in this traditional action of washing

112

that you begin to think you have kept the whole Law of God Himself. (See note on v. 8.)

3. This story was very interesting to the Christians of Rome for whom Mark was writing. Even in A.D. 65 some of them were not quite sure if it was right for a Jewish Christian and a Gentile Christian to take Holy Communion together. This story assured them that it was indeed right.

v. 6a. You double-dealers . . .

A "double-dealer" or "hypocrite" sometimes means someone who pretends to be different from what he really is; e.g., a preacher who lives a bad life privately; but Jesus did not accuse the Pharisees of being like that. He meant, "You honestly *think* that you are successfully keeping God's commandments, but *really* you are failing miserably. You are satisfied with yourselves and therefore you cannot improve." That was hypocrisy (John 9. 41).

The Pharisees were satisfied with themselves because they were successful in keeping a number of little traditions, but forgot the great Law of loving one another.

Note: It is possible that as we are reading this, we are guilty of hypocrisy by saying, "Thank God I am not a hypocrite."

v. 6b. This people honours me with their lips, but their hearts are far from me;

These words from Isaiah 29. 13 do not, of course, teach that God does not want us to honour Him with our lips (Eph. 5. 19). They mean: "Do not honour God with hymns and prayers *instead* of loving Him in your heart." Hymns must be an outward sign of the love we have for Him.

v. 8. You give up the commandment of God, and hold fast to the unwritten law of men.

This verse sums up the teaching of vv. 1–13.

Jesus did not say that it was wrong for the Jews to have unwritten laws. Nor is it wrong for Christians to have theirs. But He said three things:

1. Do not pay *more* attention to your traditions than to God's Laws.

But we Christians often do. Two women in an African congregation wanted to have their children baptized. One was well known for her unkind tongue, the other was a good woman, but had not contributed much to Church funds. The first woman was allowed to have her child baptized, the second was refused. Of course Christians should contribute freely to the needs of God's Church! But in this case God's own great law about loving our neighbours was clearly considered to be less important than a rule about Church contributions.

2. Do not make your traditions of *equal* importance with God's Law. This is what we do when we say about a decision of some Church committee or about a rule of our own congregation, "This is certainly God's will". This is behaving as if we were God. We must try continually to distinguish between the rules of the Church and God's own will. Paul does this in 1 Cor. 7. 12a. The Church is not the same as the Kingdom of God.

The words of Jesus in Matt. 16. 19, "I will give you the keys of the Kingdom", do not mean that our voices are always the voice of the Divine King Himself.

Note: What has been said above does not mean that lawlessness is ever right. When decisions have been taken by those in proper authority, we must keep them. Then, if we sincerely believe that the decisions are not right, we can do our best to have them changed.

3. Do not *force others* to keep your traditions.

This is what the Pharisees did. See their question in v. 5. Jesus said they were "putting burdens on people's backs" (Luke 11. 46). Christians also do this. We have a rule which we (and others before us) have found helpful, and we tell others that they cannot be real Christians unless they keep the same rule. Some Christians were forbidden by their Church council to attend Holy Communion because they smoked cigarettes. Members of the council were right to abstain from smoking if they believed it was wrong for themselves, but they had no right to make this into a law which everyone else had to keep.

v. 11. This money of mine might have been useful to you, but now it is Corban.

1. This is the second example of "man's tradition". In this case, by keeping it, the person actually broke one of God's Laws. This is the sort of thing to which Jesus was referring: A man made a vow to

114

" 'You think that you are successfully keeping God's commandments, but really you are failing miserably.' That was hypocrisy." (p. 113).

African spectators at a sports event in Rhodesia are permitted by the white authorities to enter the "Golden Circle" enclosure. But tickets for the enclosure are so expensive that only the richer white spectators can afford them. So this part of the enclosure remains empty except for a few white children, while the Africans are crowded together outside.

"It seems as if Jesus is refusing to help anyone who is not a Jew." (p. 119)

Did He really refuse? What was His attitude to people of another race?

At meetings of the United Nations Assembly and its Councils the attitude of each representative to other nations is very important. He must faithfully represent his own nation, but at the same time share in a united effort to create peace and justice in the world.

give some money to the Temple in Jerusalem at some future time. But before he had given it, his parents both fell ill and needed his support. But the man said the words of this verse, i.e., "I cannot keep the Commandment about honouring my father and mother, because I have already vowed to give the money to the Temple." ("Corban" probably means "set apart for God".) Most Jews would tell the man to break the vow in such a case, but there were some Pharisees who said he should keep it. To this Jesus said, "Remember God's *own* commandments and do your duty to your parents."

Note: There are some who say that "Corban" was an oath and that evidently someone had said to his parents in a fit of anger, "Corban! I will never support you"; and that some scribes said he ought to keep this terrible vow, since he had made it.

2. This teaches us not to escape the ordinary duties of life (e.g., the duty of loving our neighbour and family) by doing some service for the Church. That was the sin of the Priest and Levite in the Good Samaritan Parable. It is like the girl who spent so long saying her prayers that she could not help her mother to prepare the food; or the man who made large contributions to his Church, but neglected to clothe his children properly. God is not more pleased with prayers or gifts to the Church than with an act of kindness to a neighbour. He is the God of life at home and in the office, and not only the God of the Church.

v. 13.   You make the word of God of no effect . . .

1. **Word of God** here does not mean the words of the Bible, but the Will of God or the Mind of God. It is, of course, true that a sure way of finding out the will of God is to read the Bible, but God's will existed long before the words of the Bible existed. We need to "go behind the words to hear His Word".

2. **Of no effect:** i.e., "You make it impossible for people to hear and obey the commandments of God." Every leader in the Church must pray that he may not be guilty of this. Yet it is easy to preach too much about the many Church rules and thus to hide from the people the great Laws of God Himself.

See picture facing p. 114.

Mark 7. 14–23 : Evil Comes from Within

See also Matt. 15. 10–20

INTRODUCTION

These verses (and especially 14 and 15) answer the question which the Pharisees asked in v. 5.

The teaching is in three parts: a. things you eat or touch do not harm your soul (vv. 15–19a); b. all kinds of food are equally "holy" in God's eyes (v. 19b); c. your own thoughts are what harm you most (vv. 20–23).

This teaching was important for the Christians for whom Mark was writing. Some were Jews by race, and some were Gentiles (i.e., not Jews). Gentiles were sometimes being told by Jews that they must avoid certain sorts of food.

NOTES

v. 15. Nothing that goes into a man from outside him can make him unclean, it is what comes out . . .

1. Jesus meant, "No food can hurt your soul. Food comes in through the mouth, goes into the stomach, leaves the body, and finally goes into the latrine (v. 19). All that time it never touches your soul and so cannot hurt you yourself". This was new teaching for the Jews, who thought that in God's eyes some foods like pig's flesh were evil. (See note on 7. 2.)

2. **What comes out:** Nothing which comes to a man from outside can harm him nearly as much as the evil thoughts and words that "come out" of him. (See note on v. 20.) But many people wrongly think that they are harmed most by things outside them, e.g., by an unhealthy house, by the bad example of a parent, by the insults of a neighbour, or by a curse someone has put on them.

v. 19. He made all food clean.

1. Mark wrote this note to show us how new and extraordinary this teaching of·Jesus was. (See note on 2. 22.)

In vv. 1–13, Jesus surprised the Jews by saying, "You must distinguish between: a. man's tradition; b. the written Law. The

116

written Law is far greater." Now, however, He says in vv. 14–23 that there is something even greater than the written Law, namely the will of God Himself. He says, "In the Old Testament (Lev. 11) you were told that certain foods are 'unclean'; but I tell you that in God's eyes all food is clean." (This was terrible in the ears of the Pharisees: they regarded every word of the Written Law as showing exactly the Will of God.)

2. This helps us to-day to read and use the Old Testament in the right way. God does not want us to obey every word of it, e.g., He does not want us to offer the sacrifices laid down in Num. 29. 8. We are to read it in such a way (i.e., with prayer) that we can see the real will of God for us. It is the spirit of the written Law we are to see and obey, not the letter (Rom. 7. 6).

v. 21.   Out of the heart of a man, evil thoughts come . . .

1. **Evil thoughts:** They can harm us, because if we think about evil, we become evil. The more often we make a picture in our minds of doing wrong, the more likely we are to do wrong. What we think about when we are alone, especially just before sleeping or just after waking, makes our character what it is. That is why we pray at the beginning of the Communion service "Cleanse the *thoughts* of our hearts . . ." (See also Phil. 4. 8.)

2. **Exploitation** (In the A.V. "covetousness"): This is the sin of making use of someone else to get some gain for ourselves while the other person suffers, e.g., paying a labourer wages which are too low.

3. **Jealousy** (In the A.V. "wickedness"): This means hoping that someone else will do wrong.

4. **Envy** (In the A.V. "evil-eye"): Probably Jesus meant, "If you hate someone and wish to cast an evil spell over him, it is yourself rather than the other man who is harmed".

5. **Abuse** (The A.V. says "blasphemy", but that is not correct): The insults and slander we speak against others hurt us more than words spoken against us.

6. **Pride:** This harms us because it prevents us from receiving correction from others (see Prov. 15. 5).

7. **Senselessness** (In the A.V. "foolishness"): This is the sin of treating worthless things as if they were precious.

117

Two points may be noted:

1. It is harder to get rid of evils which are in ourselves than those which come from outside. The Pharisees only said, "Wash your hands." Jesus said, "Wash your hearts."

2. It is so hard that we need God's special grace to help us to do it (Ps. 51. 2). That is why He died for us. We have to be *made* clean, we cannot of ourselves become clean.

Mark 7. 24–30 : The Woman from Syro-Phoenicia

See also Matt. 15. 21–28

INTRODUCTION

Jesus now travelled north into the country between Tyre and Sidon which was inhabited by Gentiles, not Jews. It was not the first time He had gone outside Jewish territory. (See note on 6. 14–16.) He seems to have gone chiefly in order to be quiet, to pray, and to prepare Himself for the suffering that He knew would soon come. (There may have been other reasons also why He left Galilee: Herod, and also the Pharisees wanted to arrest Him, and the ordinary Jewish people wanted to make Him a national king.)

There are two important questions that a reader of this story asks:

1. Was Jesus unwilling to help this woman because she was a Gentile? (See note on v. 27.)

2. Did He heal her daughter without seeing her? (See note on v. 29.)

NOTES

v. 24. He could not be hidden.

Jesus was not a magician like someone in a folk-story who can make himself invisible. He was a man like ourselves and He was unable to escape from the people when they heard that He was in their village. See 5. 30; 6. 5; 9. 16; 13. 32; for other things which He could not do, because He had willingly become a man and was limited in what He could do, as we are (Phil. 2. 7.)

118

v. 26. The woman was heathen, a native of Phoenicia in Syria . . .

The word which is translated "heathen" probably means "Greek". She spoke the Greek language and worshipped heathen gods as the Greeks did. Jesus spoke with her, which shows that He knew at any rate a little of her language in addition to His own languages of Hebrew and Aramaic.

The verse also tells that she was a Phoenician. This great nation had a large colony in N. Africa, but its own country was in Syria.

v. 27. It is not fair to take the children's bread and throw it to the house-dogs.

1. **Children, house-dogs:** The woman knew that Jesus was using the word "children" to mean the Jews, and "house-dog" to mean Gentiles. At first it seems as if Jesus is speaking rudely or is refusing to help anyone who is not a Jew. (According to Matthew's account, He first refused to listen to her, and then said, "I was sent only to the lost sheep of Israel"). But He was not.

2. Why did He speak in this way?

a. It was not because He despised women. Passages like 1. 30, 31; 5. 40–43; 10. 7, 8; John 4. 1–30 show that He, unlike other Jewish teachers, treated women with the same care that He showed to men.

b. It was not because He despised Gentiles. He cured the Gentile madman of Gerasa (5. 1–20), a Gentile Centurion's servant (Luke 7. 1–10), and a Gentile nobleman's son (John 4. 46–54). Thus, He was showing by His actions that He had no "race-prejudice".

c. It was not because He was tired or unwilling or had to be persuaded to change His mind. Nor does He change His mind in these days when we pray to Him. Prayer is not trying to persuade God (see 11. 24).

d. It was because He was, at that moment, thinking over a difficult problem: He needed to be quiet and alone; therefore He must not attract attention by doing miracles or by teaching. But when He did miracles and taught people, He had to give His attention to the Jews first. God had chosen this one race (the Jews) and planned to make Himself known to all the world through them. It was not because God had "favourites" or because Jews were better than other nations, but simply because it was His method (and still is) to reach *all* through a *few* (see Matt. 10. 5; Rom. 1. 16;

2. 9–11). So Jesus wanted to train His few disciples before He was arrested, so that they could continue His work afterwards.

Yet His plan was that all nations should be brought under the rule of God, as He said in 13. 10.

3. Thus, when He spoke to the woman, it was as if He were saying, "It is my plan to teach and heal only Jews at this stage of my work, but, of course, I will heal your daughter: it is a sign that God loves all nations." Perhaps the words of v. 27 were a well-known proverb and surely Jesus spoke them in a way which would not offend her.

4. Two lessons of this verse are:

a. No man does effective work for God unless he limits his work (as Jesus did). Every successful student knows this. Someone who is in charge of a congregation limits himself to work with those people to whom he is committed instead of travelling round the whole country.

b. God's will is that *all* nations are to be brought under His rule. No nation is holier than another in His eyes. (Eph. 2. 13.) No national Church may keep for itself all its best Christians, for some are needed to go and work amongst other races. We are all expected by God to pray for and help other nations, especially for their Christians.

v. 29. For that word, go home; the evil spirit has gone out of your daughter.

1. **For that word:** It was because of the words and the love of the woman for her daughter that Jesus healed the girl. According to Matthew, Jesus said, "You have great faith." The woman had faith in these ways: a. she trusted Jesus; b. she was unselfish; c. she was persistent; d. she used her intelligence. (See Additional Note, p. 91.)

2. **Evil spirit:** (see note on 1. 23). Here, as in vv. 25, 26 and 30, this means "demon", not devil.

3. **Has gone out:** The woman asked Jesus to heal the girl. Jesus, by saying these words, cured her, although she was absent and could not see Him. It is impossible to say *how* He did this; but we can understand that, since He was in perfect fellowship with God the Father, He could, by His prayers, release the power of God to cure a sick person. It did not matter where that person was. (See also John 4. 49–51; Luke 7. 6, 7, 10.) This is what happens when we pray

120

for someone to-day. We know that God has the power and the desire to heal and bless people wherever they are. By our prayers we are able to help them to receive that power.

See picture facing p. 115.

Mark 7. 31–37 : The Deaf Man Cured
INTRODUCTION

The Journey

After the healing of the girl near Tyre (vv. 24–30), Jesus and His disciples went a long journey, perhaps lasting several months. It was across wild country and He would have opportunity to teach them without interruption.

The journey is not described very clearly. Probably they travelled north to Sidon, then south across the river Leontes, then eastwards over the Jordan at a place near its source, and finally through the group of towns called Decapolis (see 5. 20), and so reached the east shore of the lake of Galilee. At some point on the journey, He cured this deaf man.

The Cure

The healing of this man was *like* other miracles in several ways: his friends brought him to Jesus (2. 3), He took the man apart privately (5. 40), and told him not to tell anyone (1. 43, 44). It was *unlike* previous healings, because He used saliva or. spittle. (See note on v. 33; also Additional Note, p. 26.)

The Teaching

1. The Kingdom of God is already here; it is God, not Evil, that is in control of the world.

The Jews expected the Messiah, when He came, to make deaf people hear and dumb people speak (Isa. 35. 5, 6). This cure of the deaf man did not, of course, *prove* that Jesus was the Messiah or that the Kingdom had come; but when we already and for other reasons know that Jesus is the Messiah, this story strengthens our belief.

2. God can and does take away deafness and dumbness of spirit. Many of us are *deaf* in spirit: we do not "hear" God's commands to

121

us nor the cries for help from our neighbours. Many are *dumb*: we do not praise God wholeheartedly, because we are not grateful enough; we do not speak to others to help them, because we are afraid (Eph. 6. 19, 20).

The Church has often used the word "Ephphatha" (v. 34) in the Baptism service (and has even used saliva) to show that Baptism is a time when God cures us of such deafness of the spirit.

Note: The many other lessons of this story are referred to in the notes below.

NOTES

v. 32. Deaf and almost dumb . . .

The man was deaf, and because he had not heard his own voice for a long time (perhaps never), his speech was almost impossible to understand. His "dumbness" was probably the result of his deafness.

Perhaps the reason why we are often "dumb" in the service of God is that we are "deaf" to Him. Once we have really "heard" His voice (that means, we have become sure, perhaps at a time of prayer, that He is present and is telling us to live for Him) then we shall be ready to speak and live and work for Him in our daily activities.

v. 33. He took him out of the crowd apart, . . . spat, and touched his tongue.

1. **Out of the crowd:** Probably He did this because the man needed to be quiet before he could be cured, but it may have been in order to prevent the crowd knowing about the miracle.

There are times in every man's life when God can only help him if he is alone and quiet. Many of us live in a crowd all our lives: we may be born as one of a big family, or we work in a big college or factory or office. Perhaps this is why we find it hard to "hear" God. There is a city in Europe where a river runs underground, but you can only hear the noise of the water if you stand in the street alone, after the crowds have gone home.

2. **He . . . spat:**

a. When Jesus used saliva, He was doing what Jewish doctors often did, though they more often used it for eyes. (See Mark 8. 23; John 9. 1–7, for other times when He used it.)

122

Note: Saliva was, and still is, also used as magic. This was forbidden by Jewish religious leaders. Jesus certainly did not use it in this way.

b. He knew that if He used something that the man could see and feel, it would help him to believe in Him, but the power that cured the man came from Jesus; it was not in the saliva itself.

c. Just as Jesus used a common thing (saliva), so God usually blesses us by means of ordinary things. He usually speaks to us through the voice of a neighbour, not through lightning, and He heals us by means of an ordinary doctor's medicine. (We often forget, when we take medicine from the doctor, that it is God who is healing us.)

d. Jesus knew that this man would be helped in this way; but He cured other people in many other ways. So God treats each of us according to our own special needs: He knows that each one of us is different.

v. 34. Looked up to heaven and sighed and said to him, Ephphatha.

1. **Looked up:** This was one of the many signs that Jesus used at this time: it showed the man that the power to heal him came from God. (See note on 6. 41.) In the same way, Jesus put His fingers in his ears, a way of saying, "These are going to be opened". He used signs because the man was deaf, but all through His ministry He did the same (9. 36; 11. 7; 14. 22).

a. Christians use signs in their worship, e.g., we kneel to pray: some make the sign of the cross with the hand. There is a danger that we may forget the meaning of our signs, just as there was a danger that the actions of Jesus might be regarded as magic by the deaf man. But we need signs, and by using them we follow the practice of Jesus.

b. Why did He sigh? Perhaps because He was deeply unhappy when He thought of all the deaf people who had no one to heal them. (See also Mark 8. 12; John 11. 33, 38.)

2. **Ephphatha:** This is an Aramaic word, like the words in 5. 41; 7. 11; 15. 34. Jesus spoke naturally and in His own vernacular. This was not a magic word: people using magic used strange and usually unknown languages. (See note on 5. 41.)

v. 35. His ears were opened and his tongue loosed . . .

"His tongue loosed" meant "loosed from the power of Satan".

(The English still use the word "tongue-tied" for someone who cannot or is ashamed to speak freely.)

Jesus is to-day still curing not only those who are deaf in spirit (see Introduction above), but those who have lost the proper use of their ears. But just as He was able to heal this man because his friends brought him (v. 32), so to-day Jesus usually cures a deaf man through our work for him. As Christians, we try to show them great sympathy, and take a leading part in collecting money for them and for their families and the hospitals where they may be cured.

v. 36.   The more he forbad, the more they spread the news.

(See note on 1. 45.) By speaking about it and thus disobeying Jesus, they made it harder for Him to escape the notice of the Pharisees and harder to find quiet in which to train His disciples. When we disobey Him, we do not see at the time how much we are spoiling His work.

Mark 8. 1–10 : The Feeding of the Four Thousand

See also Matt. 15. 32–39

INTRODUCTION

For the teaching of this story, see notes on the Feeding of the Five Thousand (6. 30–34 with 6. 35–44). The lessons of both stories of feeding are the same.

It is sometimes asked whether Jesus did *two* miracles of feeding, or whether there was only *one* miracle (of which Mark gives us two different accounts).

Some think that there were two miracles. Mark says so in 8. 19, 20. If this was so, it shows how slow the disciples were to trust Jesus. According to 6. 35–44, they saw Him feed the crowd, but in 8. 4 ("Where can anyone get enough bread?") they have forgotten it. This is just what happens to-day. We know, for instance, that Jesus has very often changed bad people into good, yet we frequently forget this and talk as if bad people (ourselves or others) must always remain bad.

Others think that Jesus did only one miracle of this kind, and that two reports of it reached Mark, one saying that there were "about 5,000 there", the other "about 4,000". (It is very unlikely that anyone would actually count the crowd.) Luke seems to think this, for he only tells us of one feeding and this is what probably happened. The two accounts in Mark of the one miracle make us doubly certain that that miracle really took place.

Mark 8. 11–13 : The Demand for a Sign

See also Matt. 16. 1–4

INTRODUCTION

The Pharisees knew that Jesus had done miracles. But they refused to believe that He was sent by God, or to listen to Him seriously unless He first did some much more extraordinary thing for them. Jesus refused.

NOTES

v. 12.   Why do the people of this age ask for a sign? . . . no sign shall be given them.

We ask, Why did Jesus say this? Were His miracles not "signs"?

1. It was because the Pharisees ("people of this age") asked for the wrong kind of sign.

a. In one way, miracles were "signs": when a man already loved Jesus and wanted his sins to be forgiven, then the miracles were signs to him that Jesus had power to take away all kinds of evil. That man had "faith" or "eyes to see". He first had "faith"; it was afterwards that the miracles became signs to him. (See John 2. 11.)

b. The Pharisees said, "First do a remarkable miracle or "sign" for us, and afterwards we might "have faith in you". It was this sign that Jesus refused to give. He had been tempted to make people believe in Him by such means, but had overcome the temptation (Matt. 4. 5–7; and note on Mark 1. 13).

2. It was because he wanted men to follow Him for the *right reasons*, i.e.:

a. In *Faith*, i.e., to take a risk and to obey Him without having seen any extraordinary event such as His coming down out of the sky. See Additional Note, p. 91.

b. Of their own *Free-will*. If He had done a "sign", they would have been forced to regard Him as a wonderful person.

c. With *Love*. If He had done a "sign", they would have looked on Him as a magician: He wanted them to regard Him as their Saviour who loved them.

3. *Ourselves:* Many people to-day are unwilling to follow Jesus in faith. They say: "If He stopped all the fighting in the world to-morrow, then I should be sure that he is God, just as I am sure that rain comes from the clouds. But I will wait until He does something like that before I become a Christian." Those people will wait for ever, because "no sign shall be given".

God has already sent us His Son, who lived a life of perfect goodness, and then after His death, rose again. If we are unwilling to follow Him after all that, then nothing more will convince us.

Mark 8. 14-21 : The Anxiety of the Disciples about Bread

See also Matt. 16. 5-12

INTRODUCTION

There are really two parts in this story: a. Jesus' words about the Pharisees (v. 15 only); b. His words about anxiety (v. 14 and vv. 16-21).

Perhaps this is what happened: after Jesus had refused to give the Pharisees a "sign", they planned to arrest Him. (That is why He and the disciples hurriedly left that side of the lake without making the usual preparations.) In the boat He began to talk about the Pharisees, and said that they were like leaven in bread. (See note on v. 15.) As soon as He said that, one of the disciples remembered that they had only brought one loaf with them, and they began to worry about the shortage of food. So Jesus taught them again not to worry, but to trust Him.

NOTES

v. 15.   Be on your guard against the leaven of the Pharisees and the leaven of Herod.

When bread is being made, "leaven" (sometimes called "yeast") is mixed with the flour; then it is all put into a warm and dark place. After a little time, the leaven makes the bread rise and swell. Jesus said that the Pharisees and the friends of Herod were like leaven amongst the "bread" of the Jews: they influenced them harmfully and very strongly, e.g.:

1. **The Pharisees:** Their teaching made the Jews think that it was more important to keep the many traditions than to obey the real will of God. (See note on 7. 6, and Additional Note, p. 43.)

2. **The Herodians:** These people were harmful in a different way from the Pharisees. They would do anything (right or wrong) which would keep Herod in his position as Tetrarch of Galilee, and did not care if their action was God's will or not. (See note on 3. 6.) They were like some people of to-day who, in an election, vote for any candidate who promises to get them a good government job, no matter whether that candidate is a good or bad man.

v. 16.   They began to say to one another, We have no bread.

They were anxious and said, "Whatever shall we eat?" Like all anxious people, they forgot two great truths (see note on v. 18):

1. Jesus *can* do for us much that we cannot do for ourselves;

2. He loves us and *wants* to give us what we need.

The teaching which they needed and which all anxious people need is given more fully in Matt. 6. 25–34; Luke 12. 6–12. (See also Phil. 4. 6.)

Jesus did not teach that there is no need to make preparations. Of course students must prepare for examinations, and mothers are right to make clothes for babies that are not yet born. He did *not* say, "Take no thought" (as the A.V. wrongly says), but, "Do not be anxious". (Matt. 6. 34.)

v. 17.   Are your minds quite stupid?

Jesus was not blaming them for being disobedient. He was pointing out that they were still stupid and blind in heart. Their minds were closed. They, like the whole Jewish race, had been given the Son of

God, but they were too "blind" to see who He was. (See Isa: 6. 9, 10; Jer. 5. 21; Ezek. 12. 2; and Additional Note on the "blindness" of the disciples on p. 173.)

v. 18.   Do you not remember?

Part of the disciples' mistake was to forget. Perhaps that is why so much of our worship of God must be a remembering of what He has done. Reading passages of the Bible helps us to remember: the Holy Communion Service is called in the words of the Service itself "a perpetual memory" (i.e., memorial) of Christ's death. (See John 14. 26b.)

Mark 8. 22–26 : The Blind Man Cured

See also John 9. 1–7

INTRODUCTION

Mark has put together two stories of Jesus meeting "blindness". In 8. 14–21 it was the disciples' blindness of heart: in vv. 22–26 it is the blindness of a man's eyes that He took away.

This story is like the story of the deaf man (see Introduction to 7. 31–37). He took the man into a private place, He used saliva, He put his hands on him, and He told him to say nothing. Its teaching also is similar:

1. Jesus overcomes evil in the body. He cured the man's body because of His love and power. To-day He still cares for all who are blind and cures many through His servants on earth.

2. Jesus overcomes evil in the soul. In 8. 17–18, He spoke of the disciples' blindness of heart; but He was all the time curing it, and in 8. 27–30, we read how one of them "saw" the truth that Jesus was the Messiah. Jesus offers new "sight" to ourselves in our blindness of heart.

3. Jesus overcomes evil in the whole world. When He cast out blindness, He was showing that the "Kingdom" or "Rule of God" had begun in the world. So God has already started to overcome the world's evil. Here is hope for us: evil is not the master.

128

This is the last of the many stories contained in chaps. 6. 1—8. 26 which show how Jesus trained His disciples and taught and healed people, chiefly outside the territory of Galilee. After this, a great event occurred (8. 27–30) and a new part of Jesus' life and work began.

NOTES

v. 22. They came to Bethsaida, and a blind man was brought . . .

1. **Bethsaida:** This was on the east side of the river Jordan near to the place where it flows into the lake of Galilee. Thus it was outside the territory of Herod Antipas.

2. **Was brought:** The man's friends showed their care for him by bringing him to Jesus. There are many ways in which we can show our care for blind people: a. By bringing them to Jesus in prayer; b. by showing kindness to any who live near us; c. by persuading the Government or others to give them help when necessary; d. by preventing people from becoming blind. Many children are born blind because one of the parents had Syphilis. Many others become blind because they are not kept clean, and disease attacks them.

v. 23. He spat on his eyes and laid his hands on him . . .

1. **Spat:** See note on 7. 33.

2. **Laid his hands:** This way of healing the sick was used not only by Jesus, but also by Christians after His Ascension (Acts 28. 8). To-day there are many in the Church who use it. They are people who know how to pray, and who are sure that God wants everyone to be "made whole". It is God who heals: the power is not in the healers themselves. The act of laying on the hands is an outward sign to the patient that the loving God is near, and that His power can enter him to heal. (Sometimes the patient recovers only after hands have been laid on him more than once. This is what happened to the blind man in vv. 23, 25.)

Note: There are others who are not Christians who also can heal by laying on hands. This is not surprising (9. 38–40).

v. 24. I can see men, they look to me like trees . . .

1. This shows that Jesus cured the man gradually. He could not see at all at first; then he could see men, but not clearly; in v. 25 he can see perfectly. (Matthew and Luke, who used Mark's Gospel

when they were writing theirs, did not copy this story. Perhaps they thought that it was dishonouring Jesus to say that He did not heal the man as soon as He touched him in v. 22.) But a sudden cure is not more useful than a gradual one. Jesus saved the man from his blindness: that was the important thing.

2. Jesus also may cure blindness of heart gradually. The first time in our lives that we know that He loves us is a wonderful moment, and we see life in a new way. We often call this "conversion", but it is only a beginning, and we shall need Jesus to "touch" us many times before we shall see clearly His Majesty and His will for us.

v. 26.   Do not even enter the village.

This was said to stop the man from telling his friends about the wonderful cure. (See note on. 1. 44.)

Mark 8. 27–30: Peter's Declaration of Faith

See also Matt. 16. 13–20; Luke 9. 18–21

INTRODUCTION

Part 2 of Mark's Gospel

The whole section of Mark's Gospel which begins at 8. 27 and ends at 10. 45 can be called "Part 2" of his Gospel. From the time when Peter declared that Jesus was the Christ or Messiah (v. 29), He did His work in new ways: a. He now taught His own disciples rather than the crowds; b. He gave very little time to healing; c. He taught them about Himself; d. He especially taught them about His own death (see 8. 31; 9. 31; 10. 33). For this reason this part of the Gospel is sometimes called "The Way to the Cross".

The story of chapter 8. 27–30.

Jesus and His disciples now travelled northwards towards Caesarea of Philip, so-called because it was built by Herod Philip, the brother of Antipas. It was about twenty five miles from the lake of Galilee. On the way they talked together, and Jesus asked them if they knew

130

who He really was. (Luke says that He prayed before He did so.)
Then Peter, probably speaking on behalf of the others, made his
great declaration, "You are the Christ" (or Messiah). We see in the
next section (8. 31–33) what Jesus' answer was. He said, "Yes, I am;
but the Messiah must suffer before He reigns", and (in 8. 34–9. 1,
the other great lesson He taught them at this time), "My followers,
too, must be prepared to suffer."

NOTES

v. 27. Who do the people say I am?

See note on 6. 14. According to the disciples, some said that He was
Elijah or John the Baptizer (prophets who only prepared for the
Messiah; see Mal. 4. 5; John 1. 20–23). So many people to-day speak
of Jesus as "one of the greatest men who ever lived, like Socrates",
and Muslims treat Him as one of the great prophets. But the New
Testament shows that He was more than that (Matt. 12. 14, 42).
He did for mankind, by His living and His dying, what no one else
has ever done. He is *the* way, not one of many good ways (John
14. 6).

v. 29a. But you, who do you say that I am?

1. This is the most important question that has ever been asked.
Who was Jesus? Was He only a very good man? Or was He mad?
Or was He a deceiver? (See note on 3. 21a.) Or is He God and alive
now? None of us can escape giving one of these answers.

Some say, "Why did Jesus not tell them plainly who He was?"
The answer is that: a. even if He had done so, they probably would
not have believed it; b. it is no use telling people certain things:
they have to find them out for themselves. (Students do not become
good teachers by listening to lectures on methods, but by watching
good teachers and by practising teaching.) The disciples had lived
with Jesus and watched Him, and very slowly they had been finding
out who He was. (See Mark 4. 41; 8. 17; John 6. 68, 69, etc.) By
asking this question Jesus made them make up their minds.

2. **But you:** Jesus asked the disciples to decide *for themselves*
who He was. He asks the same of us. (See also John 18. 4.) It is
not enough for us to know what others think about Jesus, or what
the Creeds teach, or to worship Him in church because our friends

do so. We must decide what *we* believe. When trouble or persecution comes, it is only those who have decided for themselves to obey Jesus as Lord who stand firm.

v. 29b. You are the Christ.

1. **The Christ**: See Additional Note, p. 133. The Jews had for a long time been waiting for God to send someone who would obtain freedom for their nation. The person was called "Messiah" (or "Christ" by those who spoke Greek). Peter and the disciples were the first to see that Jesus was this Person.

2. *Peter's "faith"*: Peter took a risk when He said this, because he could not prove that Jesus was the Messiah in the same way that he could prove that Andrew was his brother. He said it in faith. Every time a man of to-day, e.g., a candidate for Baptism, says, "I believe in Jesus Christ", he is taking the same risk. (See Additional Note, p. 91.)

3. *The first step:* When they called Jesus "Messiah", it was only the first step. They did not yet know that He was much more than Messiah, that He was really God's own and only Son. (It was a long time before they knew that.) They only knew a little about Jesus, but what they knew was true. Many of us are in the same position: we have made a start in following Jesus, and if we are humble and faithful, God will certainly show us more about Himself and how we can serve Him.

Note: **On this rock:** According to Matt. 16. 18, Jesus replied to Peter's Declaration, "On this rock I will build my Church". Three different answers have been given to the question, "What did Jesus mean by the 'rock'?"

1. The "rock" refers to the belief in Jesus as the Messiah, and Jesus meant, "Your belief is like a strong foundation, and one on which I can now build my Church of believers".

2. The "rock" referred to Peter, and Jesus meant, "Since you, Peter, know who I am, you shall be the leader of the Church".

Either of these interpretations is possible.

3. There is a third answer given by Roman Catholics:

The "rock" means not only Peter, but also all who, after him, become head of the Church in Rome. Thus they teach that Jesus in this verse gave authority to all future Bishops of Rome over all other Christians. But the Bible itself does not teach this, and no

Christians taught it until 350 years after Christ had spoken the words.

v. 30.   He forbad them to tell . . .

Jesus did not mean that Peter was wrong, but He did not want them to tell others that He was the Messiah, until they had learned what sort of Messiah He was. In vv. 31–33 we see that Peter was quite ignorant about that. He thought, like other Jews, that the Messiah would fight against evil with Jewish armies and God's angels.

ADDITIONAL NOTE
JESUS THE MESSIAH

1. *What does the word "Messiah" mean?*

It is a Hebrew word and means "someone anointed with oil". Kings were anointed, so "Messiah" often means a royal person.

The Greek translation of "anointed" is *christos*, so "Christ" and "Messiah" mean the same. Later "Christ" was used by the followers of Jesus as part of His name (Acts 2. 38).

2. *What sort of Messiah were the Jews expecting before Jesus came?*

For hundreds of years the Jews in Palestine had been a subject race, ruled by foreigners; yet they were God's chosen people. So they longed for someone to lead them into greatness and freedom. According to their prophets, God promised to send them a deliverer, who was often called "the Messiah".

The Jews held many different opinions about this Messiah. These are some of the beliefs often held: a. God (not mankind) will take the first step in sending him; b. Elijah will come back to prepare for him (9. 11–13); c. he will be a descendant of King David (see note on 12. 35–37); d. he will be opposed by other nations, but he will overcome them, probably by military force, and will gain freedom for the Jews; f. Jerusalem will be rebuilt and the Jews will live together there as a community; g. other nations will be subject to the Jews.

3. *What sort of Messiah was Jesus?*

a. He was sent by God, but He was more than a messenger: He was Himself God.

133

b. He did belong to David's royal family, but, unlike David, He did not use force: He did His work by suffering and by dying.

c. He did obtain freedom for others, but He obtained for them freedom from sin, rather than from a foreign enemy.

d. He obtained this freedom for the Jews, though it was not for the Jews only, but for all mankind.

e. He did found a community, but it was not at Jerusalem: His community was the Church of all believers (John 4. 21).

Thus there were many ways in which He was *like* the sort of Messiah the Jews expected: this is why Peter could say to Jesus, "You are the Messiah" (8. 27). But there were ways in which He was very much *unlike* the Messiah who was expected. This is why very few Jews could see that He was the Messiah.

4. *Did Jesus know that He was the Messiah?*

It is probable that He did, and that He first knew it when He was baptized. (See note on 1. 9–11.)

5. *Did He ever say that He was the Messiah?*

According to Mark, He said so only once, at the time of His trial (see 14. 61).

6. *Why did He tell people not to say that He was the Messiah?*

For two reasons:

a. He did not want crowds around Him. They would have made it impossible for Him to train His disciples.

b. Most Jews who heard that He was the Messiah would expect Him to use violence against the Romans. They would not understand what sort of Messiah He was. (See notes on 1. 25, 34, 44; 3. 11; 5. 43; 7. 36; 8. 26.)

7. *Did He want people to know that He was the Messiah?*

Yes, He did indeed want them to know that He was, and that God had kept His promise to send them a deliverer. Teaching like that in 12. 1–12 was given in order that His hearers might recognize Him as the Messiah before they became guilty of killing Him. But He wanted them to know what sort of Messiah He really was.

8. *Who accepted Him as Messiah?*

a. Those like Simeon (Luke 2. 25–35) who had been expecting lowly Messiah.

b. Those with faith, i.e., those who were willing to take the risk of believing in Him. These people were the Christians (see John 20. 31). But most Jews had not enough faith to recognize Him. Although the person they had been expecting for hundreds of years had come, they did not know or receive Him. The Jews of to-day are still waiting for their Messiah to come. The Christian message to the Jews of to-day is, "He has come".

Mark 8. 31–33 : The First Announcement of Jesus' Death

See also Matt. 16. 21–23; Luke 9. 22

INTRODUCTION

In v. 29 Peter had called Jesus "Messiah". In these verses (31–33), Jesus explained that the Messiah is one who will suffer and die before He reigns. The whole passage (vv. 27–33) should be read together.

NOTES

v. 31. It was necessary for the Son of Man to suffer . . . and be put to death, and after three days to rise.

1. **Necessary:** He meant that: a. it was His Father's will that mankind should be saved through the sufferings of the Messiah (see note on 14. 36); b. the Scriptures (i.e., the Old Testament) had said so (see Isa. 53; also Luke 24. 46). He did *not* mean that there was a power called "Fate", which was stronger than God and which was going to make Him suffer: there is no such power. So when His suffering came, He was not surprised.

Note: This reminds us of questions which are often asked, e.g., Was God not able to save mankind without making Jesus suffer? Did God know that His Son would have to die when He sent Him

135

into the world? But they are surely questions which only God Himself can answer.

2. **Son of Man:** See Additional Note, p. 137. This was a name that Jesus used when speaking about Himself, especially when He was talking about His death.

3. **To suffer:** No Jew had ever before taught that the Messiah would suffer and die. They regarded Him as a conqueror. It is true that passages like Isa. 53 had spoken of a "Servant of God" who would suffer for others, but no one thought that this Servant and the Messiah were the same person. So it seemed nonsense to them when Jesus taught that: a. the two were the same; b. it was because He had to suffer that He was Messiah. (See note below on v. 33.)

4. **After three days:** English readers sometimes think that this is different from "on the third day" (1 Cor. 15. 4) and that this saying of Jesus does not agree with what really happened at Easter. But in Hebrew there is no difference, as Gen. 42. 17 shows. (But probably the words "after three days" just meant "after a short while".)

5. **To rise:** This showed that the Messiah would, as the Jews had said, be a conqueror, but only after first suffering and dying.

v. 32. Peter took him aside, and began to rebuke him.

He said, "This shall never happen to you".

1. He was tempting Jesus to escape His suffering. That is why Jesus called him "Satan". (See note on 1. 13 about Satan.) Being a real man, Jesus continued to be tempted all through His life on earth.

2. He thought he knew better than Jesus. (See notes on 6. 37 and Additional Note on the blindness of the disciples, p. 173.)

v. 35. Out of my sight, you Satan; your way of thinking is not God's but man's.

1. **Not God's way but man's:** See Isa. 55. 8, 9. How very often Christians, in making plans for themselves or for the Church think in the way that the world usually thinks. They forget how different are God's ways. Even at Church meetings we often fail to listen quietly and humbly for His guidance before we begin our discussions: we wrongly think that our thoughts are likely to be the same as God's.

2. *Man tries to save without suffering:* This is one great difference between man's plans and God's. God knows that people can only be saved by those who are willing to suffer for them. Jesus knew that

He had actually to die in order to save men: it was not enough merely to teach and to heal them. It is true that most mothers and fathers know that they have to suffer in many ways in order to bring up their children in the best way, but generally speaking we men and women have not yet learnt this lesson. Most of us are enemies, not of Jesus, but of His methods (Phil. 3. 18).

The teaching of this verse is continued in the next section (8. 34—9. 1).

ADDITIONAL NOTE

THE SON OF MAN

Jesus used these words as a name for Himself. It was a title known to the Jews, although we do not know fully what it meant to them, He gave it a new meaning.

There are three special ways in which Jesus used it:

1. Someone who has the same *authority* as God (2. 10, 28). So it was almost a way of saying that He was Himself God.

2. Someone who is going to save others by *suffering* and by dying. So the name is like the "Servant of the Lord" in Isa. 53. Jesus used the name in this way especially as the time for His death drew nearer, i.e., after the events described in 8. 27. (See 8. 31; 9. 12; 10. 33, 45; 14. 21.)

3. Someone who will come *at the end of the world* as a judge (8. 38) with great power (13. 26), to overcome God's enemies and set His people free (14. 62). The name "Son of Man" had already been used in this way in Dan. 7. 13, 14.

Thus, sometimes "Son of Man" means almost the same as "Messiah". (See 14. 62 and Additional Note, p. 133.)

Mark 8. 34—9. 1 : Losing Oneself and Finding Oneself

See also Matt. 16. 24–28; Luke 9. 23–27

INTRODUCTION

The Story

In vv. 31–33 Jesus had spoken about the sufferings He was going to endure. Several days went by and then He continued that teaching by saying, "My followers also must be prepared to suffer" (8. 34—9. 1). He was now speaking to the crowd, not to the disciples alone, which shows that these words are not for a few Christians only, but for all of us. The crowd had hoped to make Jesus the leader of a rebellion and wanted Him to be a king in Jerusalem, so this new teaching was very hard to accept. But it was the teaching that they needed.

The teaching

Those who follow Jesus must be willing to give up things which most of us want to keep:

a. They must be prepared to lose their safety, and even their lives for His sake. It must be admitted that we often lose this spirit to-day, as is shown by these words which were spoken recently at a meeting of a city church: "We cannot expect our members to attend unless we provide them with a good choir and comfortable seats."

b. Followers of Jesus must "disown themselves" (v. 34) and "lose themselves" (v. 35).

c. Those who do this will "find themselves": they will find the best and happiest kind of life. It is dangerous to follow Jesus, but it is more dangerous not to follow Him.

Note: Mark was probably writing this passage at a time when the Christians were being persecuted in Rome by the Emperor Nero (about A.D. 65). If so, it must have been of special help to them.

NOTES

v. 34. If any man wishes to come after me, let him disown himself, and take up his cross . . .

1. **Disown:** This is a better translation than "deny". If I disown

138

myself, I look on myself as I would look on someone else. I love myself only as much as I love all other people. I take notice of what I want, just as I notice what others want, but not more than that. I am not my own: I am just one of God's many children. (1 Cor. 6. 19b.) If we ask, "Can anyone really do this?", the answer is that it is just what some of the happiest people in the world have done. *Note:* "Does this mean that followers of Christ should not have any ambition in life?" No, Paul had strong ambitions (Phil. 3. 14) and so have most healthy people. There is a right kind of ambition as well as a wrong kind. A Christian says something like this: "It is my ambition to become a good doctor (or whatever it is), but: a. I only want to be that if God wants me to be it; b. I hope that all God's children also will find the work in which they can be most useful."

2. **Take up his cross:** A cross was a heavy piece of wood about 8 ft long which was carried through the streets by a criminal who was going to be executed. When he reached the place of execution, he was tied or nailed to it. (See note on 15. 24.)

a. There are several ways in which followers of Jesus are *like* those criminals carrying a cross through the street: (i) they expect to suffer and are not surprised when it comes; (ii) they have given up all desire to be honoured.

b. The way in which a Christian is *unlike* those criminals is that he "takes up his cross" willingly: he is not forced to (Mark 15. 21). If we complain to God about the pains or insults we endure, it is plain that we have not "taken up" our cross.

Note: There is for some of us a third way in which we may have to be like those criminals: we may have to die for His sake. We think, for example, of those faithful Africans, men and women, in Kenya, who were killed by Mau Mau supporters. Some of them died simply because they refused to stop worshipping Jesus.

v. 35. Whosoever wishes to save his life shall lose it . . .

This verse means, "The man who aims at saving himself will ruin himself: but the man who lets himself be lost for Jesus' sake will become his true self and his best self". The word which is translated "life" here means two things: a. the whole of oneself; b. one's life on earth. (The A.V. wrongly translates it "soul".) Thus there are two main lessons.

1. *Losing:* The person who is always thinking of ways of making himself happy or important will never be the happiest or best person that he could be. But as soon as he makes someone else happy instead (i.e., when he "loses himself"), he finds that he is becoming his best self. Most of us are too afraid to take the risk of "losing ourselves": we think, "If I don't grasp all I can for myself, no one will give me what I need. It is not safe to be unselfish". Thus we are often like the man who held on to a window in a two-storey house that was on fire: his friends said, "Let go and be saved", but he would not, for he dared not jump. So many people never take that risk all their lives and so never live the full and happy life that they could have. *Note:* No book can teach this lesson, but anyone, even an entirely uneducated person, can learn it by putting it into practice.

2. *Losing one's life on earth:* The person who tries to avoid death (e.g., by pretending that he is not a Christian during persecution) will lose the life after death: the man who is willing to be killed for Jesus' sake will find "eternal life". (It is this lesson that Mark himself probably had in mind, since he was writing to persecuted Christians.)

v. 36. What good does it do a man to gain the whole world and lose his life?

V. 35 said, "You must lose yourself in order to find yourself". Vv. 36 and 37 say, "No price is too high to pay in order to find and to be one's real self". We are reminded of the man travelling in a canoe, wearing a coat in which were heavy bags of coins. The canoe began to fill with water, and he was told, "Take your coat off if you want to be saved; what good is it to keep your money if you are dead?" Jesus shows how foolish it is to allow anything at all to prevent us from finding both life of the best possible kind now, and also life in the next world (Luke 12. 16–21).

v. 38. Whoever is ashamed of me . . . The Son of man shall be ashamed of him . . .

1. People are "ashamed of Jesus", the Son of Man, when they are afraid to admit that they are His followers, e.g., when they are in the company of those who are not Christians.

2. This verse does not mean that Jesus will cease to care about those who are disloyal to Him. He never gives us up even when we

give Him up. But at the Judgement, He will not pretend that we have been loyal if we have really been disloyal (Gal. 6. 7).

Chap. 9. 1. Some . . . shall not taste death, till they see the kingdom of God come with power.

This was a message of great encouragement. Jesus had taught in 1. 15 and elsewhere that the rule (or "Kingdom") of God over men's hearts had already begun to arrive. He now said that some of His hearers would see that rule powerfully at work in their own lifetime. At the time, and also during later persecutions of Christians, this probably seemed impossible to believe, but it wonderfully took place. Thirty years later there were strong Christian congregations even in great cities such as Rome, Alexandria, and Antioch.
Note: The words "Kingdom of God come with power" do not refer to the end of the world. In 13. 32 Jesus said even He did not know when that would take place.

See picture facing p. 142.

Mark 9. 2–8: The Disciples see the Glory of Jesus (The Transfiguration)

See also Matt. 17. 1–8; Luke 9. 28–36

INTRODUCTION

In Chap. 8. 31–end we learnt that Jesus would have to die: now in .9. 2–8 we are shown that this Jesus is God's own and only Son (v. 7), who was going to His death of His own free-will.

The Story

No one knows exactly what took place at this time, but it is possible to discover some of the important events. About a week had passed since Jesus told the disciples that He would have to suffer and die, and that they must be prepared to suffer too (8. 31–35). In order that He and they might offer themselves in obedience to God and might pray for guidance and strength, He went away with the three who best understood His teaching. They climbed some of the way up Mount Hermon, which is so high that it nearly always has snow on part of it. There they were able to be alone and quiet. While they were praying, the disciples saw a vision. Awe came over them as they saw Jesus shining white, then Elijah and Moses, and then a cloud. Last of all, they heard a voice. Then the vision came suddenly to an end.

The Vision

a. Was it a vision? Matthew says plainly that it was (17. 9). A vision is not a dream; it is something seen or heard by people who are fully awake, often when they are saying their prayers. Isaiah (6. 1) and Ezekiel (1. 1) saw visions, and in the Acts we read of many visions (9. 3 with 26. 19; 10. 9-11; 16. 9). Many have since those days done great work for God as the result of visions they saw.

b. Are visions sent by God? Can we trust what we see in a vision? Sometimes, but not always. For it is possible for someone to see a vision just because he is sick. Therefore those to whom this happens should ask, "Does this teach me something that I know Jesus Himself would want to teach me?" If it does, it is to be trusted and followed, and in such a case we can surely say, "God sent me this."

The Teaching

Through their vision, the disciples were shown two great truths about Jesus Himself.

1. They saw Jesus as He really was: a. they saw Him shining with a bright light: it was as if until then they had been wearing dark glasses; now the glasses were taken away and at last "they saw His Glory" (Luke 9. 32; see also 2 Cor. 3. 15-end); b. then they saw a cloud, which in the minds of the Jews, was a sign of God's presence (see Ex. 13. 21; 24. 15); c. lastly they heard the voice telling them that Jesus was God's own and only Son. (See notes on v. 7.) In these three ways they saw Him as He really was, and they fell down and worshipped (Matt. 17. 6). That is the best thing that we too can do after reading this story.

2. They learnt that He was greater than either the Jewish Law or the great Prophets. In the vision He remained after Moses (the Lawgiver) and Elijah (the Prophet) had gone. (See note on v. 8.)

"Whoever loses his life for my sake shall save it" (Mark 8. 35).

In this match between Ghana (wearing double bars on their shirts) and Sudan (single bar), a Ghanaian player is about to pass the ball to another Ghanaian. He must first lose possession of the ball in order that his team may defeat Sudan and he himself be part of the winning team.

"He was telling them that the Son of man was to be given over into the hands of men" (Mark 9. 31).

This young American has led a public protest against the policy of his country's government which he believes to be "warlike". As a result he is arrested and beaten by riot police.

NOTES

v. 2. A change came over his appearance;

See Introduction. Did Jesus' appearance really change or was it only in their vision that it seemed to change? We cannot really answer that question, but note:

1. Since Jesus was God's own and only Son, it would not be surprising if His appearance did really become different from that of other men;

2. All three disciples saw His changed appearance;

3. Perhaps it happened at that time because He had, in His prayer, completely offered Himself to do the will of His Father, and was filled with peace and joy;

4. The faces of many men and women have been seen to shine (see Ex. 34. 30). George Fox, the saintly founder of the Society of Friends, was being stoned by students whom he was addressing. Suddenly they noticed that his face shone, and became silent.

v. 4. Elijah together with Moses appeared to them . . .

Elijah was the great Prophet, Moses the great Lawgiver. (See note on v. 8.)

1. **Elijah:** Jews believed that when the Messiah came, Elijah would come with him (see Mal. 4. 5). So when Peter saw Jesus accompanied by Elijah in the vision, he knew he had been right in calling Jesus "Messiah" (8. 27).

2. **Appeared to them:** Did Moses and Elijah really come back from the grave? No. Since it was a vision that the disciples saw, we cannot say that this story teaches that dead people return to earth.

v. 5. Let us make three shelters . . .

Peter was afraid and confused by what he saw. He unwisely said the first thing that came into his mind, "Let us show honour by making a shelter for each of you." His words show that he held wrong ideas:

1. He was treating all three as equals, forgetting that Jesus was so much greater than the others.

2. He was hoping to persuade Jesus to remain with them on the mountain, and to escape from the suffering of which He had spoken (8. 31). (See Additional Note, p. 173.)

v. 7. A cloud came . . . and a voice came out of the cloud, This is my Son, my beloved, listen to him.

1. **A cloud:** This was regarded by all Jews as a sign and as a reminder of the presence of God (Ex. 13. 21; 24. 15). When at this time the disciples saw Jesus in a cloud, they perhaps asked themselves, "Can it be that God Himself is present in Jesus?" Long afterwards they could answer, "God was indeed present; for we now know that where Jesus is, God is; for Jesus is God" (2 Pet. 1. 16–19).

2. **A voice came:** The Bible is full of stories of people "hearing God's voice". "Hearing" His voice means becoming certain that God is making something known to us (rather than hearing a noise, e.g., like that of a radio). There is "hearing" as well as "seeing" in a vision (see Acts 9. 3, 4).

3. **Beloved:** means "My own and only" (Mark 1. 1; Gen. 22. 2).

4. **This is my Son:** "Do we know that Jesus is God's Son because these words were heard? Do the words prove that Jesus is God?" They do not. No words and no miracles ever made a man believe that. It is by faith that we believe that Jesus is God: so it is only after we have made that act of faith that we can understand words like these, and that we find they are true. They only strengthen a belief we had already.

5. **Listen to him:** i.e., to Him rather than to Moses or Elijah. (See note on v. 8.) It also means "Spend more time listening to Jesus Himself in prayer than to listening to friends or reading books". (We are all tempted to listen to people rather than to Jesus.) And some Christians spend so much time reading the Bible that they have no time, and no wish, to hear the living Jesus Himself. "You search the Scriptures . . . yet you are not willing to come to me" (John 5. 39, 40).

v. 8. They saw no one, but Jesus only . . .

Elijah and Moses went out of sight: Jesus remained. So they discovered that Jesus had taken the place of the great Prophets like Elijah, and of the great Law of Moses.

This does not mean that we need no longer read the Old Testament. It does mean that:

1. When we want to find out God's will for us, it is the teaching of Jesus that is our perfect guide: it is more certain even than the teaching of the Prophets.

2. The most important thing is to love and follow Jesus rather than to try to keep a number of laws (see John 1. 17). There are many who are called Christians, but who really follow a system of laws, like those of Moses. These are the people Paul was talking of in Gal. 3. 2; Col. 2. 8, 16, 17.

Mark 9. 9–13: Coming down from the Mountain
See also Matt. 17. 9–13

INTRODUCTION

There are two parts in this story:

1. *Vv.* 9, 10: As they came down from the mountain Jesus said, "Tell no one about this until after I have risen from the dead". They said, "Why do you speak about dying and rising? You are the Messiah: how can the Messiah die?" (See note on v. 9.)

2. *Vv.* 11–13: Then perhaps they continued to talk about Jesus being the Messiah, and one of them said, "But can He really be the Messiah? For we are taught that Elijah must come before the Messiah. But Elijah has only been seen in a vision, he has not come to the earth". (See note on v. 13.)

NOTES

v. 9. He forbad them to tell . . . till the Son of man had risen from the dead.

1. **He forbad:** He told them to keep silent in order that: a. people should not hear that He was the Messiah, and then try to make Him nothing more than a leader in a political rebellion; b. the three disciples should have time to understand the lessons of the vision before they taught them to others.

This good news was first known only to a few, and had to be kept secret for a time; then at the right moment it became as widely known as was possible. (See Luke 12. 3, and note on Mark 4. 22.)

2. **Son of man:** See Additional Note, p. 137.

3. **From the dead:** As in 8. 31, Jesus spoke about His death. The three still thought that the Messiah could not be defeated, could not

145

die. So He says, "You should not be perplexed, because the Scriptures (i.e., the Old Testament) say that the Messiah will suffer". Perhaps He was thinking of Isa. 53. 4, etc., but other Jews did not think that Isaiah in chap. 53 was speaking about the Messiah.

In order to save us, Jesus the Son of God had to die. There was no other way. That is what most people, e.g., Muslims, do not understand, and what Christians often forget.

v. 13. Elijah has come already . . .

1. The disciples said, "Elijah must surely come before the Messiah comes". (See Introduction.) Jesus replied, "Elijah has come", meaning that John the Baptizer had come and had taken the place of Elijah (Matt. 17. 13). And He added, "You can tell that John has followed in Elijah's footsteps because he has suffered boldly". (Compare 1 Kings 19. 1, 2 with Mark 6. 19.)

2. Did Jesus in this verse teach that the spirit or soul of Elijah had been born again into the world when John the Baptizer was born? (i.e., Did Jesus believe in "reincarnation?")

a. The meaning of the verse is made plain by Luke 11. 7: John was a prophet who did the same sort of work as Elijah and with the same courage and faithfulness to God. It does not teach that the soul of Elijah returned to the earth in John.

b. No verse in the Bible definitely forbids us to believe in "reincarnation", but there is nothing in the New Testament to show us that Jesus or His followers believed in it. There were some Jews who believed in it (see Wisd. 8. 19, 20), but most of these were probably Jews who lived in foreign countries like Egypt and Greece.

Mark 9. 14–29: The Cure of the Epileptic Boy

See also Matt. 17. 14–21; Luke 9. 37–43a

INTRODUCTION

The Story

We are told in great detail how Jesus cured this boy. Mark must have heard what happened from one who had been present.

Note: 1. Jesus and the three disciples must have travelled some distance from the mountain, for that was a lonely place, and here there were crowds (v. 14).

2. The people were surprised to see Him; perhaps no one had expected Him to return so soon (v. 15).

3. Although Mark does not say so, Jesus probably took the boy and his father away from the crowd (as He usually did), for we learn from v. 25 that they began to crowd round Him again.

The Teaching

From this story we learn that: a. Jesus could and still can drive out evil (see Additional Note, p. 26); b. his followers can also do great things, if they have faith.

NOTES

v. 14.   A great crowd round them, and scribes arguing . . .

After the peace and joy which Jesus had on the mountain, He came down to meet the noise and evil of this town: the evils of useless argument (v. 16), sickness (v. 17, 18), and lack of faith (v. 19). What a difference! (In the same way, after the joyful vision at His Baptism, Jesus had to face His temptations: see 1. 11, 12.)

After our prayers, and after times when it seems easy to believe that God is good, then our faith is tested, e.g., by hardship, or by working among suffering or sinful people.

v. 16.   What are you arguing about . . . ?

1. This is one of many questions that Jesus asked. (See also v. 21.) He asked in order to know: He did not pretend to be ignorant. When God became man, He became a real man, and there were therefore matters about which He had to ask in order to know. (See notes on 5. 30 and 12. 36.)

2. **Arguing:** the nine disciples had given up trying to cure the sick boy; they were not praying for power to do so. They were just arguing with the scribes of the town. It is still a temptation for Christians to argue and discuss instead of praying and going out into the places where their help is needed.

MARK 9. 14–29

v. 17.   He has a dumb spirit . . .

The spirit was regarded as someone who lived inside the boy, and who could speak and see (v. 20). (See note on 1. 23.) To-day doctors would probably say that the boy had epileptic fits. (The last words of v. 18 should be "becomes rigid", a common happening in such fits, not "pines" or "wastes away".)

v. 19.   O faithless age, how long have I to be with you?

This tells us something about the feelings of Jesus Himself. It gave Him pain to be amongst many people who did not have faith and to meet so many who could have been healed and saved, but who were not healed because they did not believe that God could do it. We sometimes think that because Jesus was God, it was easy for Him to live on the earth; but it was sometimes so very painful that He even longed for His time to come to an end. (See Luke 12. 50.) *Note:* "You" in this verse does not mean the disciples, but all the people of that time.

v. 23.   Power? Everything is in the power of the man that has faith.

1. The man had said, "If you have the power, please cure my boy" (v. 22). Jesus replied, "Why do you say, '*If* you have power'? That shows that you are not sure if I have it." (*Note:* The A.V. is not correct here.)

2. **Everything:** This means all those things which God has promised to give us, e.g., peace and joy (see John 14. 13). (The verse does not teach that if we are Church members, we obtain everything we should like to have!)

3. **Faith:** this word here refers to belief that: a. God loves us and wants to help us; b. He is able to do so. It means really *expecting* God to give us what we need. It does not mean faith in one's own powers (see Phil. 4. 13).

v. 24.   I have faith, help my want of faith.

1. **I have faith:** In these words, the boy's father showed the way in which we should pray: a. he was trustful; he had faith that Jesus could save his boy; b. he humbly admitted his weakness, and asked Jesus for help.

2. **My want of faith:** The man had not much faith, but he had a

148

little, and because of it, Jesus cured his son. God does not wait until we are perfect before He hears our prayers, but we must have some confidence in Him. (See Additional Note, p. 91.)

v. 29.   This kind can be driven out by nothing except prayer.

1. This was said in answer to the disciples' question, "Why could we not drive it out?". They had been able to heal before (6. 13), but had failed now.

2. In His answer Jesus meant that if they had depended more on God they could have healed the boy. (Perhaps their successes at other times had made them think that the power came from themselves.) He did not mean that if they had said one prayer, they could have healed him. Here Jesus is using the word "prayer" as He did in Luke 18. 1. (See also 1 Thess. 5. 17.) Prayer is living all day in faith and reliance on God; it is not only words spoken to Him.

3. We to-day are in a world full of evils, great ones, like war, lesser ones, like bribery. As happened in this story, people expect the followers of Jesus to drive evils away, but we have often failed. When we try to find out why we have failed, we should ask: a. Do we really *expect* God to overcome evil (i.e., have we faith in Him)? b. when a difficulty arises, do we regard prayer as one of the most important things to do?

Note: The A.V. adds "and fasting" to v. 29. Some old manuscripts of Mark do not contain these words, but they are true. It is those who know how to control their minds and bodies who can heal and help others.

Mark 9. 30–32: The Second Announcement of Jesus' Death

See also Matt. 17. 22, 23; Luke 9. 43b–45

INTRODUCTION

1. *The Journey*

These verses (and the rest of this chapter) tell of the beginning of the long journey of Jesus to Jerusalem to die. (See Luke 9. 51.) Probably this journey took six months, from September A.D. 28 until March A.D. 29, for He did not go straight to Jerusalem. During these months He paid His last visits to Galilee, and taught in the villages of Judea and Perea (as Mark says in 9. 30—10. 31). He probably also made short visits to Jerusalem (described in John, chaps. 7–11) and taught in Samaria and other areas described by Luke in chaps. 9–18. He wanted His journey to be made in secret (v. 30) for two reasons: a. He wished to escape being arrested by Herod; b. He wanted peace in which to train the Twelve. It was not His plan to die yet, but in Jerusalem, and at a time chosen by God.

2. *The Teaching on the Journey*

In chaps. 9. 30 to 10. 52 Mark has collected together stories showing the chief lessons that Jesus taught His disciples at this time. This lesson was that the real value of a person or thing is different from the value which the world usually gives to it, e.g., the one who really saves men is One who will suffer, i.e., Jesus (see 9. 30–32; 10. 32–34; 10. 45).

NOTES

v. 31. Given over into the hands of men . . .
Jesus meant that His Father would "give Him over" to be killed, because there was no other way in which to save us. (See notes on 8. 31–33; also Rom. 8. 32.)

v. 32. They did not understand . . .
See note on 8. 17 and Additional Note, p. 173. Although they had been told about Jesus' death twice already, they still did not understand. So Jesus went on patiently teaching them, as He goes on patiently teaching us, although we are very slow to understand.

See picture facing p. 143.

Mark 9. 33–37 : "Who is the greatest?"

See also Matt. 18. 1–5. Luke 9. 46–48

INTRODUCTION

The disciples had been discussing on the road which of them were the most important, and who would have the highest places when

Jesus became King. (They still thought that Jesus would rule as King in Jerusalem.) Perhaps some of them were jealous that only three had been chosen to go up the mountain (9. 2). Jesus showed them who really are the "great" people: this teaching is in two parts:

1. *Vv.* 33–35: Those who serve others are the "great" ones.
2. *Vv.* 36, 37: Serve those who most need help.

Note: The "house" where He taught was probably Peter's, as in 1. 29, 2. 1.

NOTES

v. 33.   What were you arguing about . . . ?

Jesus asked this question (as in v. 16), but this time He knew the answer. Perhaps He had heard them talking on the road. But they were too ashamed to answer Him.

Often we cannot help being ashamed when we remember that God has heard our conversation, e.g., when it was about things we want for ourselves.

v. 34.   Which of them was the greatest.

The disciples wanted to hold positions in which they would receive honour from others; they wanted to give orders and to have power over others. If they could do these things, they thought they would become important and "great". This is what most people think to-day. Even leaders in the Church (who ought to have the spirit of Jesus in them) sometimes feel jealous when others are chosen for high positions. The teaching which the disciples needed, and we need, is in v. 35 and, more fully, in 10. 41–45. (See Additional Note, p. 137.)

v. 35.   If anyone wishes to be first, he shall be the last of all, and the servant of all.

1. In saying this Jesus was saying the opposite of what most people in the world think. (See note on 10. 43.) The man who is truly "great" (i.e., who is "first"), says Jesus, is not the rich man, nor the chief or ruler, but is anyone who serves others without looking for honour or praise.

Note: Jesus was not here telling them that they *ought* to serve others: what He is saying is that people who serve humbly really *are* the greatest.

2. This does not mean that a leader like a king or a bishop cannot become "great" in God's eyes. There are Christians in high positions who are truly great, because they have no wish to receive praise from others, but serve their fellow-men by undertaking hard work on behalf of others.

3. Nor does it mean that all who do useful work for others, like cleaning the roads, are "great". Such people are often humble; but they may, on the other hand, have in their hearts jealousy and a desire to be honoured and praised.

4. The Greek word which is here translated "servant" is *diakonos* (deacon). The R.V. used the word "minister". These names, deacon and minister, have been used for positions in the Church; this verse reminds us that their chief work is to be servants, not lords, of all. The same is, of course, true of all who hold authority in the Church. (See note on 10. 45; Rom. 12. 16.)

v. 37. Whoever receives one little child like this in my name receives me . . .

1. In vv. 33–35 He told them to serve others: in vv. 36–37 He said, "Serve especially those who are young or weak". Not only did He teach this by word, but He Himself also put His arms with affection round one small child.
Note: The teaching here is different from that of 10. 13–16, where we are taught to *be like* children.

2. By treating children in this way He was doing what great teachers before Him had not done. Of course, even in the days before Christ came, parents cared deeply for their children and others often treated them very well. But even a father going a journey with a young child might leave the child to carry the heaviest load. When we see children being looked after with great love and care to-day (e.g., in schools and hospitals), we know that one reason for this is that Jesus cared for them.

3. **Child:** This meant not only young boys and girls, but all people who are unable to protect themselves, and all who have the greatest need to be served: it included new Christians and those who are weak in times of temptation (9. 42; Rom. 14. 1; 15. 1; 1 Cor. 8. 13).

4. **In my name:** This means "because I have told you". (See note on v. 38.)

5. **Receives me:** When we are humbly serving one who is in need

152

we are at that moment doing a service to Jesus Himself. In fact if I say that I serve and love Jesus but do not really give help to a neighbour in need, that shows that I do not really love Jesus (Matt. 25. 40; 1 John 4. 20). Then in v. 37b, Jesus added, "And if you do me this service, you are serving my Heavenly Father Himself".

Mark 9. 38–41 : The Healer who was not a Disciple

See also Luke 9. 49, 50

INTRODUCTION

This healer had not been given a command to heal by Jesus, nor did he work with the disciples. Yet he healed the sick and he said that he did so by the power of Jesus ("in your name", v. 38). How should he be treated?

Jesus' teaching was: "Be glad about the success of others: if others do good, they do so by God's help. My Church is not a body which fears the success of others because it thinks about its own power. The Church is the servant of all."

Thus this is another of the stories which Mark gives us to show how differently from the world Christ and His Church think and work.

Note: It is important to see what Jesus did *not* teach in these verses:

1. He did not say that it was good to do Christian work in separation from other Christians (see John 17. 10; Rom. 12. 5).

2. He did not say that all who call themselves Christians are on God's side.

3. He did not say that all religious people are equally right (see Acts 19. 13). Indeed, He often said that God judged between the true and the false. But God judges as Jesus judged this healer, i.e., by saying, "The true are those who are in fact driving out evil from others and overcoming evils like dishonesty and hatred in themselves".

When Christians to-day ask, "How should members of one Church treat those of another?" or "How should ordained ministers regard the work of laymen?" or "How should Christians treat those who live good lives but belong to no Church?" the answer comes from these verses: a. "Rejoice in the good that others do"; b. "refrain from speaking against them".

NOTES

v. 38.   We tried to stop him . . .

Why did they do this? Why do we to-day sometimes speak against those who are meeting or working in Jesus' name? Occasionally it may be right to do so (e.g., if they are really not engaged in driving out evil at all; if they are a trading company pretending to be a Church); but far more often we do it for wrong reasons such as these:

1. We are jealous of them and are afraid that they will have more power than we have or will have larger congregations.

2. We make the mistake of thinking that everyone should worship God exactly as we do. This mistake is a kind of selfishness or pride. There are many different right ways of worshipping and showing our love for God. In Rev. 21. 12 we read of *twelve* gates leading to the Holy City, not one only! (See Additional Note, p. 173.)

v. 40.   The man that is not against us is for us.

A different saying is in Matt. 12. 30. "He that is not with me is against me." There seems at first to be a contradiction between the two sayings, but the teaching of each verse is clear in the passage in which it comes:

1. Mark 9. 40: The meaning is: "When a man is doing good, do not stop him; he is on God's side".

2. Matt. 12. 30: The meaning is: "When a man refuses to do good and to give help in time of need, he is working against God".

v. 41.   Whoever gives you a cup of cold water . . . for the reason . . . that you are Christ's . . . shall not lose his wages.

This was perhaps said on a different occasion, for the teaching is not connected with that of vv. 38–40.
Note:

1. A small action done for the right reason is an important action.

2. The reason here is "because you belong to Christ": so the deed is done to Christ Himself. (See Matt. 25. 37–40.)

3. Such an action is a sacrament, i.e., an outward sign of love. God is not more pleased to hear us preach than to see us give a cool drink to someone in need.

4. This kind of person will get his reward. (See note on 10. 28–31 about rewards.)

Mark 9. 42–50: A Group of Sayings

See also Matt. 18. 6–9; Luke 17. 1, 2; 14. 34, 35

INTRODUCTION

These words of Jesus were not written down at the time He spoke them; those who heard Him remembered what He said (or part of it) and passed it on to others, Later Christian teachers (who perhaps had never seen Jesus) found it hard to remember this teaching, and so Church leaders sometimes collected together a group of sayings in a way that made it easy to remember them. That is what has been done here.

The saying about falling into sin (v. 42) helped them to remember the sayings about falling into sin and fire (vv. 43–48); these verses in turn lead on to the saying about fire and salt (v. 49), which reminded them of other sayings about salt (v. 50).

(If this grouping had not been done, perhaps Mark would never have heard of some of this teaching, nor should we.)

NOTES

v. 42. Whoever causes one of these little ones . . . to fall into sin . . .

This continues the teaching of v. 37, and means: "It is better to be drowned than to make some young or weak Christian lose his trust in God." (These are stern words, but of course they do not mean that Jesus wished anyone to be drowned in this way.)

1. As in v. 37, "little ones" means anyone weak in faith, but it

155

also means children. (Those living in big towns have to ask whether they are leading children into bad habits, e.g., by not providing places where they can play.)

2. This verse is for anyone whose words are listened to by others, parents, older brothers and sisters, newspaper editors, teachers, preachers.

v. 43.   If your hand makes you fall into sin, cut it off; better for you to enter into life with one hand, than to go away into the pit . . .

V. 42 was about the danger of harming others: vv. 43–48 are about the danger of harming oneself and of losing the best kind of life.

1. **Cut it off:** It is better to lose *everything* rather than to lose the full and joyful "life" of fellowship with God. Even a lizard knows that it is better to give up his tail than to let an enemy kill him. We have to "cut off" (give up) not only bad things, but often good ones too, in order to have this kind of life. Different people will give up different things. A priest gave up a high post because he knew that it was making him proud, saying, "My greatest powers are the reason for my greatest temptations." Others know that they have to give up alcohol: others that they must stop visiting their friends late at night because they become too tired to say their prayers.

2. **Enter into life:** In each case a man gives up a good thing in order to find the best thing of all, "life". That is the only reason why Jesus gave this teaching about "cutting off". It was not because He liked to see people depriving themselves of good things, nor because He is against enjoyment. It was because He knew that this is the way in which we find joy and the highest life of which we are capable. He came into this world in order that we might have such things (John 10. 10). Having this "life" is the same as entering the Kingdom of God (see v. 47): it means having eternal and joyful fellowship with God.

3. **Go away into the pit:** The word translated "pit" is "Gehenna" (In the A.V. the word is "Hell"). This was a place near Jerusalem (the Valley of Hinnom) where the city's rubbish used to be burned, and the name was later used to describe the state of wicked Jews after death.

Jesus here uses the word "Hell" or "pit" for the state of those who: a. have refused to give up the things that make them sin; b. have not "entered into life"; c. are apart from God; d. know what great

156

benefits they have lost; e. as a result, are in very great pain and unhappiness.

Note: "Hell" or "Gehenna" was different from Hades. Hades was called Sheol in Hebrew and was thought of as a resting place after death (not a place of misery or punishment).

v. 48.   The fire never goes out.

These words come from Isa. 66. 24. Jesus used them as another way of speaking about "Hell", to teach its pain and unhappiness.

The words do not teach that sinful people are punished everlastingly nor that they are destroyed for ever. Then what is the end of those who refuse to "enter into life"? It seems that God does not intend us to have definite knowledge about this. What the New Testament says clearly is this: a. God is a stern judge; b. you have the opportunity of having eternal life, through Jesus; take your opportunity.

v. 49.   Every one shall be salted with fire.

One of the many uses of fire was to clean. So this verse means: "Everyone shall be purified or made holy by enduring suffering." Christians after Pentecost found that this really was so (see 1 Cor. 3. 15b).

Note: It is when we accept suffering gladly for His sake that it purifies: to suffer with complaint purifies no one.

v. 50a.   If the salt has lost its saltness, with what will you make it salt . . . ?

Salt has many uses: a. To make things clean; b. to keep things from going bad; c. to make food taste good. If it is mixed with something else, e.g., with white sand, it still looks like salt, but no longer does the work of salt.

Jesus has given each Christian congregation its own work to do for Him in the town where it is situated, e.g., to live in love towards each other, and to remind everyone of God's will for mankind. But it is possible for its members to become too much mixed with those who do not follow Christ. In this case they may still *look* like Christians, but they no longer do the work Jesus gave them to do.

v. 50b.   Have salt . . . and be at peace . . .

Salt was also a sign of fellowship. If men ate together and put salt on their food, they showed that they trusted each other. Perhaps Jesus said these words on some occasion when the disciples were quarrelling, e.g., 9. 33, 34.

Mark 10. 1–12: Teaching about Marriage

See also Matt. 19. 1–12

INTRODUCTION

The Journey

Jesus and the disciples, on their long journey to Jerusalem, now visited Perea (the eastern part of the country now called Jordan) and parts of Judea. (See v. 1 and note on 9. 30–32. Introduction.) In one town, Pharisees, who had perhaps heard that some of His teaching did not agree with that of Moses, asked Him if divorce was allowed. Probably they planned to report Him to the authorities if He taught differently from Moses (who had allowed divorce in Deut. 24).

The Teaching

He did something more than answer their question about divorce, because He drew their attention to an even more important question, namely, "What kind of marriage does God intend us to have?" He said:

1. God's plan is for a man and a woman who marry to remain together as long as they live. (See notes on vv. 6 and 8.)

2. The same faithfulness is expected of the man as is expected of the wife. (See note on v. 12.)

3. In all this passage, Jesus is thinking of marriage as between one man and one woman. (See note on v. 8.)

NOTES

v. 5. Moses wrote this commandment for you because of the hardness of your hearts.

This commandment was in Deut. 24. 1–4. Jesus does not here say that Moses was wrong to allow a man to divorce his wife. The teaching is that at the Creation God intended all married people to stay together for life, but when they sinned greatly and had little love for each other ("hearts were hardened"), He gave permission to Moses to allow divorce on condition that the woman was given a certificate. This teaching of Moses is not for Christians, for God's Kingdom has come and, we, its members follow God's plan at Creation, not the law in Deuteronomy.

v. 6. From the beginning . . . He has made them male and female . . .

This verse and vv. 7 and 8 are from Gen. 1. 27 and 2. 24, and show us God's plan for us men and women.

1. It is His plan that men and women shall marry and have children; for it is as children in a human family that we best learn how to love others.

2. He intends husband and wife to stay together for life. (See also 1 Cor. 7. 10, 11.) This is His plan for all people. Just as any machine only goes well if used in the way that the maker intended, so all who marry must pay attention to their Maker's plan, if they want to live happily. No one should marry except with the intention of living with the same partner for life.

v. 8. The two shall become one.

1. In the A.V. we find the words "one flesh". The verse means: "they will be joined for ever in body and mind and spirit. They will be joined together even more closely than are the members of a family" (see v. 7).

2. This verse, like v. 9, shows that Jesus had in mind the marriage of one man with one woman. (See also v. 7, where the words are "joined to his wife", not "to each wife".) He never actually said "Thou shalt not marry two wives", because this was unnecessary: at the time He was teaching the Jews no longer practised polygamy, as in the days of Abraham.

159

v. 9. What, then, God has joined, let not man divide.

Did Jesus in these words teach that divorce is never right? The answer of most Christians is as follows: Yes, this is one of the few rules that Jesus ever gave. We believe this because:

1. Divorce is against the plan God made when He created us (v. 6).

2. We have found that the rule is needed. It is only when two people, at the time of their marriage, know that they will never be divorced, that they can regard their marriage as secure. If they know divorce is possible, there is often less trust between them; one may be afraid that the other will go away when difficulties arise.

Note: Some Christians would give a rather different interpretation. They would say:

1. Jesus' words were an answer to the Pharisees only and not intended to be a rule for all Christians.

2. Although divorce is against God's plan and must be firmly avoided by Christians, there may be very occasional times when it is allowed. Matt. 19. 9 is sometimes quoted by those who say this. In this verse Jesus is reported as saying that a man can divorce his wife if she has committed fornication. But it is unlikely that Matthew's account is quite correct, because if Jesus had said that, He would have been taking sides between two groups of Pharisees. (These two groups were: a. that of Rabbi Hillel, who allowed divorce even for such reasons as bad cooking by the woman; b. that of Rabbi Shammai, who allowed it only after adultery.) Surely He did not do this, for He hated the way in which they both regarded the service of God as a matter of keeping rules. It is Mark, in this verse and verse 11, who seems to give the true teaching of Jesus on divorce.

v. 11. Whoever divorces his wife and marries another, commits adultery . . .

Jesus forbids Christians to re-marry during the life of the first partner. (See note on v. 9.)

v. 12. If she divorces her husband . . .

Jesus, in these words, puts the man and the woman equally under the law of faithfulness to one another. So once again, He taught something quite different from Jewish Law. According to Deut. 24. 1–4 there was one law for the man and another for the woman:

160

he could divorce her, but she could not leave him. And still to-day, when a woman commits adultery she is often punished, while a man who has committed the same offence goes free. But a Christian who expects to receive love and faithfulness from his wife knows from this verse that she has an equal right to expect these from him.

See picture facing p. 176.

Mark 10. 13–16 : Jesus and the Children

See also Matt. 19. 13–15; Luke 18. 15–17

INTRODUCTION

In this story about children being brought to be touched by Jesus, the great lesson is this: those who want to "enter God's Kingdom" must be like children in certain ways. (See note on v. 15.)

We see also how important children were in Jesus' eyes. Although He had much to do in the last few months before His death, He spent time with them and gave them happiness. (See note on 9. 37.) *Note:* The Greek word for "those" in v. 13 shows that both fathers and mothers probably brought children to Jesus.

NOTES

v. 14.   He was indignant, and said . . . Do not try to stop them;

1. **Was indignant:** He was angry because someone (not He Himself) was being ill-treated. (See note on 3. 5.)

2. **Do not try to stop them:** Perhaps the disciples tried to keep the children away in order to give Jesus rest; or because (like many people of that time) they did not think it necessary to pay attention to children; or because they thought that Jesus was going to overthrow the Romans by force and it seemed a waste of time for Jesus to talk to children who were too young to fight. We Christian parents and teachers of to-day often make the same mistake (of stopping young people from meeting and loving Jesus). We do that whenever we set them a bad example or fail to take enough trouble to teach them about Jesus, whether at home or in school or in church. (See Additional Note, p. 173.)

v. 15. Whoever does not receive the kingdom of God as a child, shall never enter it.

1. To **receive the Kingdom** is the same thing as to "enter the Kingdom" (9. 47); "to enter into life" (9. 43); "to be saved" (10. 26). All these phrases mean "living the best and most joyful kind of life".

We can have this kind of life (as a gift from God) by being like children. **Receive . . . as a child** means "Receive it in the way that a child receives something".

.2. **As a child:**

a. In what way are we to be like children? We are to be as trustful and dependent on God as children are upon people older than themselves. They know that they depend on the goodness and the knowledge of others; they do not worry about the future, for they trust older people to take care of them; they know they have little knowledge and are hungry for more. So God's Kingdom is for those who know they are weak and ignorant and sinful, and who gratefully accept from God the forgiveness, strength, and guidance He offers. (See Matt. 5. 6; Eph. 2. 8.)

b. But we who are no longer children are often *not* like this. We do not like to admit that we depend on God for everything that is good. (See John 9. 41b.) So we need to turn and become like a child again; we have to be "born again" (John 3. 3).

Note: Jesus nowhere commanded us to baptize infants, but this story shows us reasons why the Church thought it right to do so very soon after Pentecost. Jesus not only said "Let the children come to me" (v. 14) and took them up in His arms (v. 16); He also taught that children have something which everyone must have before he can belong to the Kingdom, namely a trustful heart. In view of this it would have been hard to refuse to admit children into membership of the Church (by Baptism).

v. 16. He took them in his arms . . . and blessed them.

He did more than they had asked. They asked Him to touch the children, but He took them up and put His arms round them, because He loved them. A collect says, "God, who . . . art wont to give more than either we desire or deserve . . ."

Mark 10. 17–22: The Refusal of the Rich Man

See also Matt. 19. 16–22; Luke 18. 18–23

INTRODUCTION

The Story

This man came to Jesus at some point on the long journey to Jerusalem. Perhaps he was a ruler (as Luke says) or a young man (as Matthew says); certainly he was rich. He was also a good man, who knew that he was not good enough.

Note the three questions Jesus put to him:

1. Do you sincerely mean what you say? (v. 18)

2. Are you living already according to the laws of God in so far as you understand them? (v. 19)

3. Are you willing to take a step further and give up the thing that is hindering you? (v. 21)

The Teaching

This story (like vv. 13–16) answers the question "How can we have the best kind of life?" In vv. 13–16 the answer was "By being like children"; here it is, "By giving up whatever prevents you having this life". (See notes on v. 21; 9. 43.)

NOTES

v. 17.   What am I to do to gain everlasting life?

1. His life was already a successful one in the eyes of others, but he rightly wanted his life to be more than that. He was so willing to learn that he ran along the road and knelt down, like a child.

2. **Everlasting life:** He wanted the best possible kind of life for himself. In the Bible these words do not only mean a life that goes on for ever after death, but a life full of joy and fellowship with God which we can already begin to have now. (See note on 10. 15; John 5. 24.)

v. 18.   Why do you call me good? No one is good but God.

Jesus is saying two things here:

163

1. When you called me "Good master", did you really mean what you said, or were you flattering me? Are you sincere?

2. Even if it is true that I am a "good master", remember that all goodness comes from God (John 5. 19).

In these words Jesus did not, of course, deny that He was perfectly good (John 8. 46). Nor did He mean that He was not God (John 10. 30).

v. 19.   You know the commandments . . .

Commandments means the Jewish law and we see here Jesus' attitude to that:

1. Although He did not teach us to keep it all (vv. 5, 6), He certainly expects us to keep the commandments mentioned here, which are about our duty to our neighbour.

2. But such commandments are like the foundations of a house: they are necessary, but not enough (v. 21; Matt. 5. 20).

3. In this verse He meant, "If you are doing your best to keep the old commandments, then you show me that you are sincere in trying to obey God. I can show you how to reach new life."

v. 20.   I have kept all these since I was a boy.

He could make this boast because he did not fully understand the commandments. He did not know for instance, that "Thou shalt not murder" means "Go on loving and helping everyone you can, especially those who have treated you unjustly". When we know that, we cannot say that we have kept even one commandment. (That is why we can never say that we have earned everlasting life.)

v. 21a.   Jesus looked at him and loved him . . .

1. **Jesus . . . loved him.**

a. The Greek word here translated "love" is "Agape", the word which describes the kind of love which Jesus showed in all His life and death. If we have this love, we give ourselves joyfully to the service of others and are willing to suffer for them.

b. Jesus loved this man because: i. he was a childlike person who knew that he needed help (see Matt. 19. 20 and note on v. 15); ii. He could see what he was capable of becoming in the future.

2. **Loved him:** it was the man himself that Jesus loved. He had no wish to have his money, not even to use it in the service of God.

164

v. 21b.   One thing you need; go and sell all . . . and you shall have treasure in heaven.

1. **Sell all:**

a. To sell all he possessed was the step which this man had to take in order to have the best and most joyful kind of life. Jesus could see that having money in some way stopped him from loving God and loving others fully.

b. There have always been Christians who knew that they could not follow Christ without giving away *all* their possessions. St Francis is one who did this, after reading this verse.

c. But Jesus did not give this command to everyone. It is not an evil thing to have money or possessions, but these become evil to us if they keep us from God. (See note on v. 23.)

d. There is, however, teaching in this which is for everyone: i. There are times in our life when, in order to obey God, we have to live without something which we enjoy; e.g., a well-educated man or woman may be called by God to work in a lonely place for a small salary in order to help the people of that place; a Christian may feel it necessary to resign from a political party (to which his friends belong), because it is working in an un-Christian way. ii. This is something more than keeping the Ten Commandments; it is the result of loving God whole-heartedly; General Booth (founder of the Salvation Army) said, "From the time I gave my heart to Christ, He had all of me." iii. These actions are daring; they are taken only by those who are willing to take a risk, i.e., those with faith. iv. But we do not "gain everlasting life" merely by one action like this; it is only the first step in following Christ.

2. **Treasure in heaven:**

a. "Heaven" sometimes means the sky, e.g., 7. 34. More often it means "fellowship with God" (as here). "Treasure in heaven" thus means a joyful life of fellowship with God. It can begin now and will continue after death.

b. This is a promise of a reward. (See notes on vv. 28–31.)

v. 22.   He went away sorrowful.

1. The man was willing to do much in order to find this new kind of life, but he wished to choose what he would do and would not do. He was like a man who asks a doctor for medicine, but when given it, is afraid to take it!

2. By not obeying Jesus, he kept his possessions and continued to be regarded by others as a successful man; but he lost a close friendship with Jesus, the joy of working with a group of disciples, and the full, joyful life he had asked for.

3. So Jesus did not succeed in making him a disciple, in spite of His love for him and although He was the Son of God.

If Jesus failed to convince a man, it is quite wrong for us to be discouraged when we fail. Of course the failure is often due to our own fault; but it may be due to the unwillingness of those we are trying to help.

Mark 10. 23-27 : Teaching about Possessions

See also Matt. 19. 23-26; Luke 18. 24-27

INTRODUCTION

This story is one of many stories which Mark has collected in chaps. 9 and 10, and which teach the same lesson, namely, that the true value of things is often the opposite of the value which most people give. (See Introduction to 9. 30-32.)

The teaching here is this: people think that it is easy for those who have possessions to have the best kind of life; but really it is very hard indeed for them.

NOTES

v. 23. How hard it will be for the rich to enter the kingdom of God . . . his disciples were greatly astonished.

1. **Astonished:** They were surprised because their own ideas about this were so different from the teaching Jesus now gave. They (and other Jews) had thought that:

a. If a man had many possessions, it was a sign that God was pleased with him (Gen. 24: 35). But Jesus taught almost the opposite of that!

b. Rich people were surely more holy than poor people because they had more money for Temple sacrifices and more leisure in

166

which to attend services. (But for Jesus a "holy" person was a child-like one (v. 15), not the one who went to church the most times.)

c. Although it was not easy for a rich man to be good, yet it was not very difficult if he was generous to the poor.

2. **How hard:** Jesus' teaching was:

a. It is almost impossible for rich people to "enter the Kingdom" (v. 25).

b. "Rich people" means anyone who has any possessions. (We need to note this, for we usually call "rich" anyone who has more than we have.)

c. It is hard for these reasons:

i. We so often lean on them and depend on them for our happiness. When we lose them, we find we cannot live happily without them. This is what is meant by "trusting in their wealth" in v. 24. (But we should note that these words are not found in many of the copies of Mark's Gospel.) We need to learn to lean on God Himself, as His children, and so have that fellowship with Him which is Life at its best.

ii. We may pay so much attention to possessions that we lose our desire to worship God or to serve others. Something always takes first place in our hearts, either God or possessions: both cannot (Matt. 6. 21, 24).

iii. We get power over others if we have possessions; a man with power finds it very hard either to serve others humbly or to have sympathy with them.

Note: It has sometimes been thought that these verses (especially v. 25) teach that no Christian should own anything privately. Some have therefore given what they have to the group to which they belonged (as in Acts 2. 44), or to their monastery or "ashram" (as in India); others have lived in poverty and depended on others' gifts. This is good, but Jesus has not told us *all* to do this; it is impossible for everyone to depend on the gifts of others! Nor is evil always got rid of by these means; for even the members of a group can be spoiled through the property which the group owns. This happened to many of the monks in England in the days when there were a large number of monasteries there.

v. 25.   It is easier for a camel to pass through the eye of a needle ...
This was His way of saying that "entering in" was almost impossible.

(v. 27 shows that it was not quite impossible.) This must have made people laugh. So with a joke and by speaking about ordinary things that were known to everyone, He made His teaching unforgettable.

v. 26.   Then who can be saved?

See notes on v. 15 and 5. 34. "To be saved" means the same as to "enter the Kingdom of God", i.e., to be given the power:

a. to overcome evil desires which tempt one to rely on possessions rather than on God;

b. to live the full life that God has meant us to live, both now and in the future.

v. 27.   With men it is impossible, but . . . with God all things are possible.

1. The meaning is, "A man with possessions can be 'saved', but only with God's help and because of His 'grace' (His generosity)." The last few words are encouraging: God never commands us to do anything without also providing the strength we need to do it (see 1 Cor. 10. 13; 2 Cor. 12. 9a; Phil. 4, 13).

2. The words do not, of course, mean that when we become Christians, we can do everything. If we try to live without eating, we shall die like anyone else. Nor does it mean that God Himself can do anything. God has chosen to behave in a certain way and He does not break His own rules, e.g., He will not force anyone to repent who refuses to do so.

Mark 10. 28–31 : Teaching about Rewards

See also Matt. 19. 27–30; Luke 18. 28–30

INTRODUCTION

The New Testament gives much teaching about rewards. The teaching is that:

1. Christians are promised rewards (9. 41; 10. 21).

2. What they do now makes a difference as to what reward will be theirs in the future (Gal. 6. 9).

We are not helpless, or in the hands of "Chance" or "Fate". We are free to choose to do right or wrong.

Jesus gives further teaching about rewards in these verses, and shows that the best reward of all is the joy of fellowship with God, i.e., "everlasting life" (v. 30).

NOTES

v. 29. If a man has left house . . . for my sake.

Rewards are not given to those whose chief reason for becoming a Christian is to gain them. They cannot be earned or deserved. They are given to those who follow Jesus and give up friends or possessions for the sake of Jesus and because they love Him, that is, "for my sake".

v. 30. He shall receive a hundred times as much now in this life, houses and brothers . . . with persecutions, and in the age to come everlasting life.

1. **A hundred times as much:** The rewards are very great. What we shall receive is of far greater value than the things we have given up (Rom. 8. 18). We are promised very great joy; because we know of the coming joy, we can live joyfully now.

2. **In this life, houses and brothers:** Rewards are given now, e.g., a man who becomes a Christian can already enjoy the fellowship of brotherly people in the Church (Eph. 2. 19).

3. **With persecutions:** This shows that the best reward is not regarded as desirable by non-Christians. It is not a thing that can be touched or seen (such as the rewards promised to Muslims in the Koran). Thus, no one can say, "My business will prosper and my family will increase because I am a Christian". Such things are not the rewards, for we are told to expect a life with "persecutions".

4. **In the age to come:** Rewards will be given in the future. The friendship we now have with God will continue after our death and in the new kingdom of God.

v. 31. Many are first that shall be last . . .

This means: "Rewards are not given to those who are expected by most people to receive them", e.g., "You think that the rich will be rewarded: actually it is the poor who are more likely to get a

G   169

reward. Turn your own thoughts on this upside-down, and then you will be thinking as God thinks." (See notes on 9. 35, 10. 43.) Sometimes the human race does gradually learn to judge men as God judges them. Once John Bunyan was a despised and imprisoned man: to-day everyone knows of his greatness, and very few know the name of the king who imprisoned him. The "last" is truly "first".

Mark 10. 32–34: The Third Announcement of Jesus' Death

See also Matt. 20. 17–19; Luke 18. 31–34

INTRODUCTION

Now began the last part of the journey to Jerusalem. Jesus walked alone in front: behind were the disciples and a larger group behind them. After a while He told them (for the third time) that He would soon be killed. (See note on 8. 31.)
Note: It is asked: "Did He know exactly what would happen to Him (as vv. 33, 34 suggest)?" Probably He did not, for He did not claim to have this kind of knowledge. (See note on 12. 36; 13. 32.) What He certainly knew was that He must soon die.

NOTES

v. 32. Jesus walked in front of them, and they were astonished and . . . afraid.

1. **Jesus . . . in front:** (See note on 1. 17; Heb. 12. 2.) Just as He was in front of the others on the road, so He was far beyond them in His understanding, e.g., He knew that He could not save others except by dying in Jerusalem: they did not yet know that. (Later they understood and themselves suffered for His sake.)

This has happened ever since: e.g., Jesus must have wanted Christians to do away with slavery long before they actually did so. We shall never "keep up with" Him, but we must:

170

a. continue to try to do so, i.e., try to see things as He does;

b. never pretend that we have already done this.

2. **They were astonished . . . afraid:** Those who watched Him as He walked nearer to His death and who saw His face, began to feel that something terrible was going to happen. They were surprised, because they did not understand why He had to die, and they were afraid; for if He went away they would be without their Master, but they loved and trusted Him so much that they still followed Him.

We may often be surprised and afraid when trouble comes, but we shall, like them, still follow Him. (It should be easier for us to trust Him, for we know that He rose after death and is never defeated: they did not know that at that time.)

Mark 10. 35–40: The Request of James and John

See also Matt. 20. 20–23

INTRODUCTION

This story is completed in vv. 41–45. The two main lessons are:

The Mistakes of the Disciples

The two disciples were selfish (see note on v. 35) and thoughtless. They promised to endure suffering without considering what they were promising. (See note on v. 39 and Additional Note, p. 173.)

The Patience of Jesus

Although they went wrong, there was good in them, e.g., they promised to endure suffering. Because they sincerely wished to do right, Jesus was patient and encouraging.

It is in this way also that God is saving us, i.e., by patiently making the little bit of good in us grow. (That is also how we help others, too.)

But how much patience Jesus must have had! The disciples continued to have so many wrong ideas although they had been with Him for a long time.

NOTES

v. 35.   We wish you to do for us whatever we may ask.

1. This request is exactly the opposite of the kind of prayer which Jesus taught us to pray. The request was, "Do for us what we have decided is best." But the Christians' prayer is, "Thy will be done", i.e., "we are willing to do whatever you want us to do".

2. Their prayer was also a selfish desire to hold more important positions than the other disciples when Jesus became King in Jerusalem. (Luke in chap. 19. 11 shows that they still expected that. See also Mark. 10. 37.) It is not wrong to have ambition, but this was the wrong kind of ambition. (See notes on 8. 34 and 10. 43.)

v. 38.   Can you drink the cup which I am drinking, or pass through the waters . . . ?

1. A "cup" was often thought of as holding a bitter drink (Isa. 51. 17; John 18. 11): "waters" were thought of as dangerous (Isa. 43. 2). So the two words together mean "suffering and danger".
Note: The word for "waters" is translated as "Baptism" in the A.V.

2. We are often told to "be like Jesus": here is one way in which every single Christian can be like Him, by suffering willingly (2 Cor. 1. 5; Col. 1. 24; Matt. 10. 25).

v. 39.   They said to him, We can.

1. There was some good in this answer—"Yes, we can, we are prepared to suffer with you" and, after Pentecost, both of them did. (See Acts 4. 1–3; 12. 2: James was killed by Herod.)

2. But they still did not really expect that it would be necessary for either Jesus or themselves to suffer. It was thus easy to say, "We can", but when Jesus was arrested, they ran away. There are two kinds of hope: these disciples had the wrong kind and said, "We do not worry: evil may never come"; those with *true* hope say, "We do not worry: evil may come, but with God's help we shall overcome it" (see 2 Kings 6. 16).

v. 40.   To sit at my right hand . . . is not mine to give; it is for those for whom it has been prepared.

The meaning is: "You cannot become leaders in my Kingdom simply by coming privately to me and asking for high positions ('not mine to give'). God has long ago planned that places of leadership are for people of a certain kind." (In vv. 42–44 He explained what kind.)

But note:

1. **Not mine to give:** This does not mean that Jesus thought of Himself as inferior to or less than God the Father. Jesus was fully God. But while He was on earth He was obedient to His Father. (See 13. 32 and John 12. 50b.)

2. **Those for whom it has been prepared:** This does not mean that God long ago planned to make some of us good Christians and to send others of us to hell (see 1 Tim. 2. 4). We are *all* free to become the sort of people whom Jesus describes in vv. 42–44, but we do not all choose to do so.

ADDITIONAL NOTE

THE BLINDNESS OF THE DISCIPLES

In his Gospel Mark gives us a large number of stories which show the blindness and stupidity of the disciples, and it is useful to study them. They are found in 4. 38–40; 5. 31; 6. 37, 52; 7. 18; 8. 4, 17–21, 32, 33; 9. 5, 6, 32, 34, 38; 10. 13, 35–40; 14. 10, 37–41, 50; 14. 66–73.

It is surprising that Mark reported all these stories about the disciples: some of them were leaders in the Church at the time when he was writing. We think especially of Peter. Surely he did not intend to attack them.

1. *Why did Mark tell these stories?*

The chief reason seems to be this: Mark wanted to show that no one came to know or believe in Jesus by nature: people only came to know Him by an act of "faith". Clever and important people often did not see who He was: these stories show that the very disciples who lived with Him did not understand Him. It was not until Jesus rose and the gift of the Spirit was given that they made this act of faith. Then they became strong believers.

As for ourselves, Jesus has risen for us and the Spirit is offered to us. We are free to make our act of faith and to "see Jesus".

2. *What do we learn from these stories?*

a. These stories give us encouragement. We see that Peter and the other disciples were ordinary people like ourselves: they were slow to learn and unwilling to trust God. But in spite of this, they were accepted by Jesus and finally made into trustful servants of God.

b. The sins of the disciples were the sins of the Church for which Mark was writing. It was important for readers (and it is important for us) to notice these sins in order to overcome them.

c. As we read these stories, we feel quite sure that Mark's Gospel is a true story. Some non-Christians have said that Christians invented the Gospel stories after the death of Jesus and that the stories were untrue. But if the Christians had done this, they would certainly not have described the weakness and stupidity of the disciples, such as Peter, in this way. They would only have written stories which described the strength and goodness of the disciples.

Mark 10. 41–45: Teaching about Service

See also Matt. 20. 24–28; Luke 22. 24–27

INTRODUCTION

The other ten disciples were angry and jealous when they thought that James and John might get the greatest positions. So Jesus again taught them all what true greatness is. (The ten who were jealous were no better than the two who were selfish; they all made the same mistake.)

The teaching is: a. We must be willing to think and act differently from the rest of the world (vv. 42–43a and see Introduction to 9. 30–32); b. the person who serves others the most is the greatest person (vv. 43b, 44); c. Jesus Himself was the greatest servant, and more than a servant, see John 13. 1–15, and the note on Mark 10. 45.

NOTES

vv. 42, 43. Their great men exercise power over them. But it is not so with you.

1. He was saying, "The greatest honour is usually given to those who have the most power over others". Even unjust landlords, or

rich men who pay insufficient wages are called "great", but this is the opposite of what is really true. In a certain bookshop each book had a label with a price written on it. The owner of this shop went outside for a moment and a boy changed round the labels so that big, valuable books were now labelled 2d. each, and little notebooks were labelled at 15s. We have behaved like that boy. We have called the rulers the great ones and the servants the lesser, but in truth and in God's eyes those who serve are usually the "great" and those in power are usually the least important. (We say "usually" because some who serve do so unwillingly and are therefore not "great"; and some of those in power truly serve others and are "great".)

2. **Not so with you:** We must act and think the opposite of what the world thinks, even though we live in the world (John 17. 16 and John 3. 13). A writer who lived about a hundred years after Mark said that Jesus' teaching was "Unless you change your 'down' to 'up', you shall not enter my Kingdom".

3. But because we live in the world, we act and think as the world does unless we are constantly being corrected by God's Holy Spirit.

v. 44.   Whoever wishes to be first among you must be the slave of all.

1. **Wishes to be first:** It is right to have ambition and right to desire to be a leader and to be "first" (see note on 8. 34), but we often forget what a leader is. This verse tells us.

2. **Slave of all:**

a. In v. 43 the word is "servant" for which the Greek word is *diakonos* (see note on 9. 35). But here the Greek word is *doulos* which means "slave". Christians are often called slaves in the New Testament when they have willingly given themselves up to serving God and other people. Paul is: i. slave of God (Phil. 1. 1); ii. a slave of others (1 Cor. 9. 19). (From this it is clear that Christians are not slaves in the way that Jews were the slaves of Pharaoh; for we are slaves willingly, but the Jews were forced to serve.)

b. How can we be "slaves of all" today? i. Christian congregations must become the slaves of the others in their neighbourhood, if they are to lead the neighbourhood. (See 2 Cor. 4. 8–11.) Sometimes they forget that they are servants of those outside and are too much engaged in defending or adding to their property. ii. "Minister" means "servant". But ministers are often tempted to seek for power over others and to expect to receive honour in public. One who was taking up new work found that the house provided for him was the largest in the village; he said, "You are kind to provide such a house, but you make it hard for me to be the 'slave of all'." iii. We cannot be slaves of all until we have been "born again"; for when we were born as helpless babies, we were served *by* all. As soon as possible we have to turn right round and become servants *for* all.

Note: Jesus is not here saying that we *ought* to be slaves of all, but that those who serve *are* in fact the leaders of the world.

v. 45. The Son of Man came not to be served but to serve, and to give his life to set many free.

This verse comes near the end of chap. 10. In chaps. 11-15, we are given the story of how Jesus went to His death in Jerusalem. So these chapters show what this verse means. Jesus did not only teach what "greatness" is: He showed it by the way He lived and died.

1. **Son of Man:** This means Jesus. See Additional Note, p. 137.

2. **Give his life:** So Jesus was prepared to die when He went to Jerusalem; He was not killed by accident.

3. **To set many free:** The A.V. words are "to be a ransom for many".

a. This shows that His dying would make a difference to us. He did not explain how this can be so. He just said it was so (Isa. 53. 5).

b. By dying, He would set us free from the power that evil has over us. ("Ransom", as in the A.V., was the money paid to the owner of a slave to set him free.) We are by nature under the power of evil, and need to be released. (See 14. 24; Rom. 6. 17, 18; Gal. 1. 4.)

c. This is something which we cannot do for ourselves. He died "for" us. We cannot earn our freedom by trying to do good as some slaves could earn their freedom by collecting enough money (Luke 17. 10).

d. **Many:** It is wrong to say that all men cannot be set free because Jesus only says "many" (not "all") in this verse. "Many" is the answer to the question of Luke 13. 23, "Will there be many saved or only a few?": It means "*all* who are willing to accept freedom".

"Therefore a man shall be joined to his wife" (Mark 10. 7).

Is marriage necessary in order that a man and a woman may have a happy family like this one in India? If it is necessary, what sort of marriage must it be? What guidance can be found in Jesus' words (Mark 10. 1–12)?

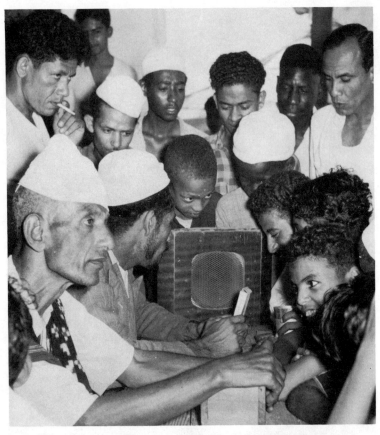

"By what authority do you do these things?" (Mark 11. 28).

By what authority do these people in a Mombasa coffee shop conduct their lives? Where do they get their ideas? Whose opinions do they regard as "authoritative"?

Mark 10. 46–52: The Cure of Bartimeus

See also Matt. 20. 29, 34; Luke 18. 35–43

INTRODUCTION

The Events

This happened on the last day of their journey to Jerusalem. Jesus had come from Perea, had crossed over the Jordan, and was passing through the hot, tropical town of Jericho. There was a crowd of pilgrims (probably going to Jerusalem for the Feast) and some of them told this blind beggar that Jesus was present and that there was a rumour that He was the Messiah. The beggar daringly called out to Jesus, using the name, "Son of David" (a title of the Messiah) and was cured.

What Mark intends us to learn

1. This is a story of Jesus (because of His compassion) healing the blindness of a man's eyes; but it is also a sort of parable of the way in which He was curing the spiritual blindness of the disciples. (We read of their "blindness" in vv. 35–45; Jesus is the bringer of sight and light in both stories: see John 8. 12; 9. 40, 41.)

2. Isaiah (Isa. 29. 18; 42. 1, 7) and others had taught that when the Messiah came, he would cure the blind. So Jesus is seen as Messiah in this story: the Rule of God over all evil has already begun. Here is even greater good news than the curing of one blind man!

(This story does not, of course, "prove" that Jesus was Messiah, for others had cured blind men too; but when we believe, for other reasons, that He was Messiah, this story strengthens our belief. See introduction to 8. 22–26.)

NOTES

v. 49.   Jesus stood still and said, Call him . . .

Here Jesus put into practice His words of v. 45a and showed how much He loved people:

1. He was near the end of His life on earth: there was very little time in which to train His disciples, yet He willingly stopped to help

someone in need. (So the Christian minister goes about among his people slowly enough to notice who needs his help.)

2. He was the Saviour of all the world, but He stopped to heal one uneducated person who was thought unimportant by others (v. 48a; Luke 15. 4).

v. 51. What do you wish me to do for you?

1. Although Jesus knew what the man needed, He wanted him to express his need in words. So God, who knows what we need before we pray still wants us to utter our prayer (Phil. 4. 6b). This is because He wants us to take an active share in what He does for us.

2. Jesus had asked the same question from James and John in v. 37. Their answers may be compared:

James and John: "Give us important posts."

Bartimeus: "Help me to see more clearly."

Bartimeus' answer shows the right way to approach God (rather like the parable in Luke 18. 9–14).

v. 52. Your faith has saved you.

1. **Your faith:** If Bartimeus had not had faith, he would not have been cured. This faith was shown:

a. By daringly treating Jesus as having great power (he treated Him as the Messiah), before he knew for certain who He really was, or whether He would agree to stop on the road (v. 47).

b. By continuing to call out to Jesus, although others strongly discouraged him (vv. 47, 48).

c. By taking all the action himself that he could (v. 50).

Everyone can show his faith in God in these three ways. (See note on 5. 34 and Additional Note, p. 91.)

2. **Saved you:** Although we are only told that Jesus cured his eyes, it may be that He cured him in spirit also, for he followed Him (v. 52). Certainly Jesus' aim was to save men, both in body and in spirit: to "save" meant to "make them whole". (See note on 5. 34.) That is God's aim to-day. He is working to heal divisions between people; to heal their bodies and their minds; and to rescue them from the disease called sin, which is spoiling their lives and separating them from Himself. All this is "saving"; all this is "healing". He wants the *whole* of a person to be well.

178

Mark 11. 1–11 : The Entry into Jerusalem

See also Matt. 21. 1–9; Luke 19. 28–38; John 12. 12–19

INTRODUCTION

Chapters 11 *and* 12

These chapters describe the kind of thing that Jesus was doing in Jerusalem during the time before He was arrested. Verses like 14. 49 make us think that this time was probably much longer than a week. We are not certain when the riding into Jerusalem took place, but the arrest was certainly in April.

During this time Jesus wanted to give the Jews their last opportunity to change their minds about Him, and to accept Him as their Messiah. We can see this most clearly in 11. 1–11; 15–18; 27–33; 12. 1–12; 35–47. But the leaders did not accept Him: their desire to destroy Him increased.

The story in 11. 1–11

On their long walk from Jericho to Jerusalem, Jesus and His followers probably rested at Bethany, about two miles from Jerusalem. It is likely that they were tired, as the journey is mostly uphill and takes about twelve hours to walk. At Bethany He sent two of them to fetch a donkey from a village near-by, probably Bethphage. (This was a mile from Jerusalem, and, like Bethany, on the Mount of Olives.) It was not the first time that He had been here and He seems to have known someone who owned a donkey.

They brought it and He got on it. Then He rode into Jerusalem; probably pilgrims who had come for the Passover Feast accompanied Him. They went down the Mount of Olives, across the valley of the Kedron river, and through the gate in the city walls. As He rode He was given a welcome such as might be given to a king, both by the pilgrims from His own part of the country (Galilee) and other pilgrims. When it was evening, He went back into Bethany. This was: a. in order to prevent anyone killing Him in the dark streets before He was ready to die; b. so that He should have opportunity for quiet prayer.

Why did He ride a donkey?

It was in order that the people who had the faith to see that He was

Messiah should know that He was a lowly Messiah. Mark has given us this story chiefly that we also might know this. (See note on v. 2.)

NOTES

v. 2. You will find a young ass tied, that no one at all has ever sat on.

1. **You will find:** Jesus was not taken by surprise in the things that happened. He made His own plans and kept to them. In this case He seems to have known someone who owned a donkey and to have arranged to borrow it when He needed it. So when the two disciples found the donkey it was not by chance, nor was it a miracle.

2. **A young ass:** If He had wanted to show that He was the general of an army (i.e., the kind of Messiah that most Jews were looking for), He would have ridden a horse. When He rode a donkey, it was a sign that He intended to do His work of saving mankind by gentleness, not by violence. But it was also a sign that He was Messiah. The Jews knew the words of Zechariah (9. 9 and 14. 4) that the Messiah would ride a donkey on the Mount of Olives. Jesus intended to teach all this by His actions rather than by His words.

3. **No one at all has ever sat on . . .** The donkey was young and had not been ridden before. Thus Jesus was lent an animal that was in perfect condition, one without the sores and diseases from which older animals suffer. They gave to Him something unspoilt, just as the Jews, when they sacrificed to God, killed an animal that was unspoilt. (See Deut. 21. 3; also 1 Sam. 6. 7; Luke 23. 53.) It is with this desire to offer the best to God that many Christians say their prayers early in the morning before their minds are tired. This is also why many receive Holy Communion before eating.

v. 3. The Master needs it, and will send it back . . .

The owner knew Jesus and perhaps called Him "Master". He said he would lend Him the donkey when He wanted it, and Jesus promised to return it when He had used it. "The Master needs it" (or words like that) was said to the owners of a boat (4. 1), and to the owner of a room (14. 14). God says this to us concerning our talents and possessions and time and minds. Like the owner of the donkey, we offer them to Him so that they may be used for the very best purposes.

v. 8. Many others spread their clothes on the road . . .

The crowd spread their clothes on the donkey and on the road, and scattered leaves and little branches in front of Him. Why did they do this?

1. A few surely did it because they knew Him. They wanted to show their love for Him so much that they forgot that their own clothes would be spoiled by the dirt. So, at times of prayer, Christians worship best when they forget themselves for a moment and think of God Himself.

2. Some did it because they had heard of His miracles and were curious to see more (John 12. 9).

3. But most of them did it because they hoped that He was going to lead a rebellion against the Romans. (See note on v. 9.)

v. 9. Victory, God bless him that comes . . .

1. When they shouted this, they were saying words that all Jews knew well. They are from Ps. 118. 25, 26, and this psalm was used at the Feasts of Tabernacles and of the Passover. At both these festivals the Jews praised God for setting them free from slavery in Egypt. After they had been conquered by other nations, these festivals became times of praying for freedom. So by shouting this, the crowd were saying, "Here comes the One who will lead rebellion against the Romans. The Kingdom of our ancestor David is going to be restored."

Note: "Hosanna" (which is translated "Victory" here) means "Save us", i.e., save us from the Romans.

2. Were the people wrong to ask Jesus to help them to get political freedom? Are Christians to-day wrong if they pray to God for self-government for their country?

a. Christians are right in praying for anything which they believe to be best for their country. But when they do this, they have to remember two things: i. it is God who knows what is really best for them (we often make the mistake of thinking that what we *want* most is what we *need* most); ii. when they pray for their own country, Christians must pray that other countries may also have what is best.

b. The people were wrong to expect Jesus to do this for them, because He had come for a different purpose. He had come to set all mankind free, not the Jews only. He had come to free them from the power of sin, not from the power of the Romans. A Christian is still someone who knows that the kind of freedom Jesus offers is worth even more than freedom from foreign rule.

c. They were wrong to try to use Him to do their will, instead of finding out His will and doing it. In our prayers we may make the same mistake: we tell God what we want Him to do for us, instead of dedicating ourselves to do for Him what He wants.

3. **Him that comes:** Jesus has come and does come in many ways: a. to earth, when He came as a baby; b. to Jerusalem, as in this verse, when He came on a donkey; c. To the disciples at Pentecost, because when the Holy Spirit came, this was Jesus Himself coming; d. To Christians to-day when He comes into their hearts, whenever they are ready to receive Him, and when with faith they receive the bread and wine at the Holy Communion; e. When He comes at the end of the world in His Glory.

Jesus comes: our whole duty is to receive Him.

Mark 11. 12–14: The Fig-Tree without Figs

See also Matt. 21. 18–19

INTRODUCTION

This story, which begins in vv. 12–14, is completed in vv. 20–21. It is not easy to know exactly what Jesus did on this occasion, because Mark does not tell us the whole story. The event took place some time just before Jesus was crucified. (See Introduction to 11. 1–11.) These five verses should be read together and are taken together in the commentary here.

The Story

As we have already seen, we cannot say exactly what took place, but the following is what probably happened:

Jesus and His disciples were on a journey and were hungry. Suddenly Jesus saw a fig-tree with leaves on it, and they were all astonished. There were two reasons for their surprise: a. it is rare for fig-trees to have leaves at that time of year; b. fig-trees bear leaves and figs at the same time, but this one had nothing but leaves.

Note:

1. Jesus did not expect to find figs on the tree at the wrong time of year, as some people think after reading this story: He had been brought up in the country; He loved nature and knew all about plants, trees, and seasons. (See Matt. 24. 32.) What He now said was: "Look at this tree. It has leaves earlier than other fig-trees; it makes one expect that it has early fruit too. But it has no fruit: it is diseased and will never have fruit."

(Then, although we are not told that He did so, it is possible that He added such teaching as this: "Our Jewish religious leaders are like it. Their words and customs make one expect that they will lead good lives also. But they do not. In their present condition they never will.")

Another day, early in the morning they saw the same tree, and it was dying. Peter said, "Jesus has killed it by His words " (v. 21). Note that this was Peter's explanation: we are not told that Jesus explained it in this way.

2. Two other suggestions have been made about this story:

a. Jesus told a parable about a fig-tree (Luke 13. 6–9) and afterwards people wrongly said that He had Himself found a tree without figs. But Mark's account was written only twenty five years after the event, and it is likely to be correct.

b. When Jesus said, "Let no one ever eat . . ." it was a curse; He killed this tree with a curse in order to convince the disciples that He was God and to teach them the lesson that if people do not practise their religion in daily life, they will fail to obtain eternal life.

But nowhere are we told that Jesus used curses either on people or things, or used magic to convince people that He was God. (See 8. 12.) For the real lessons contained in this story, see the notes on vv. 13–14 below.

3. It is not likely that the teaching in vv. 22–25 was given at the same time as the events which are recorded in vv. 12–14, and 20–21.

NOTES

v. 13.   Nothing but leaves . . .

It is a bad religion which shows "leaves", but no "fruit". The "leaves" of religion and of a Church to-day are its regulations, buildings, creeds. When we see these, we naturally expect to see the "fruits" also, i.e., forgiving those who injure us, looking after those too weak to help themselves, working honestly, having the peace of God in our hearts. But the Jewish leaders, and often Christians too, had nothing but "leaves" (Isa. 5. 4, 7; Luke 6. 46; Jas. 2. 14, 17). This is the first lesson contained in the story.

v. 14.   Let no one ever eat fruit from you.

These words do not mean that Jesus was angry with the tree, because He was hungry and found no figs to eat. From Matt. 4. 2–4 we learn that He did not act in this way. In these words Jesus was saying that a religion or a Church without "fruit" is already becoming useless: it is already dying. This is not a curse, but a terrible warning (Matt. 7. 19, 26–27; 21. 43). This is the second lesson contained in the story.

Mark 11. 15–19: The Clearing of the Temple Courtyard

See also Matt. 21. 12, 13; Luke 19. 45, 46; John 2. 14-22

INTRODUCTION

The Place

These events did not take place in the Temple building itself, but in an open courtyard. This was the Court of the Gentiles, which was part of the thirty acres of ground around the Temple itself. Only Jews could go into other parts of the grounds, but into this court-yard non-Jews (Gentiles) could go. But the Jews had begun to use it for other purposes:

1. They bought and sold the animals and birds which the people offered as sacrifices in front of the Temple. Offerings bought in the ordinary market were very often rejected by the priests as being in some way not perfect. So others were sold here by traders who made very high profits indeed. A pair of doves was the offering of poor people and cost about 9d. in the market-place: in the Temple courtyard it sometimes cost 15s.

2. They changed money there. The money used during the Roman

rule had on it the picture of the heathen Roman Emperor's face, so no one was allowed to bring it into the Temple. These coins had to be changed by Jews for old Hebrew coins before they could pay their tax to the Temple. The money-changers, like the traders, made huge profits.

3. They used it as a quick way of getting from the eastern part of the city to the Mount of Olives, even when carrying goods, which was forbidden by law.

The Story

Jesus came into this courtyard, and stopped the buying and selling and money-changing. (See note on v. 17.) He quoted some words from Jeremiah (7. 11) to remind them that this was the Gentiles' court-yard and that God cared deeply for the Gentiles, and not for the Jews only. (See note on v. 17.)

The result of His action was that: a. the Jewish leaders, who had hated Him for a long time (3. 6), now determined to kill Him; they were afraid that if He continued teaching they might lose their power and influence (v. 18); b. the people were astonished at His courage, His authority, His caring for the Gentiles; and probably they were delighted that He had attacked the religious leaders.

Why did Jesus do this?

Of course Jesus wanted to do away with injustices; but it is likely that His *chief* aim was to call upon the Jews once again to change their minds and to accept Him as their Messiah. Most of them did not, but there were surely a few people who had the faith to see that He was doing what Malachi (3. 1–6) said would be done by the Messiah.

Note: John 2. 14 says that this happened at the beginning of Jesus' ministry. But it is more likely that Mark is right in saying that it happened only a little time before He was arrested. It may have been one reason why they did arrest Him.

NOTES

v. 15. He . . . began to drive out those that were selling . . .

1. *His anger:* It was caused by the hurt done to others, not by hurt done to Himself. It was kept under control. Thus Jesus shows

that there are times when we ought to show anger (see Eph. 4. 26). But very often our anger is not of the kind that He showed.

2. *His use of force:* He did use force, but it was not force that made them obey Him. One man could not send away a whole crowd of traders, even if He did drive away their animals with a whip (John 2. 15).

3. *His authority:* They obeyed because He acted with an authority that was His own (1. 22) and with a goodness that only evil people could fail to see. Although most of them did not know it, He was the Messiah, and they felt the power of His Spirit. Because He is God's Messiah and His Son, He has authority to judge all men.

This shows that we cannot argue that, because Jesus knocked over market-stalls, therefore it is right for Christians to take part in warfare. It is not from this story that we shall learn if it is right or wrong to use modern weapons.

4. *His defence of unprotected people:* It was mainly pilgrims who were being cheated, not only by the traders, but by the important family of Annas, the father-in-law of the High Priest. Jesus attacked them, because they were wickedly misusing their position as religious leaders; it is not surprising that they planned to kill Him.

We learn from this story that: a. just as Jesus defended those who were badly treated, so it is His Church's duty to do the same to-day; b. leaders of religion who use their position badly are severely judged.

v. 16. He would not let anyone carry any goods through the temple.

There was already a law against doing this, but it was not being kept. Those who broke it were doing something that religious people are often tempted to do: they were using religion for their own convenience, because they used the Temple grounds as a quick way to their houses. We do that when we go to church with the chief aim of meeting our friends or listening to music. Our chief aim should be to worship God humbly and to offer ourselves to Him: religion and church services were not given by God to save us trouble.

v. 17. A house of prayer for all nations? But you have made it a robbers' cave.

The Jews used the Gentiles' court for their own purposes, not for the purposes for which it had been built. In the same way the Jews were continually failing to treat other races (Gentiles) in the way God had intended. God wanted the Jews to share their knowledge of Him with other races (Isa. 56. 6–8), but they had taken God's blessings without sharing them. So Jeremiah (7. 11) said they were as bad as robbers who hide in a cave.

Christians must avoid doing this. We who rejoice in what Jesus has done for us must: a. speak of this good news to non-Christians; b. make it possible for them to believe by the way in which we live. *Note:* Jesus was probably not accusing them of cheating when He said "robbers' cave"; but the pilgrims were, of course, very often cheated.

Mark 11. 20–26 : Teaching about Faith

See also Matt. 17. 20; 21. 20–22; Luke 17. 6

INTRODUCTION

This section of the Gospel has two parts: Part 1 is the end of the story of the fig-tree. (For comment on it, see the notes on vv. 12–14.) Part 2 (vv. 22–25) contains teaching by Jesus. The two parts are often printed together, but it is likely that the teaching (on faith) was given at a different time and not connected by Jesus with the fig-tree. Matt. 17. 20 says this.

The sayings about faith in vv. 22–25 may not have been given at one time, but the subject of all of them is the same, i.e., the person who lives and prays with real confidence in God.
Note: In these verses the phrase "have faith" occurs once, and "believe" twice, but it is the same Greek word for both of them. "Having faith" is the same as "believing": they both mean having confidence in someone.

NOTES

v. 22. Have faith in God.

1. Have faith: The Bible gives us two reasons why we can have complete confidence in God: a. He loves us and desires to give us

187

all we need (Luke 12. 32); b. He is able to do so. (See Luke 12. 28 and Additional Note, p. 91.)

2. **In God:** Many people put more trust in themselves or in their friends than they do in God. Others have more confidence in their possessions, or in a certain way of being governed, than they have in God (Ps. 118. 8, 9). This verse says that God is the One on whom we can completely depend.

v. 23. Whoever says to this mountain, Be lifted up and thrown into the sea . . . it shall be done . . .

1. It is possible that Jesus said this on the Mount of Olives. From this hill one can see the Dead Sea fifteen miles away.

2. But Jesus was not talking about removing the Mount of Olives. This was His way of saying, "Do you really trust God? If so, you will be able to do good things that seem impossible to do. You will be able to remove evils as big as mountains." Others may say it is impossible for anyone: a. to overcome his habit of bad temper; b. to forgive the person who ruined his reputation; c. lead an opponent of Christ to believe in Him; d. have joy during sickness. But God has promised to make such things possible. A person who has faith receives power by praying.

3. The verse does not mean that Christians pray with faith instead of working with faith. The two go together. Nor does it mean that we let God do the work instead of doing it ourselves; for, as God works, we also work. A group of Christians in America used to look after a hundred homeless children. The children grew older and needed a playing field, but the only ground they were offered was land on which were many old houses, disused and owned by no one. They had no money to pay for the clearing away of the houses. So they prayed for money and began knocking the houses down brick by brick. People said they were mad. But God put it into the minds of some people to send money, and of many others to come and help with the work; and He put courage into the hearts of the organizers. Within two years the new ground was being used. These people had "faith". (See Additional Note, p. 91.)

v. 24. All the things you pray for . . . believe that you have received them, and you shall have them.

1. **All the things you pray for:** This means all the good things;

188

i.e., we shall receive things that God knows we need. (We are not promised that we shall receive everything that we think we need: God knows far better than we do what is best for us.) To pray for such things is called "praying in Jesus' name" (John 16. 23b, 24a).

2. **You have received them:** This means that we can receive them, because God is already offering them to us. Because of His love, He is always offering what we need even before we begin to ask Him (Isa. 65: 24), e.g., when we or our friends are sick, we ask God for good health. We do not have to persuade Him to come down nor beg Him to do something which He had not intended to do before. We know that He desires our health; so, expecting to receive His gifts, we pray in words such as "God, we believe that Thou art already pouring forth into us Thy healing grace". If we pray like this, we are joining in what God has already begun to do.

Note: This verse does not, of course, mean that we should deceive ourselves that we have received something which we know we have not received. That would be "pretending", not believing. Believing is "having faith".

v. 25a. Whenever you stand praying, if you have anything against anyone, forgive him . . .

1. **When you stand:** Jesus, like most Jews, stood for prayer (Ps. 134. 1). But sometimes they knelt (Dan. 6. 10); Jesus fell on the ground in Gethsemane (Mark 14. 35); David sat for prayer (2 Sam. 7. 18). It is not very important in what position we pray; but the following words show that it is very important that when we pray, we forgive our fellow-men.

2. **Forgive him:**

a. As we pray, it is not enough that our hearts are filled with faith in God (v. 24): they need also to be filled with love and forgiveness towards other people. A person who has faith prays not only with faith towards God, but also with love towards men (see 1 Cor. 12. 2b).

b. What is forgiveness? A has been injured by B, but he forgives B by treating B as if he had not injured him. What B has done still hurts him and he does not forget it, but he gives up his right of taking revenge. He wants the best things for him.

c. Why is it necessary to forgive others when we pray to God? Because: i. prayer is joining ourselves in spirit to God; ii. God Him-

189

self is love (1 John, 4. 7, 8); iii. if we are unloving or unforgiving, we cannot join with God, just as oil and water cannot mix (1 John 4. 20).

v. 25b. Forgive him, that your Father in heaven also may forgive you . . .

a. Although Mark does not record the Lord's Prayer, this shows that he probably knew it. (See Matt. 6. 9–15.)

b. It does not mean that God refuses to forgive us until we have learnt to forgive others completely. He does not reckon up our sins like a clerk keeping accounts. He wonderfully offers us forgiveness, even when we have behaved badly towards others.

c. It does mean that if we receive forgiveness from God, though we do not deserve it, we must offer forgiveness to others when they do not deserve it. (See Eph. 4. 32; Matt. 18. 21–35; especially vv. 32–33.)

V. 26 is printed in some Bibles, but it is absent from most manuscripts and was probably not written by Mark.

Mark 11. 27–33: The Question about Authority

See also Matt. 21. 23–27; Luke 20. 1–8

INTRODUCTION

The Four Questions

This is the first of four stories about the Jewish leaders attacking Jesus. They wanted to make the ordinary people lose faith in Him, and they tried to do this by asking Him difficult questions. (The three other questions are in 12. 13–17; 12. 18–27; 12. 28–34.) All this time Jesus: a. never tried to give an answer simply in order to please the people: He spoke the truth; b. showed that He was the Messiah, although He never used the word; c. was judging the religious leaders, although they thought that they were judging Him; d. Overcame His questioners. (These are like the stories of driving out demons; they show Jesus as victorious in His fight against evils.)

190

The Story

Three groups of people, all members of the Sanhedrin Council, usually unfriendly towards each other, united to attack Jesus. They were: the chief priests, the scribes, and the "elders". (See Additional Note, p. 226.) They were angry because of His action in the Temple (vv. 15–19), and wished to catch Him. If He said He had taken that action because He was the Messiah, they would tell the Romans to arrest Him as a "rebel": if He said that He was an ordinary human teacher, they could show that He had no right to stop the buying and selling allowed by the chief priests. His words in reply were a stern judgement on them: He gave no answer.

NOTES

v. 28. By what authority do you do these things?

1. Their question was evil, because they did not want to know the answer. They had already decided to put a stop to His work. They did not say, "Let us listen and see whether His life is in accordance with God's will". Their consciences would have shown them His goodness, but they had become deaf to their own consciences; they were deaf, because they were jealous and afraid.

2. It would have been a good question, if they had asked it with a desire to learn. It is necessary to find out if a person who is talking in an unusual way is doing so by God's authority and by His will, or not (Deut. 18. 18–22). Disorder comes when people speak in God's name with no authority, except their own feelings. So it is not wrong for an inquirer of to-day to ask the question from Jesus, "How shall I know if you are really God?" We should note that they will not usually find the answer simply by reading a verse of the Bible. Most of us became Christians by boldly treating Jesus as God, in faith. Thus we discovered the answer to our question by our own experience (see John 17. 7). But this is just what the Jewish leaders would not do.

3. Although it is good to ask the question "By what authority?" when someone is teaching, most Jews asked this too often. Instead of asking, "Is it good to do this or that?" they would say, "What did the Law say about this?" Like Muslims of to-day, they looked back to a written Law of the past. They did not allow the Spirit of the living God to guide them in the present. Church leaders may be

tempted to do this, and to say, "The Church has never done this in the past: therefore it is wrong to do it now." But Christians believe in the Holy Spirit. There is no verse in the Bible which forbids slavery, but two hundred years ago a group of Christians were sure that the Spirit was leading them to abolish slavery.

v. 30. The baptism of John, was it from heaven or from men?

1. Jesus asked another question instead of giving an answer. But He did not do this in order to escape from a difficult question: in these words he was judging those who asked the question. Jesus' question was, "Do you think John spoke a message from God or spoke only his own thoughts?"

With these words He was saying two things: a. "You will agree that John was regarded by our people as a true prophet of God. But you leaders did not treat him as such. Our nation will not accept you as suitable people to judge whether I am a true prophet or not!" b. "John called Me the Messiah." (See 1. 8; John 1. 36.) "If John was a true prophet, then it is true that I am the Messiah and have authority from God Himself. But you will not accept Me. How can God accept you?"

2. He gave them no answer, because they were not willing to follow either His words or their own consciences. Jesus has no answer for us if we continue to call something good in our lives which we know to be bad, or to call someone bad whom we know to be good. How can we hear Him, if we refuse to hear our own conscience? How can we pray if we are dishonest even with ourselves?

3. The question shows how skilful Jesus was in the use of His mind in discussion. He was a real man, and His intelligence was developed and put at the service of His Father. (See Luke 10. 25–37 and notes on 12. 30; 13. 11.) May our minds be trained and put at His service.

4. We see how He used questions as a means of teaching and convincing His hearers (see 2. 9, 19; 3. 33; 10. 18; 11. 29; 12. 35). We often learn by being encouraged to think out our own answer to a hard question. According to the Bible God frequently drew men to Himself by questions. He gave them freedom in answering, e.g., Mark 8. 29; Gen. 3. 9; Jonah 4. 4; Acts 9. 4.

See picture facing p. 177.

Mark 12. 1–12: The Story of the Wicked Farmers

See also Matt. 21. 33–46; Luke 20. 9–19

INTRODUCTION

The story

Jesus told this story in Jerusalem during the weeks before He was arrested. When the Jewish leaders heard of it, they were even more determined than before to kill Him. (See note on v. 12.) Here Jesus describes things that sometimes actually happened at the time when He told the story. A rich man owned a vineyard. As he was going to live in another country for a few years, he engaged some farmers to act as his tenants. Instead of paying rent in money, they agreed to send him part of the grape harvest each year. But when he sent messengers to collect his share, these farmers ill treated them and even killed some. Then he sent his son, but they killed him too. Finally they were found guilty of murder, and new tenants were put in charge of the vineyard.

Jesus' chief aim

In telling the story the aim of Jesus seems to have been this: to show that He was God's Messiah, and that He had been sent to bring the Jews to repentance and to obedience to God. In the story, and especially in v. 6, He was giving them one more opportunity to accept Him.

The meaning of the story

When Jesus told a parable, He used it for teaching one single lesson. (See Additional Note, p. 68.) But this story is different: it is an allegory (as is Bunyan's Pilgrim's Progress). Some of the people and things in the story (but certainly not all of them) stand for the sort of people that really existed, and exist now:

a. The vineyard (v. 1) is like the Jewish people. (This was easy for Jewish listeners to understand because Isa. 5. 1–7 was well known.)

b. The owner (v. 1) is like God in this way: He had chosen the Jewish people and given them all they needed for producing fruit. (See note on 11. 14.) But the owner is *unlike* God in several ways, e.g., he went away from his vineyard; God never left His people, nor does He ever leave us.

193

c. The tenant-farmers (v. 1) are like the religious leaders of the Jews.

d. The slaves or messengers (v. 2) are in one respect like the prophets who were sent by God to remind the Jewish leaders of their duties: they were often ill-treated or killed. (See Jer. 7. 25, 26; Luke 13. 34a.)

e. The new owners, to whom the vineyard was given (v. 9), are like the people of other nations, who became the Christian Church and God's new Chosen People. (See Matt. 8. 11, 12; 21. 42.)

Note: In this way other teaching is given in addition to the main lesson noted above. This "other teaching" is noted in the Summary.

NOTES

v. 1.   A man planted a vineyard . . .

The preparations he made are those which can be seen in Israel or Jordan to-day, i.e., a "fence" (a stone wall to keep out thieves and animals), a "winepress" (a place where the juice of the grapes was collected after they had been trodden down by the labourers), a "watch-tower" (of sticks and clay, from which men could guard the grapes while they were getting ripe, and under which they could shelter).

v. 6.   He still had one left, his only son . . .

Jesus was referring to Himself in this verse. He knew that He was God's Son.

Note: "Only" means "own and only and loved". As in 1. 11; 9. 7, He was not *a* son, but *The* Son.

But not even His nearest friends understood this. Christians only understood it after He had died and risen. What they could do, and what He wanted them to do, was to accept Him as their Messiah. But the Jews thought of the Messiah only as God's messenger, not as His Son.

v. 10.   The stone that the builders refused, Is now the corner-stone.

These words come from Ps. 118. 22, 23 which was used at Passover time. Jesus was saying, "I shall be killed, and it will seem that my work has failed, and that I am like a useless stone. But in fact I shall be used by God to save mankind by dying, and I shall be raised up to live in God's presence" (Phil. 2. 7, 9).

Christ's followers, too, are often especially useful to God when they seem to the world most useless. (See 8. 35; 10. 43; 1 Cor. 1. 27.)

v. 12. They knew he had spoken the parable against them . . .

1. The story had been told in the presence of the chief priests or their messengers. Some probably regarded Him as just a bad man attacking the authorities; there were others who knew that He spoke the truth, and that He was calling on them to change their ways. They deserve praise for having seen that it was themselves whom Jesus was warning. Religious leaders to-day often read the Bible and say, "My people need this warning", rather than, "I need this": all of us, hearing a good sermon, are tempted to think that it suits other people rather than ourselves.

2. Those who knew that they deserved this warning were all the more guilty of sin when they continued to plan His death. After we have had opportunity of following Jesus, we are either better or worse than we were before. This is the meaning of Luke 20. 18 which Jesus spoke at this time. If we accept Him, He is a "stepping-stone" leading us to God. If we reject Him, He becomes a stone over which we have fallen.

3. This is a warning to ourselves. We Christians have been given even greater opportunities of knowing who Jesus is and growing in loyalty to Him: we have the Bible; we know He was sent into the world for us; that He rose again and sent His Spirit and founded His Church. We have been given all that we need for making the decision to follow Him wholeheartedly.

SUMMARY

The central teaching of this story was noted in the Introduction. Other important lessons from it are:

1. *God expects us to be stewards:* See v. 1c. The Jewish leaders are like tenants or stewards, and were expected by God to "produce fruit". This means acting with justice and sharing their knowledge of God's mercy with non-Jews. But they had been bad stewards. We are expected to be stewards of our time, our property, our children, our land, and of the Gospel (to pass it on). These things do not belong to us.

2. *God is our judge:* He leaves us free to obey or disobey Him,

O   195

just as the owner left the farmers to themselves. But the day comes when we have to give account to the "Owner" when He comes (v. 9). So the story is a warning to us as it was to the Jews. The Jews were told that disaster would result if they refused to hear Jesus. They did refuse, and crucified him. Disaster followed. Their race ceased to be the Chosen People of God, and Jerusalem, which all Jews had regarded as their home, was destroyed in A.D. 70.

3. *God is patient:* He went on sending prophets to the Jews, as the "owner" kept on sending one slave after another (vv. 4, 5, 6). (See 1 Tim. 1. 16.) God keeps on giving us opportunities of being sorry for sin and of serving Him better: He regards none of us as hopeless.

4. *God is not defeated:* Although the Jewish leaders killed Jesus, God's plan for saving mankind was not spoiled. The "owner" having been cheated by the first group of farmers, found others to take their place (v. 9). So God called on non-Jews to do the work which He had first given to the Jews.

God will get His work to-day done when He wishes. If His Church does not listen to Him, perhaps He will use other people to do it. Two hundred years ago there were very few Christians in India. The ancient Church of that country, which is said to have been founded by Thomas the Apostle, had not spread beyond a small area in the south: its people got on so well with their heathen neighbours that they did not concern themselves with making converts. At the same time, God offered the Church of England an opportunity of preaching the Gospel in India, but that opportunity was not taken. So God passed over these two organized groups of Christians and raised up a poor shoemaker, William Carey, to become the pioneer of missionary work in that country. God was not defeated: Christianity has now spread all over India.

"You do not understand the power of God" (Mark 12. 24).

In 1965 the funeral took place of Queen Salote of Tonga in the Friendly Islands of the Pacific, and her reign of 47 years came to an end. There was an end, but it was not the end. Followers of Jesus believe that God has the power to give new life after death. God re-creates what He once created.

"It is not yet the end" (Mark 13. 7).

"We must not think that these troubles are themselves the completion of God's work on earth; they come before the completion. Therefore we are to get on with our work faithfully." (p. 217)

Twice a week throughout his working life this Guatemalan farmer carries a load of 200 lbs 8 or 9 miles to market through rough and hilly country.

Mark 12. 13–17: The Question about Head-Tax

See also Matt. 22. 15–22; Luke 20. 20–26

INTRODUCTION

The head-tax

This was a tax which every Jew in Judea had to pay. Judea, of which Jerusalem was the capital, had become a colony of Rome in A.D. 6, i.e., about twenty four years before this incident. The head-tax money was sent to the Roman Emperor for the general funds of the Empire. (The Emperor was at this time Tiberius Caesar.) The tax was hated, because it showed that the Jews were a subject nation. (As well as paying this tax, the Jews had to pay other heavy taxes to the Romans, and a tax to their own religious leaders for the upkeep of the Temple.)

The trap question

The Jewish Council or Sanhedrin sent men to talk with Jesus. They were envious because the people admired Jesus so much, and they wanted to get Him to say something that would make Him less respected. They said, "Is it right to pay the head-tax?"

Some of the men who came to Jesus were Pharisees, and some, Herodians. The Pharisees always treated the Romans as enemies; so if Jesus said, "Pay these taxes", they would accuse Him of being friendly with the enemy, and the people would pay less attention to Him. The Herodians co-operated with the Romans as long as Judea was part of the Roman Empire. (See note on 3. 6.) If therefore Jesus said, "Do not pay these taxes", they would report Him to the Romans as a rebel. So the two groups thought that they had trapped Jesus.

Jesus' answer

In His answer Jesus boldly said, "Pay the tax". But His words in v. 17 mean much more than that: "Give what you owe to the Roman Emperor in exchange for law and order, but remember that in everything you are answerable to God who has given you everything that is good." This answer astonished those who had questioned Him. It is likely to have angered the Pharisees, and to have disappointed people who hoped He would lead a rebellion. But it was of

H 197

great interest to those Christians in Rome for whom Mark wrote this Gospel: it showed clearly that a Christian is not disloyal to the State.

NOTES

v. 14. You are a sincere man; you are not afraid of anyone . . .

This was said in order to deceive Jesus. They wished to pay Him compliments so that He would talk freely. They did not really respect Him.

But the words are true. Jesus was absolutely sincere. He was not moved aside by the fear of what others were thinking. Their two other remarks were also true: "You have no favourites; you teach what really is the way of God."

Note: The A.V. translation, "Carest for no man", is misleading.

v. 15. He saw through their double-dealing . . .

Double-dealing or "hypocrisy" means saying one thing and believing something different.

Jesus always saw through this. He knew what went on in men's minds (John 2. 25). So does God, "unto whom all hearts be open, all desires known, and from whom no secrets are hid" (the prayer in the Communion service).

v. 16. Bring me a silver coin . . .

There were two sorts of coins generally used in Judea: 1. The copper coin used in that part of the Roman Empire; 2. The silver coin used all over the Empire.

The head-tax had to be paid in the silver coin. It was called *denarius* and was a day's wage for a labourer. (The A.V. translation, "penny", is misleading.) On the *denarius* was the image or picture of the Emperor's face and his name. Wherever people used coins which had on them the face of the Emperor, they acknowledged his authority.

Someone went to fetch a *denarius*, probably because He was in a Temple courtyard; a coin with the face of a heathen Emperor on it was not to be found there.

v. 17. Give Caesar what belongs to Caesar, and give God what belongs to God.

In this verse "Caesar" stands for the State or government in control.

Caesar was the title given to all Roman Emperors at that time. The teaching is:

1. *We have duties both to the state and to God:* It is as if Jesus were saying "The image on the coin shows that it belongs to the Emperor, so give it to him: the image on your soul shows that you belong to God (see Gen. 1. 26, 27), so give yourself to Him.

2. *The taxes we pay are not a gift to the state, but a debt we pay back:* In the Greek of v. 15 they said, "Shall we *give* the tax?", but here Jesus says, "*Give back*". We receive the benefits of a government, e.g., roads, law-courts, etc. Christians admit this and pay for them by taxes: in fact a man becomes a more loyal citizen than he was before when he becomes a Christian (Rom. 13. 1–7).

Note: This does not mean that Jesus thought that the Romans were right in all their methods of taxation or in their treatment of the Jews. He was not on the side of the stronger nation against the weaker. He was not saying that it is always wrong to rebel. He meant, "So long as a government is in power, pay for what it gives you, even when you think it treats you unjustly."

3. *The verse does not mean that in one part of life we should obey the State, and in another we should obey God:* It is entirely wrong to say, "In politics and war I shall give my loyalty to Caesar (the State); in my Church work I shall be loyal to God." We owe loyalty to God in every part of life. (See note on 12. 29.) We do our duty to the State as part of our duty to God. God is over all.

4. *So there are times when a Christian cannot obey the State:* e.g., when the State commands him to do what is against God's laws. (See Acts 4. 19; Rev. 18. 1–4.) The State itself is judged by God. This presents difficult problems. e.g.:

a. a Christian chief in some parts of the world is expected by his advisers and the people to offer sacrifices to the tribal spirits so that the crops will grow; but if he did so, he would show a lack of trust in God the Father of Jesus Christ. b. a Christian is elected a member of the town-council, but is told that its meetings are held during the time of Sunday morning service; c. a Christian lives in a country which declares war on another country, and he believes that God desires his country to suffer rather than to kill.

In all such difficulties, this verse and 13.11 guide us.

Mark 12. 18–27 : The Question about Life after Death

See also Matt. 22. 23–33; Luke 20. 27–40

INTRODUCTION

The Question

The Sadducees told Jesus a story which perhaps he knew already, about seven brothers. Each one married the same wife and shortly afterwards died. Then they said, "We know you teach that there is a life after death. If there is, whose wife will that woman be after she has died?"

This question, like those in 10. 2; 11. 28; 12. 15, was not asked in order to know the truth, but as a way of attacking Jesus. They wanted to make people laugh at Him. Why did they want this? Because they were afraid. They knew that unless He was stopped from teaching, He would urge them to change their ways; and they were not willing to do that. Also, the people would pay more attention to Him than to themselves. People to-day often ask questions about religion for the same reason. They ask, "Who was Cain's wife?" in order to avoid having to think seriously about Jesus' words, "Follow me".

The Sadducees

Those who asked this question were the most powerful of all the groups or "parties" in the Jewish Council, or Sanhedrin. (Other groups were the Pharisees and the Herodians: see Additional Note, p. 226.) The high-priest was always a Sadducee. This was the group that controlled all matters concerning the Temple, and it was partly through the profits of the trading in the Temple courtyard that they had become rich. (See note on 11. 1.) They hated the Pharisees, who placed such importance on the traditions that had grown up in addition to the Old Testament books. They said that they could not believe in life after death because it was new teaching, and had not been believed in in the days of Moses. We can see why they chose this question to ask Jesus.

Jesus' answer

He knew that they asked this question in order to make people

200

laugh at Him. But He gave in His answer clear teaching concerning life after death. (See notes on vv. 24b, 25, 26.)

Note: When the word "resurrection" is used in this story, it means life after our bodies have died. It does not here refer to the raising of Jesus from the dead at Easter nor to the raising of the faithful at the Last Day.

NOTES

v. 19. His brother shall marry the woman and raise a family for him.

This was a Jewish law (Deut. 25. 5). It was done in order that: a. the first man's property should remain in his family; b. his name should continue. Most Jews did not believe in a life after death, so they were very anxious that their name should continue on earth. This custom is still practised in parts of the world to-day. It is not itself an evil custom; but it can become evil, e.g., if the wishes of the woman are not considered.

v. 24. You do not understand the scriptures, or the power of God.

1. **The scriptures:** Jesus was saying, "You are teachers of religion, but you have not yet learnt that a Bible passage has more teaching in it than you had discovered before." (It is possible for Christians also to be regular readers of the Bible and yet fail to see the new lessons that God wants them to learn through it.) It is likely that He was thinking of Ex. 3. 6, which He later interpreted for them. (See note on v. 27.)

2. **The power of God:** We believe we shall have life after death, because we believe in God's power to give it to us (1 Cor. 6. 14). Life after this life on earth is not ours by our nature. We are raised to it by God when it is His will to do so.

v. 25. When they rise . . . they neither marry nor are given in marriage.

This means that the life after death will be a new kind of life. (See 1 Cor. 15. 35–end.) It will be more than anything we can think of while we are living on earth. The division into male and female will be no longer needed. Men and women who know the joy of marriage are sometimes afraid that they will lose such great joy after death.

But Jesus is here saying, "I promise you new and even greater joys after death."

Note: We are not told here or elsewhere in the New Testament what life after death will be like. This verse tells us only what it is *not* like. This means that it is not necessary for us to know (Deut. 29. 29a; 1 John 3. 2). What God desires is that we should trust Him so completely now that we believe that what He will give us after death will be very good.

This teaching is different from:

1. The Jewish belief in a *half-life:* When the Jews talked about "life after death", they usually thought of a place called Sheol (see notes on 5. 39; 10. 47) where their spirits went. There was no light there or joy or fellowship with God (Ps. 115. 17).

2. The belief (held by most Muslims) in a *continuation* of this life, i.e., that it will be in a different place, but of the same kind as this life, and that there will be wives to marry and food to eat.

3. The belief in a *repetition* of this life: Many people in Asia and Africa believe that after death, a man's spirit is born again into a new body on earth and lives another life here. This is often called "reincarnation". Jesus did not in this passage say that this belief is wrong (see note on 9. 13). But He was talking about something quite different: He was describing the life that is lived after all life here on earth is over. It is a new kind of life, not a continuation of this one.

v. 27. God is not the God of dead men but of living. You are quite wrong.

1. The Sadducees said that what was taught in the first five books of the Old Testament was of special importance. So Jesus quoted from Exodus (3. 6) in answering their question. He said: "The story of the burning bush says that Abraham belonged to God. But he still belongs to God. People who belong to God are living, not dead."

2. When God makes anyone His friend, He keeps Him as His friend for ever. The death of the body does not kill that friendship. So we do not believe in life after death because some people have seen ghosts, or because we have seen dead people walking in our dreams. We believe in life after death because we believe in God, and because His love for us is too strong to be broken by the death of our bodies. If we belong to Him now, we believe that He never

lets us go. He never lets us become nothing after death (Rom. 8. 38, 39; John 14. 19b). This means that we need to make sure that we belong to Him now.

Note: This verse also reminds us that God does not belong to one generation only. He existed before the world began, and will exist after it has ended. He is just as much the God and Father of the twentieth century A.D. as he was of the twentieth century B.C.

3. **You are quite wrong:** In the eyes of Jesus the Sadducees were false teachers, because: a. they were denying that God had enough power to give us life after death; b. they found it almost impossible to accept any teaching unless Jews had believed it for many hundreds of years. (But Jesus taught that the Living God is continually leading men to new understanding of His will for them.)

Jesus rebuked them sternly. He could be very gentle, especially with sinners. He could also be angry and severe, when it was needed. Leaders in His Church to-day have sometimes to speak with the same sternness, especially when people deny that God has power, e.g., when they say, "Human nature cannot be changed."

See picture facing p. 196.

Mark 12. 28–34 : The Question about the Greatest Commandment

See also Matt. 22. 34–40; Luke 10. 25, 28

INTRODUCTION

The Question

The scribe who asked this question was probably one of the Pharisees, but he was not trying to trap Jesus. He really wanted to know the answer. A scribe's daily work was to explain the law of the Jewish religion, and especially the unwritten traditions which had grown up in addition to the laws themselves. (See note on 1. 22.) There were a great many laws and traditions. Scribes could recite the 365 actions they had to avoid and the 268 they had to perform. It was natural that they should discuss among themselves, "Is there one commandment which is more important than all the rest?" Some used to say "Yes"; but others taught that all were equally important, and that it was just as bad to offer a sick dove in a sacrifice as to steal your neighbour's wife. This is the question the scribe asked Jesus.

Jesus' answer

1. "Yes. There is one commandment more important than the rest, the commandment of love." V. 30 is about loving God, v. 31, about loving people. But the two verses go together and mean, "Thou shalt love" (Rom. 13. 10b). What does it mean to love? (See note on v. 31.)

2. "Loving God and loving other people go together." We do not even need to ask which is the more important: both are equally commanded. The words "The first is" (v. 29) do not mean that it is the more important. This was new teaching for most Jews. They knew "Love God" from Deut. 6. 4 and "Love your neighbour" from Lev. 19. 18, but the two were hardly ever put into a single commandment.

Two sorts of people need this teaching especially:

a. Those who say that being kind to neighbours and family is the important thing, and that the worship of God is only for people who feel they need it. (But in practice those who help their neighbours best are those who have in worship been filled with God's spirit.)

b. Those who say that the duty to God is more important than the duty to others. (See note on 7. 11, 12.) Many Hindus say this, and even Christians sometimes think it. But 1 John 4. 20 shows that the best way of loving God is to act with love towards other people. These verses show that there is only one God, and that we must love him in all our activities, and with our wills, feelings, and thinking.

The scribe understood all this, and Jesus told him that he was "not far" from accepting the rule of God in his life (v. 34).

NOTES

v. 29. Hear, O Israel, the Lord our God is one Lord.

1. Jesus' answer was mainly a quotation from the Old Testament: a. He began by reciting from Deut. 6. 4, 5. These verses were called the Shema by all Jews. The Shema was said every day, was written

204

out on very small pieces of paper and worn on the forehead, and was written on the doorposts of houses. Jews still do all this to-day.
b. In the next part of His answer (v. 31), He quoted from Lev. 19. 18.

Jesus thus used the Old Testament very greatly, even though He gave new interpretations to many passages. It was His Bible. Christians, therefore, cannot do without it.

2. **The Lord our God is one Lord:** These words are part of the Shema, quoted by Jesus. They are translated in the New English Bible, "The Lord your God is the only Lord", i.e., God is one; and in all the different things we do in our lives we have the one and the same God to serve. People of every race and generation need this truth. e.g.:

a. Jews in the time of Elijah used to sacrifice to Baal when they wanted their farms to succeed, but to Jehovah in wartime. It was many years before the Jews knew that no gods existed except the One God.

b. In many tribal religions still practised to-day, women sacrifice to one spirit when they are bearing children, but to different ones in a smallpox outbreak or a thunderstorm.

c. Educated people of to-day sometimes worship the Father of Jesus Christ when in Church, but in wartime give greater loyalty to the nation than to Him. In the same way, they may worship their possessions while trading, and their bodies when marrying.

v. 30. Thou shalt love the Lord thy God with all thy heart . . .

We must love God with the whole of ourselves. That is what the word "heart" meant to all Jews. (Thus it does not mean our "feelings" only, nor the part of the body through which blood flows.) The three words that follow, "soul", "mind", "strength", are simply a way of emphasizing this lesson.

One way in which we can see the meaning of loving God with the "whole" of ourselves is this:

1. To love with our *wills*. We desire so strongly to honour Him that our desire leads us to take action.

2. To love with our *minds*. We take the trouble to think out what we believe (1 Pet. 3. 15b) and what are the needs of other people.

3. To love with our *feelings*. We fall in love and make jokes in a

way that is acceptable to God: we use our feelings of joy and sorrow and triumph in our worship of Him.

v. 31.   Thou shalt love thy neighbour as thyself.

1. **Thou shalt love:** If we love someone, we sincerely want them to have the best things that God offers mankind; we are willing to suffer ourselves, if necessary, in order to help them actively; we continue in this, even if they should injure us. Loving someone is thus not the same thing as regarding him as an attractive person. *Note:* We know what "loving" is by watching how Jesus lived and loved. (See note on 10. 21.)

2. **Thy neighbour:** When the Jews read this verse in Lev. 19. 18, they thought a "neighbour" meant "another Jew". But Jesus showed in Luke 10. 25–37 that we should love not only those of our own family or nation or tribe, and not only those who have been kind to us, but anyone who is in need of our help.

3. **As thyself:** We are commanded to "love ourselves", because we are God's children and made in some ways to be like Him. (See Gen. 1. 27; 1 Cor. 3. 16, 17.) It is wrong to neglect any of His children. Therefore it is our duty to look after our own bodies, to develop our minds, to train our souls to grow in friendship with God. (See note on 8. 34.) And just as we forgive others if we love them, so we must forgive ourselves when we have done wrong.

v. 33.   To love ... is far more than all these ... burnt-offerings ...

The scribe understood Jesus' teaching. He saw that it is more important to have in your heart love for God and for others, than to perform actions which are called "holy", or "religious", such as offering a whole animal in the Temple sacrifices. In the same way, being regular with prayer and Bible study, holding correct opinions about God, performing correct actions in Church services, are important duties, but they are less important than having love in ourselves for God and others.

v. 34.   You are not far from the kingdom of God ...

Jesus said this to the scribe because he had understood His teaching. (Compare the words in 10. 21.) Jesus gave great encouragement to those who were sincerely looking for ways of serving God.

206

But he was "not far", i.e., not yet in the Kingdom. He had understood Jesus' words, but had not yet made the decision to follow Him, and to put his whole life under God's rule.

Mark 12. 35–37: Jesus' Question about the Messiah

See also Matt. 22. 41–46; Luke 20. 41–44

INTRODUCTION

Jesus' riddle

The other questions in this chapter were asked by the people of Jerusalem, but this was asked by Jesus. It was a kind of riddle, rather like, "How can a son be also the master?" He said: "When the Messiah comes, He will be a descendant or 'son' of David. Can you explain why David also calls this Messiah 'his lord' and master in Ps. 110?"

The Messiah is greater than David

The riddle was asked to make people think more deeply about the Messiah. Nearly all Jews expected that the Messiah would be a fighting man and a national leader of the same sort as David. Jesus says something different, "Ps. 110 shows that although the Messiah is descended from David, he is far greater than David. He is David's ·Lord. He existed before David was born: his ways are very different from the ways of a great army general."

The Messiah is Jesus

Jesus was talking about Himself in these verses. He was the Messiah (see notes on 11. 27–33; 12. 1–12). But He did not openly say so, lest everyone should think that He intended to lead a rebellion against the Romans. His aim was; a. to show the people what sort of person the Messiah really was; b. to bring some of them actually to accept Him as their Messiah and Master.

Note: V. 37b says that His teaching was very acceptable to the ordinary people. This means that it was acceptable on the many occasions on which He taught during the weeks before His death, not on this occasion only.

NOTES

v. 35.   How can the scribes say that the Christ is David's son?

1. **Christ** means "Messiah". (See Additional Note, p. 133.)

2. Did Jesus in these words deny that He was descended from David? No: what He taught was that He was far more than a descendant. (See John 8. 58.)

3. Was Jesus really of David's family?

a. Yes, it is likely that He was, because Mary, His mother, was. Joseph went to Bethlehem for the census, because he was of David's family. Mary was at that time in her last month of pregnancy and would probably not have accompanied him unless she also was of that family.

b. It is also likely that He was descended from David by law, even if Mary was not herself of David's family. Joseph was certainly descended from David (Luke 1. 27). He was engaged to Mary at the time she conceived Jesus, and he married her afterwards. So Jesus was held to be Joseph's son by law, although Joseph was not Jesus' father (Luke 3. 23).

c. But we should not believe in Jesus any less if it were discovered that Joseph, but not Jesus, was descended from David. We believe in Him because of what He has done for us, not because He was from David's family. That is why we are not troubled to find that the two lists of names of His ancestors in Luke 3, and Matt. 1 are different. We do not mind very much who His ancestors were: we mind very much who *He* was.

v. 36.   David himself by the Holy Spirit said, The Lord said to my Lord . . .

Note: **By the Holy Spirit** means "inspired by the Holy Spirit". The first time the word "Lord" is used it means God, the second time it means the Messiah.

Jesus thus said that the psalm was written by David, and of course it may be so. But many people who have studied the Hebrew words used in the psalm think that it was written eight hundred years

208

after David. If they are right, would it mean that Jesus was making a mistake? If so, other important questions are asked, "If Jesus were mistaken in this, how could we believe the rest of His teaching? How can we tell which part is true and which is not?

To such questions there are these clear answers:

1. Everyone living in Jerusalem at that time thought that David wrote this psalm. Jesus was a real man and had the same knowledge as other people on matters such as this. He had the same knowledge of history and geography that they had. He says this in 13. 32. If this had not been so He would not have been a real man.

2. On the other hand, Jesus taught with perfection on questions such as "What is God like? What is His will for mankind?" On these matters He taught what no other person has ever been able to teach. He did so because He was Himself God.

v. 37.   A large crowd heard him with delight.

1. **A large crowd:** These words are sometimes translated, "the ordinary people". Jesus' teaching and His method of teaching were not acceptable to most of the highly educated, or the religious leaders or the rich or influential people. It was acceptable to the general public. The Christian message is still especially understood by ordinary people who are humble enough to listen and trustful enough to follow Jesus in practice. It is certainly not a difficult lesson that only well-educated or important people can understand. In fact it is always the rich or powerful people who find it hardest to obey the Gospel (10. 42).

2. **Heard him:** It was He (Jesus) who delighted them. Ordinary people are much more likely to receive Christian preaching with delight to-day if it is preaching about *Him*, and what He did and what He does in the lives of men to-day. They listen with much less delight to preaching about the Church or the people themselves or life's difficulties (see 1 Cor. 2. 2).

Mark 12. 38–40: A Warning Against the Scribes

See also Matt. 23. 1–36; Luke 20. 45–47; 11. 39–52.

INTRODUCTION

It is not known when Jesus gave this warning but it shows how greatly His teaching about the right way to serve God differed from the customs of the Jewish religious leaders. It was so different that they killed Him (14. 2).

In His warning Jesus attacked two special sins:

1. They wanted to be honoured themselves more than they wanted God to be honoured. (See note on v. 38.)

2. They were making profits for themselves through their position. (See note on v. 40a.)

Note:

a. Not all scribes were attacked by Jesus for these sins. He always gave praise where it was right to do so, both to scribes and to others. (See 12. 34, 43.)

b. The scribes were leaders in religion. (See note on 1. 22, and Introduction to 12. 28–34.) They possessed knowledge which most people did not have. Thus they held the same kind of position among the Jews that clergy and ministers hold in the Christian Church to-day. This passage therefore describes the temptations that come to Christian Church leaders to use their high positions in the wrong way; i.e., the temptation to work in order to gain advantages for themselves rather than to be the servants of God and of other people. (See notes on 9. 35 and 10. 43.)

NOTES

v. 38. Be on your guard against the scribes . . .

1. Why are we to guard against them? Because: a. unless we are careful, we shall imitate their wrong thinking and behaviour, just as we catch smallpox from someone who has the disease unless we take care. b. They are not trustworthy guides; they do not know how to lead people to serve God humbly, because they are not serving Him humbly themselves (Luke 11. 52).

2. In what ways did they show their sin? In four ways:

a. **Long robes** (v. 38): They wore the long robes which showed that they were highly educated, and which probably prevented them from doing manual work. This was done so that people should pay them special respect. It is probably useful for leaders in the Church to wear different clothes from other members, but it is possible to do so for the wrong reasons, e.g., in order to attract attention to themselves.

b. **To be saluted** (v. 38): See Matt. 23. 7. They felt more important than others, if they were called "Sir" or "your Reverence" in public, or had their hands kissed.

c. **Chief seat** and **best place** (v. 39): In the synagogues the scribes sat and faced the people, while the people stood for worship. At a feast they were given seats near the host. It is often necessary for those in high positions to sit where everyone can see. If a man is humble, he agrees to sit there in order not to give offence: it is not in order to be thought a "big man". He is happy if he is given a seat where no one can see him (Luke 14. 7–11).

d. **Long prayers** (v. 40): These prayers are probably their own private prayers which they said in public: they hoped that people would say, "How holy they are!" when they spent a long time praying (Matt. 6. 5–8).

Note:

1. Jesus was not rebuking the scribes for wearing long robes or sitting in the chief places, etc., nor was He giving rules about such things. He was simply speaking about their desire to receive attention.

2. Why did the scribes have this desire? Why do so many of us want people to pay attention to us? It is partly because we are afraid: we fear that unless we do things to make others respect us, we shall become of no value in the world. But Jesus said in Luke 12. 6, 7 that we are already very precious to God, and He is the only one that knows the true value of people. If we really believe this, we no longer want to push ourselves forward and we have overcome the temptations Jesus was speaking of here.

v. 40. They swallow up widows' houses . . . these will receive the heaviest sentence.

1. **Swallow up widows' houses:** Perhaps they persuaded rich widows to give them their property, saying that this was what God

211

desired; or perhaps they took very high fees from poor widows who had trusted them to look after their property. (The scribes did some of the work which lawyers do to-day.) It is certain that they made profits for themselves through the position which they had as religious leaders. This can be a temptation for leaders in any Church. This is why in many Churches to-day the leaders are not allowed to employ members of their own families for work such as repairing the church or supplying books to the Church school.

2. **The heaviest sentence:** This was not, of course, a curse of Jesus. He was saying that all those who hold positions of leadership amongst God's people are more severely judged than others. They have greater opportunity than others to help people: if by their bad example they hinder them, they will receive greater blame (Rom. 2. 17, 21, 24; 1 Pet. 4. 17). This should not prevent people from becoming leaders in the Church, but show them the necessity of asking for and receiving the strengthening of the Holy Spirit.

Mark 12. 41–44: The Widow's Offering

See also Luke 21. 1–4

INTRODUCTION

Before Mark tells us of the offering of Jesus of Himself on the cross, he describes the offering made by one poor woman.

The Story

One part of the Temple grounds was the "Court" (or "compound") "of the Women". In it were thirteen collecting boxes (with mouths shaped like a trumpet), into which women put their voluntary gifts. Jesus was outside this "court" but could see this woman making her offering from where He was.

The Teaching

It is chiefly about the way in which we should make our offerings to God. Jesus did not lay down any rule about how much Church members should give, e.g., He did not just say "give a tenth".

According to Him, the *reason* why we give is more important than *how much* we give.

The story teaches us that we are to give:

a. As a sign of our *love* for God and not in order to earn praise from others. (See note on v. 42.)

b. In such a way that it is *costly* to ourselves. (See note on v. 43.)

c. With *faith* and trust in God and without fear for the future. (See note on v. 44.)

NOTES

v. 42. Put in two farthings . . .

The Greek word is translated "farthing", because that is the smallest English coin. (In every language the name of the smallest coin should be used here.) It was such a small gift that she could not possibly have made it in order to gain the approval of her friends. Jesus saw that it was given out of the love she had for God. This contains important teaching for those who collect money for the Church. We may be tempted to ask our members to give for the wrong reason, e.g., "Give generously and your gift will be acknowledged publicly." Let us say rather, "God gave us His Son; what can we give?"

v. 43. This poor widow has put in more than all . . .

1. Jesus compared her gifts with the gifts of the others and judged hers to be of greater value. The "value" of our offerings depends on how much is left after we have given; e.g., for a young man who has only just begun to earn money, two shillings a week may be a valuable and costly offering: a man earning fifty pounds a month may not notice the absence of two shillings because there is plenty left over afterwards. It was costly for the widow to give anything at all: probably she had no one to support her. She had nothing left after giving (2 Sam. 24. 24b).

2. To say that the widow's gift was of great value is not what people of the world would say. When Jesus praised her, He was thinking with the mind of God (1 Cor. 1. 25). If we learn to think as God thinks, we shall show the same respect to a poor person who has made a small offering as we do to a rich person who has made a large gift.

v. 44. All her living.

Living means "all the money she had to keep herself alive", or, "the cost of her next meal". She could not have made the gift unless she had faith that God would look after her. She "took a risk" in making her gift. (See note on 2. 5.)

It is a sign of a strong Christian congregation that, in giving, it is prepared to take such risks. One church building in R . . . needed to be repaired extensively and a fund was begun. When nearly all the money had been collected, an urgent appeal came from a very poor congregation in another country. These people's church had been destroyed in a storm. The people of R . . . decided to send them all the money collected for their own Repair Fund ("put in all that she had") and to trust God to help them to find more money for their own church repairs.

Mark 13 : Teaching about the Coming

See also Matt. 24. Luke 21. 5–37

INTRODUCTION

The arrangement of the Chapter

Vv. 1–4: Introduction: Two short conversations between Jesus and His disciples.
Vv. 5–23. The troubles which will take place before the completion of God's work.
Vv. 24–27. The Coming of Jesus.
Vv. 28–37: How Christians are to prepare.

Mark's Purpose

Mark was writing for the small persecuted body of Christians living in Rome among the heathen of that great Empire. They were like many Christians who read this Gospel to-day, namely, a small group in a country where most people are not Christians. Such Christians see the great amount of evil in the world; they find it hard to understand why God allows it, and hard to believe that God can overcome it. So Mark collected together some sayings of

Jesus which taught one great lesson. They were probably given at different times during His ministry.

The lesson is that Christians endure suffering, because they are taking part in the same fight against evil which Jesus fought (see vv. 9–13). Jesus overcame the power of death and rose again. So the Church's struggles and sufferings on earth will have an end. This end will take place when Jesus comes for the last time and all evil is completely overcome (see vv. 26, 27).

So this is a chapter of good news.

The Coming of Jesus in Glory

What was Jesus talking about when He spoke about His "Coming"? If we read the other Gospels as well as Mark, it is clear that He was talking about more than one Coming: e.g., He said that His death on the cross would be a "Coming with glory" (see John 12. 23); but He also said that His last Coming (the completion of God's work of overcoming evil) would be a "Coming with glory". So when we read in this chapter about "the Coming", we shall understand the word in two ways at once: a. as an event that was very near at hand, i.e., the Crucifixion; b. that would not happen until the completion of God's work, His "Last Coming".

We shall understand other phrases which occur in this chapter in these two ways, e.g., the "gathering of His chosen" (v. 27).

NOTES

v. 2.   Not one stone shall be left here upon another . . .

1. Jesus meant that before long the Temple would be destroyed. (It was destroyed only seven years after it had been completed.) This was a terrible thing for the disciples to hear. The Temple was not only a beautiful building of white stone with decoration of pure gold, but it was also the central place of worship for all the Jews of the world. (It was begun in 21 B.C., was still being built when Jesus was speaking—A.D. 29—and was not completed until A.D. 63.)

2. But His words also teach that this world and everything in it will have an end. (See also John 4. 21; 1 Pet. 2. 11a; Heb. 13. 14.) We often speak as if great churches and colleges and parliament buildings are built to "last for ever" (see Ps. 49. 11). But they have an end. What does really last for ever? Only the love of God Him-

215

self and the devotion of a faithful heart to Him. (See Luke 12. 21, 33.)

Since this is so, Christians are less troubled than others when they hear that scientists can make bombs which could destroy the whole human race. The Church needs to work to prevent such a thing happening. But, if it did happen, we know that God has prepared for us a new life even better than the one He has provided for us here.

v. 5.   Take care that no one deceives you.

This verse is not a reply to v. 4. It is the beginning of a new section (vv. 5–23) which describes the troubles that must be expected before the Coming takes place.

1. Deceivers of many different kinds have always been a danger to the Church. Two kinds referred to in this chapter are: a. those who claim that they, rather than Jesus, are God's special messengers (v. 6); b. those who unsettle many by saying that they know when Jesus' Last Coming will be (see v. 32). Such deceivers may be members of the Church or call themselves Christians.

2. The way to "take care" is to take all opportunities to find out what God Himself is saying. Bible Reading is one certain way, but we need help from men in authority in the Church in interpreting it. Deceivers will meet with little success, if we look more to the Bible for our guidance and less to our dreams and to newspapers.

v. 7a.   When you hear of wars . . . do not be frightened . . .

1. **Wars:** Jesus was often telling His disciples that trouble of many kinds would come, so that when it did come they should not be surprised. They are to be like people who thatch their roofs before the rains begin. (See vv. 7b, 11, 23 of this chapter, also John 14. 28, 29; Matt. 6. 27; 1 Pet. 4. 12.) Yet often we forget this and when trouble comes, think that God has forgotten us.

2. **Frightened:** Fear is the most common of all diseases amongst mankind. God often sent messengers to say, "Do not be afraid" (see Matt. 1 20; 10. 26; 28. 5; etc.). This kind of fear goes away when we believe that God loves us and is in control of all that happens.

v. 7b.   These things must come, but it is not yet the end.

1. **These things:** i.e., deceivers, wars, earthquakes.

2. Not yet the end: We must not think that these troubles are themselves the completion of God's work on earth; they come before the completion. Therefore we are to get on with our work quietly and faithfully. This was the teaching which St Paul found that many needed in his time. They were neglecting their ordinary duties in this world, because the completion was expected; so he wrote verses like 1 Thess. 4. 11; 2 Thess. 2. 1–3. A preacher to-day is right to prepare his people for Jesus' Last Coming, but he must also attend to his own present duties, e.g., his duties to his family.

Christians therefore have a double duty: to prepare for the completion and to be faithful in the present. Most of Jesus' teaching is about our present duties, e.g., "Heal the sick". We are reminded of this "double duty" by the Holy Communion service: in it we "show forth the Lord's death until His Coming again" (1 Cor. 11. 26): we also "receive the spiritual food of His Body and Blood" in present worship and as nourishment for the doing of our present duties.

v. 9. Look to yourselves . . . . you shall stand before governors and kings for my sake, to bear witness to them.

1. **To yourselves** (see also vv. 23, 33): Although we are to care greatly for others, we have a duty to ourselves, namely to examine ourselves to see what sort of life we are living. See note on 6. 31. *What kind* of life I live matters far more than *where* I work or *what* I do for a living or *how much* I earn for it.

2. **Before governors:** They are told to pay attention to the quality of their lives, because they may be arrested by government officials. In such cases they will have an opportunity to show by the way in which they behave what is meant by "following Christ". This is so even if there is no chance to preach (1 Pet. 3. 15, 16). This happened to St Paul many times, and he took the opportunities. (See Acts 26. 1, 2; Phil. 1. 12, 13.) A Christian who serves his country as a Member of Parliament or as a member of a Town Council or of a Trade Union is often in the same situation, especially if those in authority are non-Christians or Christian only in name.

v. 10.   The good news must first be preached to all the heathen.

1. **First be preached.** This means: Before the final Coming of Jesus, make sure that as many people as possible hear the Gospel.

217

This is an urgent matter because your opportunity for preaching will not last for ever.

2. **To all the heathen** (or **all nations**): This (together with Matt. 24. 14; 28. 19) shows that Jesus was interested in the conversion of everyone, not only in that of the Jews. (See note on 7. 24–30 and also Rom. 11. 11–end; Isa. 42. 1.)

3. This verse is not giving us a time-table of events; it does not mean that Jesus cannot or will not come until every family in every village of the world has heard the Gospel. If Jesus had taught that, then we could rightly say, "The Last Coming cannot take place to-day because many have not heard the Gospel yet". But in v. 33 Jesus says that He will come suddenly and that means that He may come to-day.

v. 11.   Do not be anxious what you should say . . .

1. Being anxious means thinking, "If I do not know what to say or do, then God cannot help me to know", so it arises partly from pride. But God will send guidance, e.g., through prayer and through other people. He has promised that His Holy Spirit is ready to do what we cannot. (See John 16. 13; 14. 16–18, 26.)

2. The A.V. translation "take no thought" is misleading. This verse does not mean that a sermon will be more guided by the Spirit when it is unprepared than when it has been prepared. We are told to use our minds for God in 12. 30. It does mean that we are to give as much thought as is possible to words which we speak in His name, whether they will be spoken in the classroom or in church or in a committee. But when this preparation is done, we commit it all to God without worrying, asking Him to make our words come alive. Effort is ours: results are God's.

v. 13.   You will be hated by all for my name's sake; but he that endures to the end, shall be saved.

This is only one of the sufferings to be expected (see vv. 5. 17–19). Four things are here taught about such persecution:

1. **You will be:** i.e., It cannot be escaped. Since Jesus had many enemies, so have His true followers. (See John 15. 18–20; Luke 11. 49–51; 12. 11; 13. 34, 35; 17. 23–35.)

A Christian must be prepared for this (see note on v. 7a). A boy who had been brought up in a Christian home joined the army. He found it was very hard to be faithful there, and he complained to his chaplain of his difficulties. The chaplain said, "Did they not tell you when you were baptized that Christians are always fewer than others?"

But this was new teaching for many Jews. They believed that if they were obedient to God, He would keep suffering away from them. (See Ps. 37. 25; 91. 7.)

2. **He that endures:** i.e., It must be willingly accepted. There are other ways of behaving when persecution comes, e.g., a. with pride (in our own courage): b. with silent misery (like a sick animal); c. with complaint that God is unfair; but these are not Christian ways. We are to bear it like a man who willingly carries a heavy load on his journey home. We can do this because of our faith that God is leading us to the Kingdom.

3. **To the end:** These words mean not only "until the completion of God's work in the world", and "till we die", but also "completely". There is to be no limit to our willingness to endure, "even to the point of death" (Rev. 2. 10).

Note: The persecution referred to in this verse is persecution endured because of our faithfulness to Christ. It does not refer to other people's dislike of us because we have behaved badly. Christians, even more than others, must expect to suffer.

4. **Shall be saved:** Persecution can become the means of our being saved, because it trains us to depend on God; someone who depends on God is ready to be accepted by Him as His own, that is, as "saved". (See Luke 21. 19; Ps. 119. 67, 71.)

v. 14.   When you see the unmentionable thing set up . . .

This section (vv. 14–23) refers to the destruction of Jerusalem, not to the completion of God's work in the world. (This is clear from v. 18, which speaks of the winter. It would not matter in what season the completion of God's work occurred).

1. In Dan. 9. 27b these words are used in order to refer to the action of the Greek King, Antiochus Epiphanes. After defeating the Jews in battle in 168 B.C., he set up a Greek heathen altar in the Temple. Jesus is here saying, "This kind of thing will happen again".

2. What did happen? We do not know. But "let the reader understand" is probably a note written by Mark to the Christians of that time, meaning, "You will know what I mean by this". He was writing

219

not long before the war between the Romans and the Jews in which the Temple was destroyed. Perhaps Roman armies were already surrounding Jerusalem and it seemed likely that the holy Temple would be attacked by heathen Romans. So Mark could not say openly what he was referring to, because Christians were being persecuted at that time.

3. But the words do not only refer to what Greeks or Romans did. An "unmentionable thing" is set up whenever complete loyalty is given to something or someone instead of to God, e.g., when the citizens of a country give so much loyalty to a political leader that they have almost none for God; or when Church members pay so much attention to organizing the Church that they have hardly any attention for God Himself, whose Church it is.

v. 20. If the Lord had not cut short those days . . ."

Those days: These words refer to that time in the future when Jerusalem will be destroyed. We learn here that:

1. God can and does control the events of the world; this verse says He will reduce the number of days of suffering (see note on 4. 39).

2. He will not allow His Church ("those whom He has chosen") to be destroyed completely (see John 10. 28).

v. 24. After those sufferings, The sun shall be darkened . . .

All this section (vv. 24–27) deals with the "Coming" of Jesus. It deals with: a. His Coming to glory at His Crucifixion, a very near event; b. His Last Coming. (See Introduction to this chapter.)

1. **After those sufferings:** It is after a period of trouble that Jesus will come. Christians have sometimes expected that the world would gradually become better and better, but Jesus did not say that it would. On the contrary, when evil is at its worst, we can say, "After this, Jesus may come".

2. **The sun shall be darkened:** This does not refer to an eclipse. These words (and the words, "stars shall fall") mean that the events of His coming will be very different from anything that people expect.

v. 26. The Son of Man coming in the clouds with great power and glory.

1. **The Son of Man,** i.e., Jesus. (See Additional Note, p. 137.)

220

2. Coming with power. When does He come? He comes in glory at His Crucifixion and He comes at the "Last Coming", but the two "Comings" are connected. When He died and rose again, He was already fighting the final battle against evil. He will complete that battle at His "Last Coming".

That is why His coming is good news. Jesus has "great power" and has already begun to overcome evil. Evil which is so strong now will be completely brought to an end. So we pray, "Come, Lord Jesus" (Rev. 22. 20).

3. In the clouds: To the Jews a cloud was a sign of the presence of God Himself. (See note on 9. 7.) This means that His Coming is a gift from God, not something that Christians can cause to happen. *Note:* It is important to see what this verse does *not* tell us. It does not say: a. when the Last Coming will be; b. whether the Last Coming will be an event *in* the history of the world or will take place *after* the world has ended. It seems that in God's eyes we do not need to know these things. What we have to remember is that when Jesus comes for the last time, He will come as Judge.

v. 27. He shall gather his chosen together from the four winds.

1. Chosen: Jesus will judge and choose between good and evil. He is not only the "Lover of my soul", but the stern judge of my evil. ("He shall come . . . to judge": *Nicene Creed*.)

When does He judge? He judges whenever He comes, and He comes both at His Crucifixion and at the "End" (the completion of God's work). So He is already judging us, just as He is already offering us eternal life. (See John 6. 47 and 12. 31.) At His Last Coming He will give us His last judgement (John 5. 29). Then evil will be overcome for ever.

2. From the four winds: This shows that God's chosen will not be from one race only, but from all. No race is "God's own nation".

v. 30. The people of this present time shall not pass away, until all these things are done.

This section (vv. 28–37) is about being prepared. In some verses Jesus is saying "Be prepared for the destruction of Jerusalem"; in others, He says, "Be prepared for my Coming".

These things: These words probably refer to the sufferings in connection with the fall of Jerusalem, as do vv. 5–23. This is how Matthew understood them (see Matt. 23: 34–36). They do not refer to the Last Coming of Jesus.

Thus Jesus is not saying that His Last Coming will take place during the life-time of His hearers. (Some think that He did expect it to occur as soon as that. This is not impossible, but this chapter does not prove that He believed this.)

v. 31.   Heaven and earth shall pass away, but my words shall not pass away.

1. **Heaven:** In the Bible "heaven" can mean both "the state of being with God" and also "the sky". Here it means the sky. Jesus is saying that it is more possible for the sky to fall down and the earth to disappear than for His teaching to cease to be true.

2. **My words shall not pass away.**

a. No one but God can say this. In John 14. 10 (and also 6. 63; 6. 68) Jesus says the same thing, and we learn here that the everlasting truth of His teaching shows that Jesus is Himself God.

b. Thus His words are equally true for all ages and in every generation. This is sometimes forgotten. A student who had just entered the university wrote, "Jesus was good for me when I was a child and good for my nation when it was in its infancy, but now we have progressed beyond Him and can stand on our own feet". But Jesus is the same yesterday, to-day, and for ever (Heb. 13. 8). We need Him equally at every stage of our development.

v. 32.   The day or the hour no one knows, neither the angels . . . nor the Son, but only the Father.

It is likely that this verse refers to the day of the Last Coming of Jesus. Its teaching is two-fold:

1. *About Jesus*

a. Jesus is God's Son. In no other verse of Mark does Jesus call Himself that; but note v. 31 and 1. 1.

b. He is a really human being. It is for this reason that even He does not know when the End will come. This does not mean that He is inferior to the Father. It was of His own free will that He became man; He voluntarily deprived himself of certain powers and accepted the mind of a man. If He had known everything, He would only have been pretending to be a man.

Someone may say: "Since Jesus did not know the time of the

222

End, does it mean that His knowledge is imperfect? And if that was imperfect, can we regard His teachings as perfect?" To this we reply that on all matters about which we need to know in order to love God and men, Jesus did have perfect knowledge (see v. 31); on many matters of information e.g., facts about geography, dates of history, He did not, because no human being has.

Thus this verse, like the whole of the New Testament, shows Jesus as a. perfect God (Col. 1. 19); b. a real man (Heb. 2. 17; 4. 15). He was not partly God and partly man.

2. *About our duty*

We are called to get on with our work faithfully, since it is wrong to waste time trying to discover when the completion of God's work ("The end of the world") will come. The Church has often needed this teaching. See 1 Thess. 4. 11; 2 Thess. 2. 1, 2. Men find it hard to admit humbly that there are things which they can never know. See "You do not know" repeated in v. 35.

v. 33. Look to yourselves, keep awake, and pray . . .

The previous verses have spoken of things that we cannot do, e.g., we cannot tell the date of His Coming. Vv. 33–37 tell us what we can do: we can prepare for them.

Words used for preparing are, "Keep awake" (this verse), and "keep a look-out" (vv. 35–37). The A.V. translates both as "watch".

1. **Yourselves:** See v. 23. We must prepare ourselves before we can prepare others for His Coming. It is everyone's business to be ready, not only the business of clergy and evangelists (see "all" in v. 37).

2. **Keep awake:** Just as a watchman must be awake because thieves may come, so we must be aware of the evil in the world. Evil is anything which prevents us and others from being acceptable to God.

3. **Pray:** The best way to prepare is to be in fellowship with God, especially through prayer, so that when He comes, we know Him and He knows us.

v. 37. You do not know when the master of the house is coming . . .

1. **Do not know when:** So He may come to-day (v. 36). Therefore we do our work for Him with *urgency*. There may be very little time. We should not walk in a leisurely way towards a little child

playing on the road if we had heard a lorry coming round the corner. This is the teaching in the parables in Matt. 25.

2. **The master**: Jesus is the Master and is in control. The "Coming" is in His hands and we cannot hasten it. Therefore we work with *confidence*, and without anxiety.

These words, and also the little parable in vv. 34–36 show that if we are prepared for Jesus' Coming, we show in our lives both urgency and confidence.

SUMMARY OF TEACHING IN THIS CHAPTER

1. This earth and all that is in it will come to an end one day. (See note on v. 2.)

2. The time before Jesus' Coming will be a time of great trouble. (See note on v. 24.)

3. Christians (even more than others) must expect to suffer. (See note on v. 13.)

4. It is necessary to prepare ourselves for His Coming. (See note v. 33.)

5. Although we must be ready for His Coming, we must also do our present work faithfully. (See note on v. 7.)

6. When Jesus comes for the last time, He will come as Judge. Then all evil will be overcome for ever. (See note on v. 26.)

See picture facing p. 197.

Mark 14. 1, 2: The Plot Against Jesus

See also Matt. 26. 1–5; Luke 22. 1, 2; John 11. 47–53

INTRODUCTION

Chapters 14–16

This part of Mark's Gospel tells the story of the sufferings, death, and rising of Jesus. It is told much more fully than any other part: three chapters are given up to the events of only five days. It is clear that Mark and those who gave him information regarded this as the most important part of the story. (Probably it was the first part of

224

his Gospel to be put into writing.) Vv. 1, 2 of chap. 14 are the beginning of this story.

Why did they treat it as so important? Because they knew that Jesus had done more for mankind by His dying and rising than He had ever done by His teaching or healing. It was by His death and rising that He destroyed the power of sin over mankind, and made it possible for us to be at one with God (see Rom. 5. 10, 11). It is right therefore for great attention to be paid to this section. We can regard all Mark's previous chapters as a sort of introduction to these final chapters.

The Story

In vv. 1, 2, as we have seen in 3. 6; 11. 18; 12. 12, the Jewish leaders became more and more determined to put an end to the work of Jesus. Now a group of them met and decided to have Him killed immediately. They were the chief priests and the scribes, not the whole council of the Sanhedrin. (See Additional Note, p. 226.)

But they had a problem to solve. If they arrested Him during the Passover season, the people might take His side, and there would be a riot. If there was a riot, the Roman authorities might set up a military government and take away the power of the Jewish leaders. On the other hand, if they waited until after the Festival, it would give Jesus a chance to preach to the thousands of visiting pilgrims.

They had only one day in which to arrest Him. (They met on the Wednesday afternoon, and the Passover began on the Thursday. The "two days" in v. 1 refers to Wednesday and Thursday.) They were successful only because Judas showed them how to do it secretly.

But we see that the person who was really in control during these days was Jesus. He was killed at the time planned by Himself, i.e., the time when Jerusalem was most full of visitors.

NOTES

v. 1a. The passover and the feast of unleavened bread . . .

These were two religious festivals. The Passover (called the Pascha) was the thanksgiving for God's deliverance of the Jews from Egypt. (see note on 14. 12 and Ex. 13. 3; Lev. 13. 5.) The Unleavened Bread (called the Azume) was an agricultural festival, held at the time of year when the first green shoots of the new crop were appearing (Lev. 13. 6).

But as the Passover was on the fourteenth day of the month Nisan, and Unleavened Bread was from the fifteenth to the twenty-first, the two were regarded as one great festival season (just as we to-day might speak of "The Christmas and New Year season"). So the "feast" in v. 2 refers to the whole season. The A.V. "feast-day" is not correct.

v. 1b. Catch him by treachery . . .

They could not arrest Him in public: it had to be done by cunning and in secret.

Although the Gospel of Jesus is attacked publicly in some countries to-day, some of its worst enemies make their attacks secretly: e.g., a government declares itself in favour of freedom for all religions, but in fact makes it impossible for Christians to get promotion in their work; a head-teacher allows religious knowledge to be taught by those who are not believers; and the editor of a newspaper omits all news about the Church except when its members have got into trouble. Such "enemies" are being used by those "hidden forces of wickedness" spoken of in Eph. 6. 12.

ADDITIONAL NOTE

JEWISH RELIGIOUS LEADERS

In the story of Jesus we read of several different people or groups of people who were against Him. They were:

1. *The High Priest:* He was the chairman of the Sanhedrin, which was the highest council of the Jewish religion (14. 47, 59–65).

2. *The Chief Priests:* These were the important members of those families from which the High Priest was chosen (8. 31; 11. 27, etc.).

3. *The Sadducees:* These were the most powerful of the parties or groups within the Sanhedrin. The High Priest was always a Sadducee. (See notes on 12. 18–27.)

4. *The Pharisees:* These were a religious society: some of their members were in the Sanhedrin. (See Additional Note, p. 43.)

5. *The Herodians:* These were another group which had members in the Sanhedrin. They were friendly with Herod Antipas and with the Roman authorities. (See note on 3. 6; 12. 13.)

6. *The scribes:* These were teachers of the Old Testament Law. Many of them were Pharisees. (See Additional Note. p. 43.)

7. *The Elders:* This name was given to those members of the Sanhedrin who were not priests (11. 27; 14. 43, etc.; see also note on 14. 53; 15. 1).

Mark 14. 3–9: The Anointing of Jesus

See also Matt. 26. 6–13; John 12. 1–8

INTRODUCTION

The Story

On the Wednesday evening Jesus was having supper in a private house at Bethany, about two miles from Jerusalem. A woman came in and showed her adoration of Jesus by pouring ointment on His head. It was probably a different woman from the one who anointed Jesus in a Pharisee's house and was a "sinner" (Luke 7. 36–50).

The Teaching

This is considered mainly in notes on v. 6. By anointing Jesus the woman: a. showed her generosity; and b. treated Him as the Messiah.

Note: John 12. 3 says that this woman was Mary, the sister of Martha. Perhaps this is so, although Mark does not tell us her name. In some parts of the world to-day people have suggested that Martha and Mary were secret wives of Jesus. They say that this is why Mary anointed Him.

There is, of course, no evidence of any kind to support it. To those who say it, this should be said:

a. The Pharisees, who were looking everywhere for charges they could bring against Jesus, never made this accusation.

b. It is made only by those who:

i. do not believe that Jesus is God's Son, and want to persuade others to dishonour Him;

ii. cannot understand the action of this woman because they themselves have not received generosity of this kind or shown it to others.

227

NOTES

v. 4. Why was the oil wasted . . .

The oil was certainly precious, being made from an imported Indian plant (nard). It had cost more than three hundred silver coins, i.e., about the amount of the wages of a labourer for a whole year.

But it was not waste. When we show love, it is never wasted, whether it is shown directly to God or to one of His children. It is not wasted, even when it is not accepted or noticed. Every act of love is done unto God Himself, and He is "worthy to receive" more than we can ever give (Rev. 4. 10, 11).

Christians should not be surprised if they are accused of "waste", when they do such things as: spending Sunday morning in church rather than in bed; using the early morning for prayer rather than for extra study; going to work amongst poor and uneducated people, as Dr Albert Schweitzer did, instead of accepting important university posts.

v. 6. It is a beautiful thing she has done . . .

See Matt. 15. 28; Mark 10. 14c; 12. 34; Luke 7. 9; for others who received such praise from Jesus. Jesus gave encouragement whenever people showed love or faith.

What did He praise in this woman?

1. *Her generosity:* She broke the jar, with the result that it could not be used again. The whole of the oil was given at once. She gave without "counting the cost". (Compare Judas who bargained with the priests for his thirty silver-pieces.)

2. *Her adoration:* She gave because she loved, not because she wanted to earn a reward. V. 9 shows that she had a reward, but she did not anoint Jesus in order to obtain it. (Compare Judas whose action in v. 10 was in order to obtain gain for himself.)

3. *Her pouring of oil:* Jesus regarded her deed as more than a deed of love. First, her pouring of the oil was a sign that He was the Messiah. "*Messiah*", as we have already seen, is a Hebrew word meaning "the anointed one". The Jews anointed their kings (2 Kings 9. 1-13), and the Messiah was the great King whom they expected one day to rule and rescue the Jewish people. Secondly, her breaking of the jar was a sign that He would soon die. Jews who

went to anoint a dead body used to break the jar and put it with the body. In the eyes of Jesus, the woman was, by her action, saying to Him, "You are the Messiah; but you are going to a tomb, not to the throne of a soldier-king" (compare 8. 29). Perhaps the woman herself intended to say this by her deed. We do not know. But Jesus does seem to have interpreted it in this way.

v. 7. You have the poor among you always . . . but you will not always have me.

1. The central teaching of this saying was: "There will be opportunities for many years to give to the poor, after my Ascension. But I am here now, and this woman was right to take the opportunity of showing her love to me". God judges us chiefly by the way in which we make use of the opportunities He gives us. He is frequently saying to us, "Here is an act of service that you, and no one except you, can make, and this is the time it can be done and at no other time." (See Isa. 55. 6; Matt. 25. 1–13.)

2. But the verse is often wrongly interpreted and it is useful to note what it does *not* teach:

a. Jesus was not saying that the poor must always remain poor. Luke 1. 52–53 shows that God desires to do away with the suffering that the very poor endure. It is therefore not enough to give generously to the poor: we need to work to take away the pain of great poverty.

b. It does not teach that Christians have to choose between giving to Jesus and giving to the poor. Whenever we give to those who are in need, we are giving to Jesus Himself (Matt. 25. 40). There are special ways of giving to Him, e.g., by making a church beautiful; but we do this *in addition to* helping the poor, not instead of helping them.

c. "You will not always have me" does not mean, of course, that Jesus is absent from us to-day (Matt. 28. 20b). In v. 7 He was simply speaking of His death.

Mark 14. 10, 11 : The Treachery of Judas

See also Matt. 26. 14–16; Luke 22. 3–6

INTRODUCTION

This story of Judas' going to the chief priests is the second part of the story of the betrayal of Jesus. The first part is in vv. 1, 2; the third, in vv. 17–21.

NOTES

v. 10. **Then Judas Iscariot, one of the Twelve, went to the chief priests to betray him to them.**

Three questions are generally asked about this story. These are:

1. *What did Judas tell the priests?* For what did they give him the money? Probably he told them the place where Jesus could be found late in the evening (John 18. 2; Luke 22. 6). At Passover time Jerusalem and the country round about were crowded with visitors. (Josephus, a Jewish writer who is however sometimes guilty of exaggeration, claims there were on some occasions 3,000,000 visitors.) Many of them were sleeping outside the city walls in little mat huts. It was impossible for the priests to find Jesus unless they were told the place.

2. *Why did he betray Jesus?* What was in his mind when he went to the priests? Very many answers have been suggested:

a. He was greedy for the money. (See John 12. 6.) But thirty pieces of silver is only worth four pounds. Surely he did not lead his Master and friend to death for only four pounds?

b. He was afraid of being caught if Jesus was arrested, and thought he would escape suffering if he had done a service to the priests.

c. He thought he could trick the priests: he planned to take their money, but expected Jesus to disappear by a miracle when the soldiers came (as in Luke 4. 30).

d. But the most likely answer is that he was angry that Jesus did not fight and set up an earthly kingdom. (Most of the disciples expected Him to do that. Luke 24. 21.) So perhaps he thought he could force Jesus to fight by bringing soldiers to arrest Him.

3. *Should Judas be blamed?* This question is fully answered in the notes on vv. 17–21.

But these are only attempts to answer the questions; the Gospels do not answer them. It is plain, however, from the above that Judas was guilty either of greed, or of anger, or of cowardice, or of pride in thinking that he knew more than Jesus. Whatever answer we give, Judas is seen to be guilty.

Note: Some people are not willing to call him guilty. They feel that if we call him guilty, it means that Jesus made a mistake in calling him to be one of His disciples. But Jesus made no mistake. When Judas was called, he was capable of becoming the kind of disciple that Jesus needed as the foundation of His Church. Jesus offered him the same opportunity of serving Him and of having Eternal Life which He offers to us. We can take it, or, like Judas, we can refuse it. (See note on 3. 19 and 14. 21.)

Mark 14. 12–16: Preparation for the Lord's Supper

See also Matt. 26. 17–19; Luke 22. 7–13.

INTRODUCTION

The Story

It was the will of Jesus to have a fellowship-meal with His disciples before He was arrested. (He knew that His arrest would come soon.) He was not a stranger in Jerusalem (John 5. 11), and He seems to have made the arrangements in advance with the owner of an upstairs room. Preparations had to be made without the knowledge of Judas and His other enemies. Even the two disciples (Peter and John. Luke 22. 8) did not know the place until the man with the water-pot led them to it. They noticed the man without difficulty, because carrying water was usually women's work.

Passover Time

Mark says the meal was a Passover meal. (See note on 14. 1.) It is useful to know what took place every year in Jerusalem at the time of the Passover and the Feast of Unleavened Bread.

231

Note: A "day" according to Jewish custom began about 6 p.m. and ended at about the next 6 p.m.

14*th Day* of the month Nisan:

6 p.m. Householders prepared for the Feast of Unleavened Bread by searching the house (to make sure there was no leaven there). (See Deut. 16. 2, 3.)

3 p.m. A fast was kept for three hours. The killing of the passover lambs began in the Temple (one for each house).

15*th Day* of Nisan (The "First day of Unleavened Bread"):

6 p.m. The passover lambs were roasted (in people's homes).

Later (the same evening): The Passover meal.

3. What kind of meal was it which Jesus had with His disciples?

a. In these verses Mark says it was a Passover meal. According to him it was the fourteenth day on which they made preparations, and on the fifteenth on which the Lord's Supper was held and on which Jesus was crucified. But John says that they made their preparations on the thirteenth, and that the Lord's Supper (and the Crucifixion) took place on the fourteenth. (John 13. 1, 2; 18. 28). If this is so, the Lord's Supper was not a Passover meal; it took place a whole day before the time for that.

b. There are good reasons for thinking that John's story may be the correct one. If so, then the Lord's Supper was not a Passover. (One reason is that there is no mention of a lamb being eaten at the Lord's Supper.)

This then, is what probably happened: Jesus knew that He would be arrested before the time of the Passover meal, and so He held a special fellowship-meal with His disciples. Probably this was very like a Passover meal, and during it all must have been thinking of the Passover sacrifices which were being prepared. Whatever meal it was, it became something new through the things He said and did. (See notes on vv. 22–25.)

Note: There is thus some disagreement between different Gospel writers. But this does not make us distrust the Gospels. In a law-court two witnesses are not distrusted because they say somewhat different things about an event that occurred a long time ago. In this case we rejoice that Mark and John agree in telling that Jesus did hold a Supper, and in telling us so much else about the events of that week.

NOTES

v. 12a.   On the first day of unleavened bread, when they used to sacrifice the passover lamb . . .

It is surprising that Mark (who was a Jew) should say this, because the day of sacrifices was the fourteenth, and the first day of Unleavened Bread was the fifteenth which began at about 6 p.m. (See Introduction above.) But he was writing for readers in Rome, not for Jews. In Rome a "day" was from early morning until midnight, as it is for us. By this reckoning the two were on the same day.

v. 12b. Make preparations . . . to eat the passover.

If the disciples made the same preparations that all Jews used to make for the Passover, this is what they did: they cleaned out the room and got water ready (for washing and for drinking); they bought a lamb and took it to the Temple to be killed, and got someone to cook it; they prepared the unleavened bread, the bitter herbs, wine, cups, and the "sauce" or "soup" made of dates, raisins, and vinegar; they filled the lamps, and prepared the mats and the low seats.

These preparations were made carefully because the supper was regarded as very important. So when Christians are going to meet one another, and meet Jesus Christ at Holy Communion, and at other times of worship, they also ask, "Where shall we prepare?" (v. 12) and "How can we prepare?". Some ways in which we prepare are: by confessing our sins, by forgiving our neighbours, by praying for the leaders of our worship, and also by cleaning our church.

v. 14.   Say to the owner . . . Where is my room . . .

1. Who was the owner and what "upper room" was it? We are not told the owner's name here, but very soon after this Gospel was written people were saying that it was in the house of Mark's mother. If so, then perhaps it was the same room where: a. they saw Jesus on Easter evening (John 20. 19); b. they received the Holy Spirit (Acts 2. 1); c. Peter went after escaping from prison (Acts 12. 12).

2. Jesus asked the owner to lend his room, and it was opened for

233

Him. Christians have often compared this room to their own hearts which Jesus wants to enter. How can we prepare for Him?

a. By getting rid of what is unclean and whatever prevents Him from coming in, e.g., hatred for others, worries about ourselves ("make preparations" v. 15).

b. By making our hearts an "upper room" (v. 15) above the noise, a quiet place where He can be heard.

c. By being ready to receive all who are His followers as well as Jesus Himself ("with my disciples" v. 14).

d. By opening it to Jesus without receiving public attention. (In v. 14. the "owner" is not named.)

e. By acknowledging that Jesus is the real Lord and owner of our hearts. (In v. 14 Jesus says *my* room".)

v. 16.   Found everything as he had told them . . .

Christians have always found that His word can be trusted. The New Testament is full of His promises, such as those in Matt. 10. 39b; 28. 20b. But we do not find out this great truth for ourselves until we have first been willing to do what He has told us (John 7. 17). This is what the disciples did: they "set out" (v. 16) as He said.

Mark 14. 17–21 : Jesus speaks of the Betrayal

See also Matt. 26. 20–25; Luke 22. 14, 21–23; John 13. 21–30

INTRODUCTION

When Jesus was ready, He led the disciples to the upper room, and so the Lord's Supper began. As was the custom at such meals, there was a low table in the middle. The seats were not chairs, but more like little mattresses, on which the disciples lay, their faces towards the table. They were arranged round the room in the shape of the letter U. Jesus, as the head, was in the centre, with the disciples on each side of Him like two long arms.

It is likely that the disciples knew that something very important was going to happen. Perhaps they expected that Jesus would tell them His plans for leading a rebellion against the Romans. What happened must have disturbed them greatly. They heard Him speak of the betrayal by Judas, and His own death. They saw Him doing the work of a servant by washing their feet.

All the disciples were present, including Judas. He wanted to act as if he were still a faithful disciple. (He did not know that Jesus knew of his plot.) Perhaps he also wanted to find out where Jesus would go after supper.

NOTES

v. 18.   One of you will betray me . . .

Why did Jesus say this?

1. Because of His love for Judas. He treated Judas as an honoured friend by giving him the bread dipped in the soup (John 13. 26). These words of His meant, "I call on you, for your own sake, to repent while there is time". (They were not said in order that Jesus might escape death. If He had wanted to do that He would not have come to Jerusalem at all.)

2. Because He wanted to show Judas that He knew of his plans. The words show that nothing took Jesus by surprise.

3. They were a stern warning. He not only called for repentance but warned Judas (here and in v. 21) of the result of his sin.

Note: For note on "one of you", see under v. 20.

v. 19.   Is it I?

1. The others did not know who it was. If they had, they would surely have driven Judas away and then all hope of his repentance would have gone. The arrangement of the seating made it possible for Jesus to give him the bread without the others knowing, and even to speak to him (John 13. 27).

2. Each one searched his own heart. They did not look round to see who else it might be. (Where there is trouble among Christians, let our first question be, "Am *I* the one to blame?")

3. But they did not think that they were guilty (these words really should be translated, "Surely it is not I?"). But they were humble enough to know their own weakness. The sin of Judas was probably the sin of thinking that he knew better than Jesus. They, like all of us, were continually tempted to think in this way. (See the note on 8. 32 about Peter rebuking Jesus.)

v. 20.   One of the Twelve, dipping in the same dish . . .

Several times Mark uses these words **One of the Twelve** (vv. 10, 17, 43), as if he were asking, "How was it possible for a chosen disciple to do such a thing?" This question and its answers are important:

1. Judas must have been gradually losing his faith in Jesus for some time, and "fell" like a wall which has been gradually weakened by rain. Others besides him have begun by being devoted disciples of the Master, then have became no more than officials of the Church, and finally have left it altogether.

2. It is clearly not enough to belong to the true Church or to be one of its chief ministers or to attend its most important services. Judas was an Apostle and attended the Lord's Supper itself, and these things themselves did not save him.

3. Those who, like Judas, have had the best opportunities, are judged the most severely (Rom. 2. 17–end). A baptized Christian is judged more severely than a heathen. If a Christian refuses to forgive another, he is to blame; if he comes to Holy Communion and still refuses to forgive, his guilt is increased (see 1 Cor. 11. 27).

v. 21.   The Son of man goes, as it is written . . . but alas for that man by whom the Son of man is betrayed . . .

Son of man is Jesus. (See Additional Note p. 137.) "That man" is Judas. The verse raises again the question "To what extent was Judas to blame?" We have already seen that he was indeed guilty. (See notes on vv. 10, 11, 18, 20.) Two other facts support this: a. the New Testament writers judged him to be guilty; he is twelve times called "traitor"; b. he seems to have thought that he was guilty himself; is this not the reason why he hanged himself? (Matt. 27. 3–5.)

But other answers are sometimes given by those who have not understood this verse, and which should be noticed:

1. Some say that Judas was cursed by Jesus and that the speaking of the words "alas for that man" actually caused him to do the evil. But these words are not a curse. See 13. 17 (where they mean "Such a person is unhappy indeed", and also 1 Pet. 2. 23.) It is also said that, as Judas was "entered by Satan" (John 13. 2), we should be sorry for him rather than blame him. But Satan stands at the door of man's heart and knocks. Judas, like ourselves, was free to choose whether he would open the door to him or not.

2. Others say "it was written" that Judas would to this, that God planned it long ago, that Judas was forced to do it, and that he therefore cannot be blamed.

Note:

a. It is true that it was written in verses like Isa. 53. 12 that the Servant of God would suffer for our sins. It is also true that Jesus said that He was that Servant. But it was never said that Judas must lead Him to His death.

b. It is true that God saw in advance that sin would be so great that nothing except the death of Jesus could rescue us from it. But at the time the men who caused Jesus' death were free to choose whether to do it or not. Therefore they were guilty (Jas. 1. 13, 14).

So there are two facts stated in this verse: a. God knows about the future ("it is written"); b. man is free in his actions ("alas for that man"). An illustration may help to explain this; a teacher may set his class a test. He knows that everyone in the class will make some mistakes, and so they do. But it was not the teacher who *caused* them to do so.

3. Others say that we have been saved through the death of Jesus, and therefore must thank Judas, who helped Him to die, and not blame him. But to this three things must be said:

a. Jesus offered Himself freely: it did not need Judas to bring Him to the cross (v. 21b shows this).

b. It was not only by His actual dying but also by His love and His obedience that Jesus saved us. See Heb. 10. 8b. Judas did nothing to make Him more loving or obedient.

c. In Acts 3. 14, 15, 19 it is shown that those who caused the death of Jesus were condemned as evil by the first Christians, not thanked. God wonderfully turned this evil into a way by which the great goodness of salvation can come to men. But this does not turn guilty men into innocent ones.

It is important to note that Judas was guilty. If we think Judas was somehow "fated" or forced to act as he did, we are likely to think that we also are "fated" to do certain things, and that we cannot be blamed for such deeds. But Judas was free and we are free to choose between right and wrong. We are judged by the way in which we choose.

Mark 14. 22–25: The Lord's Supper

See also Matt. 26. 26–29; Luke 22. 15–20; John 13–17;
1 Cor. 11. 23–25

INTRODUCTION

The First Part

The Supper began with a meal of fellowship. On many previous occasions Jesus and His disciples had had fellowship by sharing the same food. Now they met in this way for the last time. This was the first part of the Lord's Supper, and it was probably during it that Jesus gave Judas the piece of bread (v. 20).

The Second Part

When this was done, He began the "second part", i.e., the short meal that was a new event in the history of the world. 1 Cor. 11. 23–25 was written less than twenty-five years after it took place, and gives the first account of it. Jesus took bread in His hands and said "Grace". Next He distributed the bread and said, "This is my Body". Afterwards He took a cup of wine, and said "Grace" again. Then He gave the wine to everyone, and said, "This is my Blood of the new agreement".

John says that, when the Supper was over, Jesus washed the disciples' feet, as a sign of His humility and of their need to be made clean in heart. He also says that Jesus gave them the teaching found in John 14–17. Luke says that the disciples understood so little of what Jesus was doing that they began to quarrel over which of them was the most important (22. 24–30.)

Note: Two facts should be remembered in studying this story:

1. The Supper took place on the same day as the Crucifixion, according to Jewish reckoning. Jesus spoke and acted as someone already on his way to die.

2. It happened at Passover time, when the Jews remembered how God had set them free from the slavery of Egypt and when they sacrificed a lamb in thanksgiving. The Supper was probably not a Passover meal (see Introduction to vv. 12–16); but Jesus and the disciples, being Jews, had this deliverance by God in their minds. Jesus dedicated Himself to be the Passover Lamb, and to die so that all mankind could be set free from their sin.

238

NOTES

v. 22a. He took bread, and said the blessing . . .

1. **Took bread:** The bread was a round, flat cake, baked hard, about six inches wide, the sort of bread that everyone used. Thus it was ordinary food which He used, not "magic bread": it was food everyone could buy, not rich man's food. The great things that Jesus did during the Supper were done by using ordinary things. So at Holy Communion the bread stands for the ordinary things of our life, our bodies, work, money, etc. The bread, like these things, has a new value and can be greatly used by God when offered to Jesus and taken by Him. (See note on 6. 41.)

2. **Said the blessing:** Probably He said the "Grace" used by the heads of all Jewish homes, "Thanks be to Thee, O Lord our God, King of the World, who bringeth forth food from the earth". (Approaching death did not prevent Him from giving thanks.)

v. 22b. Broke it and gave it to them, and said, "Take; this is my body."

1. **Broke it:** He broke it so that it could be shared by the disciples; and they all took their share. By this action He was making them able to share in and receive the blessings resulting from His death: these blessings were forgiveness, and being brought into fellowship with God. He made them sharers in His sufferings, too, as the writer of 1 Pet. 4. 12–14 explains. "Breaking Bread" was the name for Holy Communion in the days following Pentecost (e.g., Acts 20. 7), because it was the service where Christians continued to share in these blessings.

2. **Take:** But He left them free to take or not to take their share. God's gifts (e.g., forgiveness) are not ours until we have the trust and humility to take hold of them. Indeed, being a Christian is chiefly taking hold of what He offers. (See Ps. 116. 11, 12.) It is not mainly following His example or understanding His words.

3. **This is my body:**
a. These words, like "This is my blood" in v. 24, are Jesus' way of offering and dedicating Himself as the Lamb of God to die for us and for all mankind. It is as if He said, "As I give you this bread (and wine) so I give myself to be killed. By taking it, you take the

239

blessings resulting from my death". (By Jewish reckoning, the words were said on the very day on which He died.)

b. Some people, reading these words, have said that Jesus only meant that the bread (at the Lord's Supper and at Holy Communion) should remind them of His crucified body. Others have pointed to the word "is" and have said that He turned the bread into His body: they say of the bread at Holy Communion, "It ceases to be bread and becomes Jesus". (But Jesus spoke in Aramaic, and this language has no word for "is".)

Neither of these views is likely to be correct. The important thing is not what the bread is, but what Jesus *uses* it for. At the Lord's Supper and at Holy Communion He uses it for giving His followers forgiveness. Thus "body" in this verse almost means "myself": it does not mean flesh or bones.

v. 23. Took a cup . . .

1. There was one cup and one single cake of bread. St Paul in 1 Cor. 10. 16, 17 explains that Christians, by drinking from one cup and eating from one loaf, become bound together. This is one great reason for attending Holy Communion. Some years ago in West Africa two Christian chiefs, who were bitter enemies, went to the same Holy Communion service. Both knelt to receive the bread and wine. As they walked to their seats, one shook the other by the hand and said aloud, "We have drunk from the same cup. We cannot remain enemies."

2. Among the Jews wine was a common drink, partly because water was often impure. It was regarded as a gift from God for the enjoyment of mankind (see Ps. 104. 15). By taking it and using it, Jesus showed that our ordinary joys can be dedicated to Him and used rightly.

v. 24. The blood of the new bond, poured out for many.

1. **The new bond:** This means, "The blood that I am now shedding is the way by which I am making the new 'bond' (or agreement between God and man)."

a. The disciples, being Jews, knew that there was an agreement between them and God, and that it had been made "by blood"; e.g., in Ex. 24, when animals had been sacrificed, Moses poured half the animal's blood on an altar (which stood for God), and sprinkled half over the people. As blood was regarded as a sign of the animal's life, God and His people had thus shared the same life. So Moses' action and his words in Ex. 24. 8. showed that God and His people were joined in fellowship by an agreement or "covenant" or "bond".

But this bond was not strong enough. The Jews failed to obey God. Jeremiah saw that and said that a new one was needed (see Jer. 31. 31; Heb. 10. 4).

At this Supper Jesus made the new bond and abolished the old one. What was the difference between the old one and the new one? i. The old one was not effective, but the new one was; ii. in the old bond, an animal was killed, but in the new bond, Jesus Himself was killed because of His love for us; iii. the old bond was for the Jews, but the new bond was for people of every nation.

b. Just as the old bond had made the Jews into the first Chosen People, so by the new bond Christians became the new People of God (1 Pet. 2. 9, 10). The disciples had come into the room, hoping that Jesus would make their people free from the rule of the Romans: they left the room, having been made into a new People, bound firmly to God by Jesus' death. They had been made free, not from the rule of the Romans, but from the power of sin. Jesus had begun to create a new agreement between God and mankind. By this agreement, God is ours and we belong to Him. One of the purposes for which Christians come to Holy Communion is to renew their agreement with God.

2. **Poured out for many: For** means "on behalf of". Matt. 26. 28 shows the full meaning: he gives the words, "for the forgiveness of sins". Since Jesus died for us, men can be free from two things: a. guilt; b. the present power of evil.

But how can we, who live after the time of the Lord's Supper, receive these gifts? Christians have found that they do so at Holy Communion. Mark does not say that Jesus commanded us to continue the Lord's Supper, but Paul in 1 Cor. 11. 24 reports that Jesus said, "Do this". Jesus certainly intended us to continue to receive these gifts which are the result of His death, and one of the times at which He does in fact enable us to do so in a special way is at Holy Communion. This service is a taking hold of the results of His death, time after time, and receiving cleansing and new life.

It is more than a remembrance of His death, and more than a knowledge of God's presence.

3. **Many**: means, "not only for you, but for all mankind". (See note on 10. 45.)

v. 25. When I drink it new in the kingdom of God.

The verse means, "I shall never again drink wine until I drink a new kind of wine in God's Kingdom."

1. This is a way of saying that He was on the point of dying. But He was also speaking with great faith of the future, of the time when He would have overcome death and would be with God the Father.

2. Jesus, like other Jewish teachers, thought of being with God or being in His Kingdom as like being at a great supper (see Introduction to chap. 6. 35–44). But it will be a new kind of supper, with a new kind of wine. (See note on 12. 25.)

3. Matt. 26. 29 says that Jesus also said, "I shall drink it with you . . ." i.e., "You too will share with me in the joy of the Kingdom."

4. In the same way, the Holy Communion which grew out of the Lord's Supper, is a looking forward to the joy of the "great supper". At every Communion we are given a promise of a new and fuller communion with God, when His perfect Kingdom comes.

SUMMARY OF TEACHING
ABOUT THE LORD'S SUPPER

Four truths about the Lord's Supper may be noted:

1. Jesus *offered Himself* to die on behalf of mankind. (See note on "This is my body", v. 22b.)

2. He began to create *a new agreement* between God and mankind. (See note on v. 24a.)

3. He made the disciples able to *receive* the gifts resulting from His death. (See note 1 on v. 22b.)

4. He intended us to *continue* to receive such gifts. (See note 2 on v. 24.)

See picture opposite.

At the Last Supper Jesus "dedicated Himself to die so that all mankind could be set free from their sin." (p. 238)

One morning in April 1945 the door of the concentration camp at Mauthasen in Germany was opened, and those who had been imprisoned by the Nazis were free to go. But some were too ill to get up, and others could not believe that they were really free.

"They crucified Him" (Mark 15. 24).
On 11 June, 1963, a Buddhist monk, the Venerable Thich Quang-Duc, burnt himself in a public place in Saigon in Vietnam, in order to call the attention of the world to the sufferings of his people.

In what ways did his death differ from the death of Jesus on the Cross?

Mark 14. 26–31 : Jesus Speaks of Peter's Disloyalty

See also Matt. 26. 30–35; Luke 22. 31–34; John 13. 36–38

INTRODUCTION

When the Supper was over, Jesus and eleven disciples sang psalms together and then went out of the city. They went down the hill and across the valley of Kedron, till they reached the foot of the Mount of Olives. Then Jesus told them that He was about to suffer. He said He would suffer alone because none of them would remain loyal to Him. He knew that they did not understand: a. how much they needed God's help in difficult times; b. how to accept it. Peter and the others showed by what they said that they certainly did not understand this. They did not believe that Jesus was going to die; they still expected Him to take power as a great king.

NOTES

v. 26. When they had sung a hymn, they went out . . .

1. Singing together to God joins Christians to Him and to each other (Acts 16. 25). It is obviously especially fitting for those who are about to face danger, as were Jesus and His friends.

2. But on this occasion the "hymn" was really psalms, probably Ps. 115–118. These were the Hallel or Praise Psalms which were sung at the great festivals. Ps. 118 seems just the sort of psalm that Jesus Himself would want to use at that time. (See especially vv. 6, 8, 13, 17, 18, 27–29.)

3. They were leaving the peace of the Supper to go out into the trouble and temptation of the world outside. (See note on 9. 9.) In the same way at the end of Holy Communion the worshippers go out from church ready to suffer with people who are suffering, and work in other ways for Christ in His world.

v. 27. You will all fall; for it is written . . .

"Fall" here means "be made to stumble". Jesus is saying that they will all lose confidence in Him; they will think He is wrong because He does not fight when He is arrested.

1. The words show that Jesus knew well what all human beings

are like. He knew the disciples better than they knew themselves. This is why Jesus is the only reliable One to follow. Communists say that people do what is right if they are in the right surroundings: Jesus says that mankind goes wrong, even in the best surroundings, unless guided and strengthened by God.

2. The words are not, of course, a curse. They state what is true. Nor does "it is written" mean that it was fated that they should fall. The words come from Zech. 13. 7. Jesus is saying that God had known long ago that this would happen. God was not taken by surprise, nor was Jesus Himself, at any of the events of that day.

v. 28.   I will go before you . . .

1. **I will go:** The words show that Jesus would not be defeated by His death. He was planning a meeting after He had risen. (But the disciples did not believe either that He would die or that He would rise again.) They show, too, that He wanted to have fellowship with Peter and the others after they had discovered their own weaknesses.

Mark does not describe any meeting in Galilee (see note on 16. 7), but Matt. 28. 16 does.

2. **Go before you:** This is the translation of a word used to describe a shepherd walking in front of his sheep to their place of feeding. (See Ps. 23. 2b; Gen. 33. 14.) So Jesus said He would go first to Galilee and they would follow. He never asked His followers to do or to endure anything except what He had first done Himself (see John 10. 4).

v. 29.   Even if they all fall, yet I shall not.

1. *Peter's sincerity:* In saying this Peter was showing his sincere will to be loyal to Jesus. His words are like the words of a brave Scottish soldier who was captured and told to have nothing more to do with his king: "You can take my head from my shoulders, but you will never take my heart from my king." V. 43 shows that Peter went nearer to Jesus during His trial than the other disciples.

2. *Peter's mistake:* In other respects Peter made serious mistakes:

a. He seemed to think he knew better than Jesus. (See note on 8. 31, 32.) This is shown by his repeating his words even more strongly in v. 31.

b. He had not learnt to know himself (Ps. 139. 23). He thought

244

he was strong in the very matters in which he was really weakest (1 Cor. 10. 12).

c. He did not yet know how much he needed God's help. It was not until he had disowned Jesus that he learnt this (vv. 66–72). Many people only learn to rely on God after they have failed badly.

d. He was not prepared for so many evils and temptations in the world. He made his promise in the company of Jesus and His followers: but amongst the soldiers and their friends he forgot it.

When we make promises in church (e.g., at Baptism), we should do so knowing the temptations that attack Christians outside it, and asking for His help. Instead of repeating these words in v. 31, Peter should have asked Jesus, "Then show me what to do and how to avoid sin".

Note: All the disciples said the same (v. 31). Why does Mark draw attention to Peter? It is because at the time when Mark wrote (about A.D. 64), Peter was head of the Church, and so courageous that he was martyred. Mark is saying: "If someone who fell into these errors could be changed into a great leader, there is hope for everyone who goes wrong and accepts God's forgiveness."

v. 30. Before the cock crows twice, you will . . . disown me.

Jesus meant that it would happen very soon. He was speaking at about 10 p.m. and cock-crow would be at about 5 a.m.

Note: The cock-crow was also a name sometimes given to the blowing of the bugle by Roman soldiers in the barracks very early in the morning. So perhaps the words mean, "before the bugle has sounded for the second time". For the word "disown", see note on v. 68.

Mark 14. 32–42 : Jesus in Gethsemane

See also Matt. 26. 36–46; Luke 22. 40–46; John 18. 1

INTRODUCTION

At the foot of the Mount of Olives was Gethsemane (which means "a garden of olive-trees"), with a stone wall round it. Jesus came to this with His eleven disciples. John 18. 2 says they had often been there before. First, He said to them all, "I need to pray". Then He took three of them a little further on, and told them His deep distress. Lastly He went forward and prayed alone.

This, so far as we can see, was a time of fight against the temptation to escape suffering. But the others did not understand this. Three times Jesus came and found them asleep. During His prayer, He won His "fight", and offered Himself in complete obedience to His Father. The third time that He came to His disciples, He said, "Are you still sleeping? (v. 41.) You have slept enough. Come with me as I face my enemies." The lanterns of those sent to arrest Him could now be seen behind the trees, and He went to meet them with peace in His heart.

Note:

a. We can only know a very little of what Jesus was thinking and suffering during this time. But we do know something. The three disciples were near enough, before they fell asleep, to hear words He spoke, and they have recorded them, and we know from other sayings of His what kind of prayers He used to offer to His Father.

b. This is one of the stories which make us sure that the Gospels are true. The first members of the Church surely did not *invent* a story like this, which shows clearly the weakness of the disciples and the distress of Jesus.

NOTES

v. 33.   He took Peter and James and John with him . . .

He took them for two reasons:

1. He was a real human being and wanted their fellowship.

2. He wanted them to pray with Him and for Him, as He began His struggle. He always gave them the opportunity of doing Him service, even though they so often disappointed Him.

But having needed them for a period, He later on needed to be away from them (v. 35a). In the same way, a Christian needs both to pray with others, and at other times to be away from them and to be alone with God. It was said of someone, "Death was the first important thing he ever did alone". That should not be; prayer alone and prayer with others are both necessary.

v. 34.   My soul is sorrowful, almost dead with sorrow . . .

This is one of three phrases describing Jesus' great suffering of mind.

V. 33, says He was "struck with awe" (i.e., filled with surprise and terror), and "greatly troubled" (i.e., weighed down with distress).

Why was He so distressed? We cannot pretend to know fully, but some probable reasons are these:

1. He thought of the evil in the world. He knew that He was soon going to take on Himself responsibility for the whole of this evil, i.e., bear it on our behalf (2 Cor. 5. 21). People often say, "Why did Jesus not face death with the same calmness that was shown by Socrates and many other brave men?" Here is the answer. He was troubled by far more than the death of His body. (But note that He did not remain troubled: He found perfect peace of mind. See note on vv. 41, 42.)

2. The very strong temptation that was coming to Him. (See note on v. 36a.)

3. The pain that He would suffer if He was crucified. (This was not the greatest reason for His distress. But He was a real human being, not pretending to be one; and this is likely to have been one reason for His troubled mind.)

4. His loneliness.

v. 36a. Abba, Father . . . take away this cup from me . . .

This is the temptation of Jesus. His struggle against it was so severe that He sweated freely (Luke 22. 44) and threw Himself on the ground.

What was He tempted to do? What were the "cup" and the "hour" (v. 35) which He was tempted to refuse? The "cup" stands for suffering (10. 38) and for His bearing of the world's sin. The word "hour" also stands for death (John 13. 1) and a time of testing. Thus He was being tempted to try to save mankind without suffering or dying. (See note on 15. 31.)

Jesus fought this temptation by prayer. It was as if He said, "Father, I am being tempted, and because I am your Son, I tell you of this". (Note that we are told the word for "Father" in Jesus' own vernacular, which was Aramaic: "Abba".) Christians faced with temptation to-day can do just what He did. Temptation is not itself sin; and by telling God of its presence and by asking for His help to overcome it we can prevent it leading us into sin.

Note: Jesus was a real human being. Heb. 2. 18 and 4. 15 show that He really was tempted to do wrong.

v. 36b. Not what I will, but what thou wilt.

1. *Obedience:* By saying this, Jesus was showing His complete obedience. In the Lord's Prayer He had taught His followers to pray, "Thy will be done". Now He Himself willingly offered Himself to do whatever God wanted Him to do, even to die.

2. *Victory:* Thus He has resisted the temptation to escape suffering. He has won a victory against the "devil", the powers of evil.

3. *How* did He win this victory?

a. By prayer (Heb. 5. 7).

b. By an act of His will and by His own decision. He had a real will such as we have, because He was a human being. Although He received God's help in prayer, He still had to make an act of His own will. He was not forced by God to do what was right, nor was His action decided by any "Fate". His will was trained to do God's will, because His whole life had been spent in fighting temptation. By giving up His own wishes, the victory was won at a "cost" to Himself. (All this is true of ourselves.)

4. What *difference to us* have His obedience and victory made?

a. It is this obedience that has made us accepted by God, i.e., has "saved" us. (See Heb. 10. 9–10b.) When He offered Himself in obedience to God, God accepted His offering, and He accepts us in so far as we are associated with Jesus in heart.

b. His victory shows what is possible for Christians. Our prayers, too, can become, "Do with me what you want", instead of "Do for me what I want". Our whole life, and not only an occasional prayer, can be willing acceptance of whatever God has given us.

This was a great encouragement to the persecuted Christians for whom Mark wrote his Gospel.

5. What *difference to Him* did it make?

a. He found peace of mind, because He had accepted God's will. The Italian poet, Dante, wrote about God, "In His will is our peace."

b. He was able to go obediently to His death on the cross, because He had already won His victory in Gethsemane and had been obedient there (Phil. 2. 8).

v. 38. Keep awake . . . the spirit is eager, but the flesh is weak.

1. **Keep awake.** Why were they told to keep awake? Chiefly, so

that they could join Jesus in His fight against evil. (The evil which brought temptation both to Jesus and to themselves.) He wanted them to join in the fight by praying.

2. **The spirit is eager:** They were eager in spirit to serve Him. He knew this and spoke of it to encourage them.

3. **The flesh is weak:** They were weak in body, and fell asleep. Why did they do so?

a. Partly because they were very tired.

b. Partly because they had not learnt how to control their bodies. Christians who want to join Jesus' work by prayer need to control their bodies. Until they do so, they cannot get up in time for morning prayers and cannot stay awake for evening prayers.

c. But the chief reason was probably that they did not understand that Jesus was engaged in a fight. (See Additional Note, p. 173.) He had fought many evils before, e.g., against disease and against the jealousy of the Jews, but now the powers of evil were making their greatest attack. If His followers had understood this they would surely have kept awake. Three Christians recently were on a motor journey in Egypt and gave a lift to a Muslim. The driver began to talk to him about Jesus, while the second one prayed for him. The third one fell asleep. He was woken up by the driver, who said, "We are fighting a battle for his soul. Why did you leave us?"

vv. 41, 42. The Son of man is betrayed . . . let us go.

1. **Son of man:** This is the name often used by Jesus to speak of Himself as God's Messiah who must suffer in order to save mankind. (See Additional Note, p. 137.)

2. **Let us go.** So Jesus still regards them as belonging to Him in spite of their weakness. (See John 13. 1b.)

Mark 14. 43–52: The Arrest of Jesus

See also Matt. 26. 47–56; Luke 22. 47–53; John 18. 2–11.

INTRODUCTION

When Judas left the Last Supper (John 13. 30), he went to the Jewish religious leaders. That was at about 9.30 p.m. His message probably was that Jesus did not intend to resist them, and that He could be found that night in Gethsemane. This was good news to them. The Passover began the next day, and they had to take Him away before it began, and before He could preach to the great crowds.

But we notice that they did not arrest Him immediately. He was in Gethsemane for a long time before the arrest (vv. 32–42). What is the reason for this delay? The probable reason is that they had certain preparations to make:

1. They had to persuade the members of their council, the Sanhedrin, to agree to their plan. (This was not easy, for some of them held Jesus in honour.)

2. As they had no power to condemn anyone to death, they had to find a charge on which the Roman Governor, Pilate, would condemn Him.

3. They had to persuade Pilate to judge the case very early in the morning. In order to do all this, it is likely that meetings with Pilate and with members of the Sanhedrin were held.

It was therefore about 11.30 p.m. when Judas led the crowd of men (probably hired by the chief priests) into Gethsemane. He kissed Jesus to show them whom to arrest. But no kiss was necessary, for He stepped forward to meet them. His followers still did not understand that He was going to His death willingly. One of them attacked the High Priest's slave, and was rebuked by Jesus (John 18. 11). They were all so frightened and discouraged that they ran away. A young man did try to go with Jesus, but he had to run away to escape being arrested. (It has been suggested that this young man was Mark himself, and that if it had not been so, he would not have mentioned the incident.)

NOTES

v. 45.   He went up to Jesus . . . and kissed him.

Judas may have thought that Jesus would be disguised or would try to escape. It was dark, too. So he gave this sign to the men with swords. But Jesus had refused to run away from His enemies before, and made no attempt to escape now. (10. 33.)

He kissed Him probably on the hand because this was the ordinary way in which a pupil greeted an honoured master. It was not regarded as womanish or indecent. We are given the vernacular word

(Aramaic) he used for Master, "Rabbi". Thus Judas used the outward sign of honour and affection as a means of doing dishonour and injury. The "Judas kiss" has become a proverbial phrase for all such actions, e.g., receiving the Holy Communion while continuing a quarrel with a fellow-Christian.

Judas never saw Jesus again. When he wanted to change his mind and declared that Jesus was innocent, it was too late (Matt. 27. 3–5).

v. 47. One of those standing by drew his sword . . .

1. John 18. 10 says that it was Peter who attacked the High Priest's slave, and says that the slave's name was Malchus. (But it is possible that it was not a disciple at all.)

2. Why did Jesus rebuke him as Matt. 26. 52 and John 18. 11 say? It was probably a courageous action, and they were surely surprised and discouraged by the rebuke. But he was rebuked because he thought that a good thing could be obtained by bad means (i.e., that Jesus could be freed from His enemies by cutting off a slave's ear). This error has unfortunately often been made by Christians since then, e.g., when the Church about eight hundred years ago tried to free the Holy Land from the Muslims by fighting, or when a congregation to-day raises funds by wrong methods.

There are other reasons, too, why it was wrong:

a. It was done without thought, and without the sort of prayer which prepares us for unexpected things;

b. the striker did not have enough sympathy with Jesus to know what help He needed. For the only way to help was to stay and suffer with Him throughout His sufferings (see Ezek. 3. 15b). This is exactly what they did not do: they ran away.

3. Many people say that since Jesus rebuked Peter for fighting, He intended that no Christian should fight under any circumstances. Others do not agree; they say that when He spoke to Peter He was not making a rule for everyone. A Christian must follow whichever of these two he sincerely believes to be Christ's will. But His whole teaching about fighting is not to be found in one single verse.

v. 48. Have you come out with swords and clubs . . .

These "swords" were really long daggers, not military swords. Jesus meant, "You cannot destroy me by these means". (See note on 14. 1.) This surely was very encouraging to the persecuted

251

Christians for whom Mark was writing. Jesus was taken away by force, but was victorious in rising again. So a congregation persecuted to-day by a heathen government is not destroyed, even if its buildings are knocked down, its leader poisoned, and its land taken away.

v. 49.   All this is in order that the scriptures might come true.

Jesus certainly did not mean that the Bible was a sort of "fate" which caused this to happen. What did He mean? Probably He quoted a passage from the Old Testament (as Mark has not told us which one, we cannot know for certain, but it may have been Isa. 53. 12), and meant, "This passage shows that God's servants will have to suffer in order to serve Him faithfully, so do not be surprised that suffering comes to me now".

v. 50.   They all left him . . .

1. **All:** When there is trouble, people like to put the blame on one special person. In this story, it is Peter who is usually blamed for running away, but they "all" went; and it is mankind itself that is weak and fearful and in need of being saved and strengthened. (See Rom. 3. 12. "All have fallen away, everyone has gone wrong . . .")

2. **Left him:** They ran away because they were: a. afraid of being arrested; b. astonished that Jesus did not resist arrest; c. deeply discouraged because it seemed that God had failed to protect Jesus. Although He had often told them that He would be killed, they had never believed Him. So now they hid themselves, probably in Jerusalem.

Mark 14. 53–65 : Jesus before the High Priest

See also Matt. 26. 59–68; Luke 22. 63–71;
John 18. 12–14, 19–24

INTRODUCTION

The Events

Between midnight on Thursday and 7.30 a.m. on Friday Jesus was taken and questioned by many different people. Vv. 53–65 describe the questioning by Caiaphas, the High Priest.

This took place at about 1 a.m. at the High Priest's house. (This house had a courtyard into which Peter came.) The High Priest was Chairman of the Sanhedrin, and had called members to meet. It is not certain how many members were here; Mark says that they all came, but the full meeting does not seem to have taken place until the next morning (15. 1a). It was not a trial. They were not allowed to hold a trial on this kind of case at night. Nor could they pass a sentence of death. What they were doing was to try to find a charge on which Pilate, the Roman Governor, would condemn Jesus to death. Three attempts were made:

1. First, some charges were brought of which we have no information (v. 56).

2. Then Jesus was probably accused of witchcraft. (See note on v. 58.) But witnesses disagreed, and this charge was dropped.

3. Then a new charge was made, that He called Himself the Messiah (v. 61). Jesus did not deny it, and He was accused of blasphemy. They decided to ask Pilate to condemn Him. Probably they hoped Pilate would think that anyone calling himself the Messiah must be dangerous and disloyal. (See note on v. 64.)

At the end of this inquiry Jesus was struck and insulted.

The Questionings

It is useful to record here all the occasions during that night on which Jesus was questioned:

1. By Annas, at about midnight. He was the father-in-law of Caiaphas, and a person of great influence. He wanted to see if it would be possible to convict Jesus. (This is reported by John 18. 12–24.)

2. By Caiaphas and some members of the Sanhedrin (as noted above).

3. By the whole Sanhedrin at about 5 a.m. At this very short trial, they all decided on the charge (15. 1a).

4. By Pilate at about 6 a.m. (See notes on 15. 1–15.)

5. By Herod, the Jewish ruler. (This is reported by Luke 23. 8–12.)

6. By Pilate again at about 7.30 a.m. (Luke 23. 13–16.)

NOTES

v. 53.   They took Jesus away to the high priests . . .

It was the religious leaders and not the Roman government who were chiefly responsible for killing Jesus. (See Additional Note, p. 226.) There was only one High Priest, Caiaphas, but his father-in-law had once been High Priest. "High Priests" here refers to both of them.

What made them want to kill Jesus?

1. Hatred: He had attacked what they did in the Temple court-yards. (See notes on 11. 15–19.)

2. Fear: They were afraid that they might lose their power (15. 10). It was by consent of the Romans that they were appointed and ruled. If Jesus' preaching made people rebel against the Romans, they would lose their position.

3. Blindness of heart: They really thought that they spoke with God's voice, and that when Jesus preached against them, He was preaching against God. They were like modern Christians who say, "Whoever criticizes the Church is criticizing God." But it is possible for a Church to misunderstand God's will: it is possible for its leaders to commit great sin.

v. 56.   Their evidence did not agree.

By Jewish law no one "prosecuted" an accused person. If there was an accusation, it was made by witnesses. But only one witness could be in court at a time, and if the statements of witnesses did not agree, they were not accepted. This was the rule of Deut. 19. 15–19, and is also Muslim law to-day.

On this occasion, the High Priest had found people who were willing to speak against Jesus, but their evidence did not agree. To-day very many groups of people say that there are good reasons for not believing in Jesus, but their reasons do not agree; e.g., some say that Jesus' teaching stirs up the minds of people too much; others, that it teaches people to be too content with bad conditions. If the unbelievers of the world agreed together, Christians would be in a different position; but they do not.

v. 58.   I will myself destroy this holy place . . .

1. Jesus had not said this, but it is not clear what He had said.

Mark 13. 2 reports that He said simply, "The Temple will be destroyed". Perhaps John 2. 19–21 and 2 Cor. 5. 1 contain the words to which His accusers were referring.

2. Clearly they had taken His words and turned them into something slightly different. Falsehood is most evil when it is not far from the truth. They pretended that He had said that He possessed powers of witchcraft to destroy and rebuild the Temple: they said that He had been disloyal to the Jewish religion in other ways.

3. Although He did not ever say that He would destroy the Temple and replace it with a new one, yet it is true that the religion of following Jesus did replace the old religion of the Jews. The Church to-day is a body of people which has taken the place of the Temple.

v. 61a.   He remained silent . . .

Why did He not defend Himself? Because:

1. He believed it was His work to die for mankind. Although He loved life and never searched for ways of being killed, neither did He refuse death (Isa. 53. 7).

2. He wanted to say one thing only, something of the greatest importance, i.e., the words of v. 62.

3. He believed that what He did was more important than what He said (Matt. 11. 2–5). In the same way a Christian's behaviour during a discussion with a non-Christian is much more important than what he says to him.

4. He knew that it was useless to speak. The High Priest had already decided to have Him killed. Jesus faced facts.

5. He had control of Himself and had peace in His heart. This was because He and committed Himself trustfully into God's hands. (See note on v. 36b.)

v. 61b.   Are you the Christ, the Son of the Blessed One?

1. The "Christ" means the Messiah that the Jews were waiting for. (See Additional Note, p. 133.) "Blessed One" means God. These were really *two* questions: a. Are you God's Messiah? b. Are you God's Son? Christians know that these two are the same, but the High Priest did not know. He wanted Jesus to say, "Yes"; then he would accuse Him of blasphemy. A blasphemer was punished by death. (Lev. 24. 16).

2. But by asking the prisoner (Jesus) to condemn Himself, Caiaphas was breaking the Jewish laws. In other ways, too, those who judged Jesus broke the law; e.g., a. the Judge himself looked for witnesses to accuse Jesus (v. 35); b. Jesus was killed nine hours after the questioning had begun, but the law said the condemnation could not take place on the same day as the trial; c. They accused Jesus of "blasphemy" because He said He was the Christ and the Son of God. But blasphemy is speaking against God's name, and of course Jesus did not do that.

v. 62. Jesus said, I am; and you shall see the Son of man, sitting at the right hand of the Power, and coming . . .

1. **I am:** At last Jesus spoke and declared that He was God's Son. (In Matt. and Luke His words are, "You have said so". This is how people said "Yes" in the Aramaic language which Jesus spoke.)

Having said this, Jesus knew that He would be condemned to death, but it was He who had chosen the charge on which He would be condemned: He was in control of events, not they.

Note: If He had said, "I am not", He could perhaps have been set free. In this case He would have saved His life, but lost His followers, and we should not know His name to-day.

2. **The Son of man:** This means Jesus Himself. (See Additional Note, p. 137.)

3. **Sitting at the right hand of the Power:** This is His way of saying, "You know that the Messiah is a victorious person. I am the Messiah, and I shall be received by God (the "Power"), sitting in honour as a conqueror sits. Then you and all men shall see that what I have said is true ("and you shall see").

4. **Coming:** does not mean "coming into the world a second time". Dan. 7. 13 shows that it means "coming into the presence of God".

5. When the High Priest heard this he tore his clothes. The garment he tore was probably a waistcoat or vest which he tore at the neck. Jews often used to show their distress and anger in this way, and some Arabs still do so to-day.

v. 64. They all gave judgement . . .

1. In doing this they were like the schoolboy who judged Shakespeare and said that he thought Shakespeare wrote bad plays. It was

the boy, not Shakespeare, who was being judged, when he said that. So they thought they were judging Jesus: really it was they who were being judged. The same is true of people to-day who say things like this about Jesus, "He was wrong to be angry" (11. 15), or, "He was foolish to let Himself be killed".

2. But it was right for them to make a decision about Jesus. Every man who reads about Jesus or hears about Him has to do that, either for or against Him. But everyone should know that he is being judged according to his decision.

3. **Gave judgement:** This does not mean that they condemned Him in court. They could not do that, becase this was not a full meeting of the Sanhedrin. They did condemn Him at the full meeting at 5 a.m. (15. 1a). Also it is not likely that "all" joined in.

v. 65. Some began to spit at him . . .

They spat at Him, put a cloth over His eyes, struck Him with their fists, shouted at Him, and slapped Him with the palms of their hands. Thus they treated Him as people treat someone who is utterly despised. (See notes on 15. 16–20, which describe the second ill-treatment of Jesus.)

Mark 14. 66–73: The Disloyalty of Peter

See also Matt. 26. 69–75; Luke 22. 55–62;
John 18. 15–18, 25–27

INTRODUCTION

The Story

At about 2.30 or 3 a.m. Peter came into the courtyard of the High Priest's house, and stood by the fire. Perhaps he was accompanied by John to start with (John 18. 15). It was a very brave action to come, especially if it was Peter who had attacked the High Priest's slave (John 18. 10). He did it because he sincerely wanted to give his support to Jesus. Jesus was being questioned probably in an upstairs room.

A slave-girl saw that Peter was one of Jesus' followers, and he moved away from the light of the fire so that he could not be seen (v. 68b). But she saw him again, and so did someone else who said, "You talk Aramaic like a Northerner: it is clear that you belong to Jesus of Nazareth". Each time Peter said he did not belong to Jesus. Then a cock crowed, and Peter was filled with shame and sorrow at what he had done. Luke says that Jesus looked at Peter at that moment.

Note: This passage should be read together with 14. 27–31 and the accompanying notes.

It is most probable that the story was told to Mark by Peter himself. It is one of the many stories which show the weakness of the disciples. (See Additional Note, p. 173.)

NOTES

v. 68.   He disowned him . . .

1. To disown is to say, "He does not belong to me: and I do not belong to Him".

So Christ is disowned whenever we forget that we belong to Him, e.g., when a Christian who is spending a holiday with friends who are not Christians, stops living in Christ's way or going to church; or when a Christian living in a Muslim country finds that he gets no promotion in his work, and so stops calling himself a Christian.

2. Why did he disown Jesus? He did it for the same reasons for which we ourselves do it: a. fear; he was afraid of being arrested; b. he was not prepared (see 14. 38); c. he was alone among strangers; d. perhaps he was angry and disappointed that Jesus had not resisted those who arrested Him.

3. He added curses to his disowning of Jesus (v. 71). "Cursing" here means saying, "May God send evil on me if I am not telling the truth." This is of course against the words of Jesus in Matt. 5. 34–37.

v. 73.   He covered his face and wept.

1. The Greek word translated "covered his face" may also mean "thought about it".

2. Mark does not tell us about the feelings of Peter that made him weep like this, but it cannot be wrong to say that he felt both shame and sorrow.

a. His shame: When we feel shame or regret, we lose confidence in ourselves. Before this moment, Peter had thought he was strong enough in his own power to remain loyal to Jesus, and that Jesus was mistaken in what He was doing. But when the cock crew he remembered what Jesus had said in v. 30. His thoughts were: "It is true that I am myself too weak to be loyal; and Jesus has clearly known all that would happen to Him to-day, so that nothing surprises Him. It is He who was right, not I."

b. His sorrow (or "penitence"): He saw that his wrong had been done against Jesus Himself. This is different from shame or regret, in which we think mainly of our own weakness.

c. But after He had risen Jesus met Peter (Luke 24. 34), and entrusted him with new work (John 21. 15). Verses like Luke 15. 7, 21–24 lead us to believe that it was because of his shame and sorrow that he was ready to be restored by Jesus. This is surely the reason why Peter told this story to Mark. It is as if he were saying, "What Jesus did to me, He will do to you, because of His extraordinary love." Christians have repeatedly found that when they have done wrong, they can use the occasion for becoming more useful to Jesus Christ. It has led them to understand more clearly than before: i. their own weakness; ii. their need for God's help; iii. the forgiveness of God.

d. Peter committed this sin only because he tried to stay near Jesus. Most of the disciples were so frightened that they had no opportunity of committing the sin. His sin was a real sin, but surely not so bad as the running away of the others. Surely Jesus welcomes an attempt to serve Him bravely, even if it leads us into new temptations. A certain village newspaper was known to be printing false information, but most people took no action except to condemn it. One man joined the staff of the paper with the simple aim of changing it into a good paper. In doing this he spent huge sums of money and got badly into debt, and was severely condemned by the judge of the court. But was not the sin of all those who had not attempted anything far greater than his?

Mark 15. 1–15: Jesus before Pilate

See also Matt. 27. 1–26; Luke 23. 1–25;
John 18. 28—19. 16

INTRODUCTION

This is the story of what happened between about 5 a.m. and 7.30 a.m. on the Friday morning. We are not told all the details, and the order of events is uncertain, but by reading all the Gospels we can make a list of the events that probably took place:

1. *The meeting of the Sanhedrin: at about 5 a.m.* This was the council of the Jewish religious leaders. During the night many of the members had already condemned Jesus for blasphemy. They had decided to ask Pilate to kill Him. But the meeting at 5 a.m. was of the full council of seventy-one members. The High Priest persuaded them to take the same decision as the earlier one (15. 1a).

2. *Pilate with the priests.* Pilate met them in the open space in front of the house where he had been sleeping. He made them angry by telling them to judge Jesus for themselves (John 18. 28–31). The priests saw that they must accuse Him of crimes which were serious in Roman eyes, so they said, "He is against paying taxes to the Emperor; and He says He is a King" (Luke 23. 2).

3. *Pilate's first meeting with Jesus at about 6 a.m.* He saw Jesus privately and said, "Is it really you that claims to be a king?" In His answer Jesus did not deny that He was King (15. 2).

4. *Pilate with the priests and with Jesus again.* The priests then repeated, "If He is a king, then He cannot be loyal to the King Emperor, Caesar". Again Pilate questioned Jesus, but He was silent (15. 3–5). Pilate said: "He is innocent" (Luke 23. 4).

5. *Jesus with Herod.* He was sent to Herod, the Jewish ruler, for a short time, because Herod was the "native ruler" in charge of Galilee from which Jesus had come. But this was not a trial (Luke 23. 6–12).

6. *Pilate decides to release Him.* Pilate then said two things to the priests:

a. "He is innocent, but I will agree to have Him flogged" (Luke 23. 12–16).

b. "I will let Him go and will kill Barabbas." But the priests urged the crowd to shout, "Kill Jesus" (15. 6–15).

7. *Pilate's third meeting with Jesus.*
After this third meeting, he said again. "He is innocent. You Jews judge Him" (John 19. 6–9).

8. *Pilate allows the death of Jesus.* The priests were afraid that Jesus might be set free, so they said to Pilate, "If you do not kill Jesus (who says He is a king), the Emperor will not regard you as a loyal officer of his" (John 19. 12–15). Then Pilate had Jesus flogged, and He allowed Him to be taken away to be killed (15. 15). He himself washed his hands as a sign of having no more to do with the matter (Matt. 27. 24).

NOTES

v. 1.   The chief priests . . . handed him over to Pilate.

The chief priests and Pilate were together responsible for the death of Jesus:

1. **The chief priests:** Perhaps they and the other leaders mentioned in this verse sincerely believed that Jesus was guilty of witchcraft or blasphemy. (See note on 14. 53 and Additional Note, p. 226.) But they knew that Pilate could not condemn anyone to death for these crimes, and that it was Pilate, not the Jewish Sanhedrin, who had the power to condemn a man to death. So they said Jesus was guilty of disloyalty to the Emperor, although they knew He was innocent.

2. **Pilate:** He was the Roman Colonial Governor, in charge of the province of Judaea from A.D. 26–36. Sometimes he lived in Caesarea and sometimes in Jerusalem; he came to Jerusalem whenever he thought that the Jewish crowds might make trouble, e.g., at Passover. (See the note on v. 15a.) Pilate was a Gentile (i.e., not a Jew). Gentiles as well as Jews caused Jesus' death. In the same way, Jesus died that Gentiles as well as Jews might be forgiven.

3. *The Church and the Government:* This verse shows that the Jewish leaders were using a political leader to solve their problems for them. This is an error which the Christian Church has also made sometimes, e.g., a congregation was troubled by Jehovah's Witnesses and asked the Government to arrest the leader of the sect for them. On another occasion a pastor called in police to deal with some unruly Church members. There are times when this may be necessary; but nearly always a Church must settle its own religious matters by Christ's methods (see 1 Cor. 6. 1).

v. 6.   Pilate used to set free one prisoner . . .

1. The Jewish people whom Pilate ruled hated being under Roman rule. There were frequent riots and the prisons were full of nationalists who had used violence. It seems that Pilate tried to win favour of the Jews from time to time by freeing one of these prisoners.

On this occasion he wanted to set Jesus free. (He did not mind that the Jewish priests had asked for His death.) He thought that the crowd might ask for Him to be released, but they did not. They shouted, "Kill Him!" and asked for the release of Barabbas, a nationalist leader. (See Luke 23. 19.)

2. **One prisoner:** Only one could be released: they had to make a choice. They chose one who by violence took the lives of others instead of the One who was willing to give up His life for others. They chose the nationalist rather than the Saviour of the whole world (see John 3. 19).

v. 11.   The chief priests stirred up the crowd . . .

1. **The chief priests:** Their sin was great because they knew that they were misleading the crowd. This is the sin of many to-day, e.g., of those who use radio and newspapers to encourage large numbers of people to do something which is wrong, e.g., a. by persuading them to waste their money, by advertising useless things; b. by stirring them up to hatred of another country.

2. **The crowd.**

a. Who are they? Some were probably idlers, those people who are often seen sitting outside an important person's house. Some may have been paid by the priests to shout, "Kill Him!" Some were probably supporters of Barabbas. These people did not really want Jesus to die: they wanted Barabbas to be free.

b. Their sin was chiefly in condemning without taking thought someone about whom they knew almost nothing. Crowds often do behave like this, and when men are in a crowd, they do things which they would never do if they were alone. So it is not true to say (as is sometimes said in U.S.A.) "A hundred million people cannot be wrong", or, "The voice of the people is the voice of God". It was the people who called for the death of Jesus. Very often Christians can only do right by acting differently from the crowd, as did Peter in Acts 5. 29.

262

v. 14.   What has he done wrong? . . .

1. *Christ's perfect goodness:* This question is like the question of Jesus Himself in John 8. 46: "Who can show me guilty of sin?" Jesus is the only Person who ever lived who could ask that question, knowing that He really was sinless.

2. *Christ's loyalty to the State:* But when Pilate asked this question, he was really saying this: "Although Jesus calls Himself King, He is not guilty of treason against the Emperor Caesar." It was so. The priests and Pilate both broke the laws of the State when they condemned Jesus to death: Jesus kept the laws.

The Christians in Rome for whom Mark wrote this Gospel were being unjustly accused of disloyalty to the State. So now they could show people this story in the Gospel and explain that their Founder Jesus was regarded as a loyal citizen by the Governor. His followers, too, should be loyal citizens, e.g., praying for the head of their nation, giving respect to his officers, keeping the laws, paying the taxes. (See 1 Pet. 2. 13–17. and note on Mark 12. 17.)

v. 15.   Pilate wishing to satisfy the crowd . . . handed Jesus over, when he had had him whipped . . . .

1. **Pilate:** We need to notice two things about Pilate:

a. *His difficulties:* It was difficult for Pilate to know what to do because he was trying to satisfy many different people:

i. He had to satisfy the Jews; not only the crowd (as this verse says), but also the religious leaders. If he did not do so, it was likely that they would report him to the Emperor, and that he would be removed from his position. He had behaved very badly towards the Jews already. He paid very little respect to their religion, and had no sympathy with their nationalist hopes. On one occasion he used money which had been given for religious purposes for a water supply, and would not listen to their complaints. A riot followed and Jews were killed.

ii. He had to satisfy the Emperor in Rome. The Emperor would not be pleased if he heard that Pilate had condemned an innocent man to death.

iii. He had to satisfy his wife. She had had a dream and begged him not to condemn Jesus (Matt. 27. 19).

iv. He had to satisfy his own conscience: he knew that Jesus was innocent.

b. *His character:* There was good in Pilate: He repeatedly told the Jews that Jesus ought to be released: he was interested in Jesus (John 18. 33, etc.): he could see the real reason for the priests' hatred of Jesus (Mark 15. 10).

But there was very much that was evil:

i. He was a coward. When he released Barabbas, he was behaving like a weak headmaster of a school, who is afraid to punish a child of a member of the school committee. (See John 19. 12, 13.)

ii. He refused to accept responsibility. He asked the crowd, "What shall I do?" (v. 12), but it was his own business to decide. Although he never condemned Jesus, he "handed Him over" to others. He tried to be neutral, like a man who refuses to give evidence in court and sees the wrong person punished. But in a battle against evil, a neutral man is on the side of evil.

iii. He would not change his mind even when he knew that he was wrong (John 19. 21, 22).

iv. He was not willing to suffer anything in order to save Jesus. But those who rescue other people must expect to do so at a cost to themselves. (See note on 15. 31b.)

2. Had him whipped: It was the custom for criminals who had been condemned to be crucified, first to be flogged. It was a most cruel punishment. They were stripped naked, and tied to a pillar or a seat, and then beaten by leather whips on which had been sewn pieces of metal or bone. Many died from the flogging, many were already half-dead or blind when they were put on the cross.

Jesus must have been half-killed by it: He could not carry His cross through the streets (15. 21), and He died sooner than the soldiers expected (John 19. 33). But it is likely that even this pain was less for Jesus than the pain which He endured in His mind. (See note on 15. 34.)

Mark 15. 16–20: The Mocking by the Soldiers

See also Matt. 27. 27–31; John 19. 2, 3

INTRODUCTION

The Story

When Pilate, the Roman Governor, visited Jerusalem, he brought with him his own soldiers, men from many different countries. They lived in one part of the palace where he lived. This is where they flogged Jesus (v. 15). When they had finished, they called in the rest of the soldiers who were stationed in the palace. They had heard that He was being put to death for calling Himself a king. So, as He stood naked, they laughed at Him by putting robes on Him, as one puts robes on a king.

First, they dressed Him in a soldier's old red cloak, which was perhaps so faded that it looked like the Roman Emperor's purple robe. Next they put a crown on Him, made from little branches of a thorn-tree. Then they shouted words with which one greets a king. (When they said the words "of the Jews", they were adding a new insult: the Jews were a conquered race and no longer had their king.) After that they put a stick in His hands to look like a royal sceptre (Matt. 27. 29); they hit Him with it, and spat at Him. Lastly, they prostrated themselves in front of Him, as people prostrate themselves before a great person. (The word "worshipping" Him is not correct.)

When it was time for the Crucifixion, they took these things off Him, and led Him away from the palace, dressed in His own simple clothes.

Note: Jesus had already been ill-treated in this way by the servants of the High Priest (14. 65).

The teaching

1. *About Jesus:*

a. Isaiah had said (53. 3, etc.) that a "Servant of the Lord" would be sent by God, and would be despised by men. Perhaps Jesus believed that He was the "Servant", and accepted the suffering as part of His work as the "Servant" (Luke. 24. 25–27). He suffered truly the bodily pain, the mockery and the loneliness, but He understood that by enduring it, He was doing God's will.

265

b. The soldiers called Him "King" as a joke; but "King of kings" is exactly what He really was and is. He really is the "Lord", i.e., the One who controls our world and ourselves, and to Whom complete loyalty is due (Phil. 2. 9–11).

2. *About the soldiers:*

a. When they flogged Jesus, they were obeying orders: it is Pilate who is to be blamed, not the soldiers.

b. But they were guilty of cruelty when they ill-treated Jesus. No one ordered them to do so. Soldiers and police are not forced to live a life of cruelty, and have many opportunities to show gentleness and mercy. (See Luke 3. 13–14.) These men cannot, however, be severely judged, because there was no hatred in their action.

3. *About ourselves:*

a. We are often like the soldiers in this way: we call Him our "Lord" and sing "Crown Him", but do not treat Him as Lord, and do not do the things He wants doing in the world (Luke 6. 46). The soldiers did not know who He really was: we do know.

b. We are encouraged to follow the example of Jesus in two ways: to accept insults without returning them (1 Pet. 2. 23); and to remain faithful to God, even when others laugh at us and our religion.

Mark 15. 21–41 : The Crucifixion of Jesus

See also Matt. 27. 32–56. Luke 23. 26–49. John 19. 17–37

INTRODUCTION

The Story

Jesus, the Son of God, really died: The Gospels tell the story of the death of Jesus very briefly; their simple purpose is to say that He was killed, and that there were many witnesses. Those who read the story also ask, "Why did He die?" and other questions, and notes on these are given on p. 274. But the most important thing is that the story is true: it is not a fable.

We cannot know all the events of that day. But by reading the four Gospels it is possible to record some of the events:

At 8.30 a.m.: At about this time the Roman soldiers made Jesus carry through the streets of Jerusalem the plank of wood on which He was going to be crucified. He was too much weakened by the flogging to carry it, and so after a short time they told a stranger to do it for Him. (See note on v. 20, 21.) As Jesus walked on, He showed His extraordinary care for other people's needs (see Luke 23. 27-31). At last they came to Golgotha, which was probably a little hill on the north of the city, and outside the walls. Here they offered Him myrrh to drink (v. 23).

At 9 a.m.: Now He was crucified together with two robbers. (See note on v. 24.) As He looked down on the soldiers and others who were killing Him, He asked God to forgive them (Luke 23. 43a). But the soldiers were occupied in drawing lots for His clothes, and they and many others laughed at Him as He hung dying. (See note on v. 31.) Again He showed His care for other people by saying to one of the robbers, "You shall be with me in Paradise, to-day" (Luke 23. 43).

From noon until 3 p.m.: The sky was dark for all this time (see note on v. 33), and in the darkness Jesus called to His Father, "Why have you left me alone?" (v. 34). Again people laughed at Him and said He was calling for Elijah. According to John, He asked for a drink (John 19. 28), and someone was merciful enough to give it to Him. (Perhaps it was a soldier who shared with Jesus the wine he had brought with him.) During this time He saw John standing below and told him to take care of His mother (John 19. 25-27).

At about 3 p.m.: Now He spoke for the last time, and died. (See note on v. 37.) As He died, the Temple curtain was torn (v. 38). Finally, Roman soldiers put a spear into His side to see if He was really dead (John 19. 33, 34), and a Roman officer who had seen Him die said, "This was a son of God" (v. 39).

NOTES

v. 21.   They forced Simon of Cyrene . . . to carry his cross . . .

Whenever the Romans crucified a man, they made him walk in public to the place of his death, carrying part of the cross. Jesus began to do this, but could not. (See note on v. 15.)

1. Simon, the stranger who was made to carry it, was probably a Jew. Some think he lived in a Jewish colony in that part of North Africa now called Tripoli; others think he was from Kyrenia in Cyprus.

Jews came to Jerusalem for the Passover, just as Muslims try to make a pilgrimage to Mecca, and it is likely that Simon was doing this.

2. He did not know Jesus, and was forced to help Him against his will. In this he was like all slaves and all people of to-day who are not free to escape from work which they hate. (These are people to whom it is the Christian's duty to give special help.)

3. But it may be that after a short time he accepted the burden willingly and became a Christian. (The reason for thinking this is that his sons, Alexander and Rufus, were probably Christians. Mark certainly knew them, and Rufus may be the one mentioned in Rom. 16. 13.) If so, he is like those who have been forced into doing what they hate doing, but who, later on, accept the work, and see it as an opportunity of serving God, e.g., a young teacher who is sent to teach in a distant village school; at first he may kick against the circumstances, but later rejoices in being allowed to serve God among neglected people.

Note: It has been said (e.g., by some Muslims) that Simon changed places with Jesus and was killed instead of Him. This is said by those who do not believe that God's Son *could* die, and who try to prove that He *did* not. But all the evidence is that He did die. (See John 19. 17.) Even the Roman heathen writer, Tacitus, states that, "Christ was put to death while Pilate was Governor".

v. 23. Wine mixed with myrrh; but he would not take it.

A group of people wanted to lessen the pain of crucifixion for Jesus, and offered Him myrrh. This is a liquid that comes from a tree and helps to deaden pain. (See Prov. 31. 6.)

Why did He refuse? Probably because:

1. He wanted to keep His mind clear in order to pray to His Father for as long as possible.

2. He wanted to live and suffer as ordinary poor men do. (See Heb. 2. 9.) He had done this all His life.

v. 24a. They crucified him . . .

When a prisoner was crucified, this is what happened: first, the plank of wood that he had carried was nailed to another longer plank which, as we have already seen, was about 8 ft high. These planks formed a cross in the shape of the letter T, and were laid on the ground. Then he was stripped naked and made to lie on the cross. His hands and feet were nailed or tied to it. The board on which his accusation was written was then nailed to the top. Then the bottom of the cross was pushed into a hole in the ground, and the whole thing raised up by ropes until it stood upright. The prisoner was left to die like this, hanging by his hands, and his head falling over his chest. He died through loss of blood, pain, and exhaustion.

This is how the Romans punished slaves or violent rebels who were not Romans. When Jesus was twelve years old, He probably saw 2,000 young men crucified a few miles from Nazareth for taking part in a revolt.

Jesus Himself was nailed to His cross at 9 a.m. and died after hanging for six hours. The actual place is not known with certainty, but it may have been on a raised piece of ground which is now inside the Church of the Holy Sepulchre in Jerusalem. It was called Golgotha ("place of skull"), perhaps because it was a cemetery or perhaps because it looked like a skull from a distance. What is certain is that Jesus, the Son of God, was killed. This verse is therefore one of the two most important verses in the Bible (the other is 16. 6). The Koran says that Jesus did not die (Sura IV. 156); it is therefore important for Christians to know that He did die and to know how He died.

v. 24b.   They divided his clothes between them . . .

It was the custom for the four soldiers who crucified a prisoner to remain on duty, to prevent his friends from rescuing him. While they were waiting they took His clothes for themselves.

Christians who read about the soldiers taking Jesus' clothes have naturally been reminded of Ps. 22. 18. In the same way, the insults described in vv. 29–31 have reminded them of Ps. 22. 7, 8, and His thirst (v. 36) has reminded them of Ps. 69. 21b (Bible version). They have said: "God put it into the minds of the writers of these psalms that this is the kind of thing that happens to a true Servant of God. So things have happened as God knew they would. God is not defeated: He has always known that His Son must die."

v. 26.   The King of the Jews

When the Romans crucified someone, they wrote the accusation against him on a small board. They either tied it round his neck, or carried it in front of him to the place of crucifixion. Finally, it was nailed to the upright cross.

Pilate wrote these words on the board on Jesus' cross in order to insult the Jewish leaders. It was as if he said, "This dying preacher is the only sort of king suitable for you." The Jews complained, but Pilate refused to alter it (John 19. 21, 22).

The words also show that the Romans were saying that Jesus' crime was treason against the Emperor in Rome, although both the Jews and Pilate knew that He was innocent of this. (See notes on vv. 16–20.)

v. 27.   With him they crucified two robbers . . .

The Romans found it convenient to crucify several prisoners at a time, so Jesus was put to death with two thieves. His cross was actually between their crosses.

Throughout His ministry Jesus was in the company of outcasts and people not regarded as important by others. (See 2. 15, 16.) Whenever Christians are faithful to Jesus, they also make friends with such people. This is not in order to condemn their bad habits (such people's sins are often less serious than the sins of those who are more highly honoured). It is because we cannot help them by keeping apart from them.

Why did they abuse Him (v. 32b)? Luke 23. 39 says that only one did so. Surely it was because they compared the extreme weakness of His body (He died before they died), with the report that He called Himself a king.

v. 31.   He saved others, but he cannot save himself.

1. It may have been the priests and the scribes who said this, but the passers-by (v. 29) and the soldiers (Luke 23. 31) and the thieves all abused Him in this way. To all of them He seemed to have failed in His life's work because He could not save Himself. Since He had failed, He could not be God's Messiah.

This is the view of most people in the world. To them the greatest person is the one whose strength can be seen, and who overcomes by force those who oppose him. Muslims say that since God is

great, it was impossible for Him to become a man who was crucified.

But 1 Cor. 1. 23–27 shows that the opposite is true. Jesus is great
and strong enough to bring us into fellowship with God, just
because He was willing to die for us like a criminal. The Jews refused
to believe in Jesus because He did not come down from the cross:
we believe in Jesus just because He willingly stayed up on the cross.
If He had come down, it would have meant that there was some
suffering that He was not willing to endure for us.

2. All this is true for us, i.e., we can often only save others by
refusing to save ourselves. It is so in little things, e.g., when we go
without sleep in order to nurse a dying neighbour; and it is so in
big things. In the 1939–45 war eight sailors had escaped from their
burning ship and were in a little boat. It was so small that if anyone
else got in, it would sink. A boy swam towards them, asking to be
saved. One of the sailors said afterwards "We knew we could not
save him and save ourselves as well". One of them did jump out
and was later drowned. The boy took his place and was saved.

3. When they said "He saved others", they were speaking the
truth. Jesus had freed people from the power of their diseases and
evil spirits and sins (1. 37; 2. 10), and made them able to live fully
in spirit and mind and body (John 10. 10). That is "saving".

v. 33. There was darkness over the whole land . . .

1. The darkness was not an eclipse, because the moon was full at
that time. When it is full, it does not appear in the daytime, and
therefore cannot pass between the earth and the sun. Probably there
was a storm of flying dust. During March and April this does sometimes occur in Jerusalem in the daytime, and drivers of cars have to
use their lights on the roads. The Arabs call it a sudden "Sirocco"
(East Wind).

2. People sometimes ask, "Was this a miraculous action by God
or did it happen by nature?" To this there is no answer except to
say that it is the same God who can do a miracle and who controls
"nature".

3. But darkness, which brings rest at night, is a fearful thing at
noon. It is thus a kind of illustration or symbol of the stern judgement of God on those who killed Jesus and did not repent (Amos
8. 9).

271

v. 34. My God, My God, why hast thou left me alone?

1. It is important to remember two things in order to interpret these words:

a. We can only understand a very little of what was in Jesus' mind when He spoke them;

b. He was suffering great bodily pain at the time, so that what He said may perhaps not be the same as what He wanted to say. This is true of people who are being tortured. Jesus was a real man and was being tortured.

2. But the words probably do tell us something about *His suffering:*

a. He made Himself one with all mankind, and took on Himself the guilt of all mankind's sin. For this reason He felt separated from the Holy God, just as men feel who have done wrong. But there was this difference between Jesus and the rest of mankind: He had done no wrong (2 Cor. 5. 21).

b. He suffered in spirit even more deeply than in body. Other people have endured even more bodily pain than He had to endure: no one ever suffered in spirit as much as He did.

c. He shows how much He loved us by being willing to suffer like this.

3. *What the words do not teach:*

a. They do not teach that God left Jesus alone. The rest of the Bible makes it impossible for us to believe that. Jesus actually was God (see John 14. 11).

b. They do not teach that Jesus was filled with unbelief and despair. He prayed, "My God", even though His Father seemed to be far away. God was still there, to whom prayer could be made. God is still there for us, even when, at times of suffering, we also want to say "Why . . .?", and He will not leave us alone (Ps. 139. 7b).
Note:

a. The words come from Ps. 22. 1. As the psalms were written in Hebrew, it is surprising that He spoke these words in His vernacular, Aramaic.

b. This is the only saying of Jesus on the cross that Mark reports. Three other sayings are reported by Luke (23. 34, 43, 46) and three by John (19. 26, 28, 30).

c. This is a verse which shows clearly that the Gospels tell a true story. Disciples would never invent such words as these in order to attract more members to the Church.

v. 37.   Cried with a loud voice . . .

This verse speaks of the moment when Jesus died.

1. The cry may have been simply His breath, breathed out without words.

2. It may be that His cry was "It is finished" (John 19. 30), i.e., "I have completed the work my Father entrusted to me".

3. Or perhaps it was "Into thy hands I give up my spirit" (Luke 23. 46), thus entrusting Himself confidently into God's care.

v. 38.   The curtain of the Temple was torn . . .

This curtain separated the Holy of Holies from the rest of the Temple: only the High Priest could go past it, and He did so only on the Day of Atonement (Ex. 21. 33).

People ask "Was this a miracle done by God?" "What caused it?" "Why does Mark not record the other two strange events found in Matt. 27. 51–53?" We cannot answer these questions satisfactorily; but Mark probably reported the tearing of the curtain because it was a kind of parable of what Jesus was doing by dying:

1. He had taken away whatever separated us from God. He has "opened the kingdom of heaven to all believers" (*Te Deum*); not only the High Priest, but all can enjoy fellowship with God. (See Heb. 10. 19–22.)

2. The opening of the curtain was as surprising as a revolution which suddenly changes the customs and government of a country. Jesus, by dying, has torn away the old ways of approaching God and given us a new way (2. 21–22).

·v. 39.   Truly this man was a son of God.

The centurion who said this was an officer in the Roman army. It was his duty to see that the sentence of death was carried out, so he stayed near the cross until Jesus died.

What did he think of when he said "a son of God"? It is not certain what he meant. Luke 23. 47 says he meant "a good man", and clearly they were words of praise. This shows that he was brave enough to change his mind and to admit publicly that Jesus was innocent after all. (It is a brave man who admits it when he or his nation has been wrong.)

This Roman officer was probably a heathen and said "*A* son

273

of God" not "The Son of God". But Christians believe that He was *the* Son, the "own and only Son" (1. 11; 9. 7), not one of many very good men.

v. 40.   There were some women there . . . watching . . .

These were the women who had helped Jesus while He was travelling in Galilee. They had cooked meals and mended clothes for Him and His followers. They were: Mary from Magdala, Mary who had two sons, James and Joseph (we do not know anything about them), and Salome, who was the sister of Jesus' mother and the mother of James and John (1. 19).

It seems that they were the only followers of Jesus who were brave enough to be present when He was killed. (John 19. 25, 26 says that Jesus' mother and the disciple John were also there.) This is only one of many occasions when women have showed greater bravery and patience than men. Christian congregations have often been kept encouraged during times of difficulty by the faithfulness of their women members. They must surely be shown more respect, and allowed to take a greater share in the work of the Church than is common at present.

ADDITIONAL NOTE

THE DEATH OF JESUS

1. *What did Jesus do for us by dying?*

a. He made it possible for us to be *forgiven* by God. Our sins deserve punishment, but Jesus took this punishment upon Himself. That is why we say that He died "for us". (See Isa. 53. 4–5; 1 Cor. 15. 3.) He did at that time what we could not do for ourselves. What He did never had to be done again. A Christian is someone who knows that he has been forgiven, and that he is being treated as innocent by God, because Jesus died.

b. He won a *victory* against the powers of evil. Evil did its worst against Him (we think of the evil in those who killed Him), but it could not destroy the love in Him (John 13. 1c) and it could not prevent Him from rising again (Acts 2. 24). In this fight, Jesus won, and the power of evil was broken for ever. Evil is still powerful, but we need never be overcome by it. It is like a huge, poisonous snake which was caught and which afterwards had its teeth taken out: the snake remained dangerous, but it could no longer kill by its poison. For these reasons the death of Jesus was different from the death of any other man who ever lived.

2. *What did Jesus show us about God by dying?*
He showed that God loves us. We know that Jesus died because He loves us. But when He loved, it was God who was loving (see 2 Cor. 5. 19; John 3. 16; 14. 9).

3. *What did Jesus show us about ourselves?*
a. He showed us our own *sinfulness*. The hate and fear of the people who killed Jesus are sins which we have in us. We see what terrible results sin has (Rom. 3. 23). We see our own need to be forgiven.

b. He showed us what to do with *suffering* that cannot be avoided. He accepted it, and then used it as a means of saving us.

See picture facing p. 243.

Mark 15. 42–47: The Burial of Jesus

See also Matt. 27. 57–61; Luke 23. 50–56; John 19. 38–42

INTRODUCTION

When the Romans crucified anyone they let the body stay on the cross to rot or be eaten by vultures. But the Jews had a law in their religion that the bodies must be buried before sunset (Deut. 21. 22, 23), and a body was often thrown quickly into a big common grave. Jesus' friends wanted to prevent His body being treated in this way, but there was very little time between His dying and sunset. Also the Sabbath, on which no manual work could be done, began at sunset on Fridays. So at 4 or 5 p.m. Joseph of Arimathea went to Pilate and asked for his permission to bury Jesus privately. Pilate first made sure that Jesus was dead, and then gave permission. Joseph and his helpers carried the body to the tomb in his garden (John 19. 39). This garden was on the same hillside on which the Crucifixion had taken place. Then they bound it with many yards of wide linen bandage, having soaked the linen in oil of myrrh, which preserved the body. Finally, the tomb was closed. Mary from

Magdala and her friends did not know Joseph, and so watched the burial from a short distance away.

NOTES

v. 43.   Joseph . . . asked for the body of Jesus.

1. Joseph seems to have been one of those Jews who rightly believed that God would sent His Messiah, or would do some great deed on behalf of his nation (Luke 2. 25; 24. 21). It is possible he was a follower of Jesus. Certainly it was Jesus he wanted to honour: he did nothing for the other two who had been crucified.

2. What changed Joseph? Before Jesus' death he was like many to-day who believe, but dare not be baptized. He was a rich member of the Sanhedrin, but took no action publicly on behalf of Jesus (Luke 23. 51). Now that Jesus had died, however, he had new courage. He knew his action would anger the other members of the Sanhedrin, but he went "boldly" to Pilate. Before, he had admired Jesus: now, he loved Him and was willing to suffer for Him. It was Jesus, by dying, who changed him in a way that Jesus, by living, had not been able to do. That is why Christians must preach Christ as the Crucified One. It is Jesus "lifted up" on a cross that changes and draws people to Himself (John 12. 32).

3. He honoured the body which was torn, disfigured, and covered with blood and flies. There are people who pay little attention to their own or others' bodies, saying that the soul alone is important. But the body is part of a person, and the whole of a person is of importance. So it is right both to give honour to a dead body, and to heal a sick body.

v. 44.   He was already dead . . .

Pilate did not give the body to Joseph without first making sure that Jesus really had died. This is an important answer to those who say that Jesus never died and therefore never rose again. (See also 1 Cor. 15. 4a.)

v. 46.   Laid him in a grave . . . and rolled a stone . . .

1. **In a grave:** This was really a stone ledge carved out of the rock inside a cave. (This kind of ancient grave can still be seen in Jerusalem to-day.)

a. This grave was like the boat (4. 1), the donkey (11. 7), and the room (14. 14); it was gladly offered to Jesus for His use. (See note on 11. 2.)

b. It was also the best that could be found: it had never before been used (Luke 23. 53). (See note on 11. 2.)

2. **Rolled a stone:**

a. The mouth of the cave had to be closed up to keep out dogs, jackals, and thieves. This was done by rolling a stone (about 7 ft high) across the mouth.

b. As this stone was rolled, the Jewish and Roman authorities thought that it was the end of Jesus, and were glad. Joseph and other followers of Jesus thought so too, and were filled with misery. They could only look back to what He had done: there was nothing to look forward to. (They were like some teachers to-day who teach that Jesus lived a good life and was unfortunately killed, but who know nothing of His life among us now.)

c. But often when it is said that someone's work is ended, it really is beginning. A teacher who has worked faithfully for many years retires or dies. It is in the next twenty or thirty years that the greatest results of his work can be seen, as his pupils become parents and teachers themselves. This is true of Jesus in a special way: He is alive and active in the hearts of men and women all over the world to-day, and no one can stop Him!

v. 47. Mary Magdalene . . . saw where he was laid.

1. **Mary Magdalene saw:** The women took note of the place where He was buried. They were not likely to forget it after only two days. This is the reply to those who say that they went to the wrong tomb on Easter Day, and that Jesus' body was still dead in Joseph's tomb.

2. **He was laid:** When Jesus' body was laid in the ground, what happened to His soul? If this is asked, no one can, of course, answer with authority, but this can be said:

a. Jesus, like ourselves when we die, passed into the state usually called Paradise. This is what the Apostles' Creed means by the words, "descended into hell", but "hell" is an incorrect translation. In this way He takes from us the fear of the unknown future, the fear of what lies on the other side of death. Those who are dying can be at rest with God.

277

b. In 1 Pet. 3. 19 the writer says that He proclaimed His message to the departed souls in Paradise. This shows that God wants no one at all to remain ignorant of His love for him.

Mark 16. 1–8: Jesus has Risen

See also Matt. 28: Luke 24; John 20; 21; 1 Cor. 15. 3–8

INTRODUCTION

The story

When Jesus had been buried, everyone thought that His work had come to an end. His friends were deeply disappointed and afraid. After the interval of one day, three of the women who had helped Him during His journeys went to the tomb to do honour to the body. They were astonished to find that the tomb was empty (v. 6). They told this to others, who said they were talking nonsense. But two of them went and found that the Resurrection was true (Luke 24. 10–12).

Afterwards Jesus was seen alive. We are told He was seen by Mary from Magdala (John 20. 14), by Peter (Luke 24. 34; 1 Cor. 15. 5), by two men going to Emmaus (Luke 24. 13) and by the disciples on several occasions, the last of which was at the time of His Ascension (Acts 1. 9).

Shortly afterwards, when God had sent His Spirit, the behaviour of the followers who had been so weak and terrified, became wonderfully changed. They were now full of courage. When asked to explain this change, they said, "It is because God has made Jesus alive again" (see Acts 5. 29–30). Certainly, nothing except the rising of Jesus from the tomb can explain why their lives were so changed or why the Christian Church grew so wonderfully.

Mark's account of the events

Only the first eight verses of chap. 16 were written by Mark. Vv. 9–20 are a collection of information from other parts of the New Testament; vv. 9–18 were added about a hundred years later, and vv. 19–20 about three hundred years later.

It is not likely that Mark intended to end his Gospel at v. 8, because vv. 1–8 only tell us that the tomb was empty. The rest of his story is lost, i.e., the story of how Jesus was seen after He had risen. To learn the complete story, we must read the other accounts.

Other accounts

In addition to Mark 16. 1–8, we have the accounts in the other three Gospels and in 1 Cor. 15. 3–8. This last account was written only twenty five years after the events, and is the earliest account.

Some readers are troubled, because the accounts are different: e.g., they do not agree about the names of those who went with Mary to the tomb, or about the time when they went. But whenever a great event takes place, people report it differently. In the last great war, the Germans were defeated at El Alamein in North Africa in 1942. Recently they and the British have produced reports and films about the battle. The accounts differ greatly, but no one denies that a great battle was fought and won-simply because the accounts are different.

There is no disagreement concerning the three most important happenings connected with the rising of Jesus: a. the tomb was empty; b. Jesus was seen alive after His death; c. the behaviour of His followers became changed, because Jesus had risen.

NOTES

v. 2.   On the first day of the week they went to the grave . . .

1. **On the first day of the week,** i.e., the day after the Sabbath. They went and found that Jesus had risen. This is the reason why Christians, ever since that time, have used Sunday (which is the first day of the week) as their day of worship and rest. It has taken the place of the Sabbath. This is something which makes us sure that Jesus really did rise. Unless this wonderful event had taken place, the first Christians, who were all Jews, would never have allowed Sunday to take the place of the Sabbath.

2. **They went to the grave:** "They" means Mary from Magdala and the other women. Women had been faithful to Jesus, although men were afraid. (See notes on 15. 40, 47.)

They went with ointment with which to preserve the body. This had been done already (John 19. 39); but the women did not know

279

this. They had not been near enough to the tomb to see what was happening inside it.

v. 3.   Who will roll away the stone . . . ?

Why did they go at all to the tomb? Did they not know that the entrance was blocked? Certainly they knew that, and must have known that their journey might be useless. But they were also hopeful that they would find one or two men who would help them to move the stone away.

Since that time Christians have very often had fears that certain things might stand in the way of their finding and serving Jesus, e.g., their own weakness, the weakness of the Church, opposition from members of the family. But Christians also know that God is at work to take away obstructions just as He took away the stone. As William Carey said, Christians "attempt great things for God", because they "expect great things from God".

v. 5.   They saw a young man . . .

Who was this? Possibly it was a stranger who was standing near the tomb when Jesus rose, and to whom Jesus gave a message. But Matt. says it was "an angel"; John says it was "two angels"; Luke says it was "two men". Whoever he was, his message was found out afterwards to be true.

v. 6.   He has risen; he is not here.

1. **He has risen:** This verse does not tell us when or how Jesus rose; nor does it describe the body which He had after rising (although we know it was of a different kind from His previous body). But it does tell us *that* He rose, and it tells us *where* He rose.

Why is this so important? What does it show us which nothing else can show? Here are four great truths it shows:

a. Jesus is alive now. Christians do not merely remember Him: they worship Him as One who is living, and they welcome Him as a partner in their daily work. "Christ lives in me" (Gal. 2. 20).

b. God is stronger than any evil in the world. Men killed Jesus because evil was in them: they lied and had fear and hatred in their hearts. But this evil was found to be not as strong as God's goodness, for God took Jesus out of death (Acts 2. 23, 24). Christians know

280

that whenever they fight, e.g., against corruption, or by continuing
to show kindness to ungrateful people, they are on the winning side.
Such acts are never wasted.

c. God is stronger than the evil in ourselves (1 John 3. 20). The
same God who raised Jesus up can raise us up from a life of sinful
or careless habits. We can rise, if, in penitence, we have let our evil
ways die (see Rom. 6. 4b, 11).

d. God is stronger than death. God, who raised Jesus up, can
give us new life after the death of our bodies. We are not promised
that we shall appear on this earth again, as Jesus did, But we can
trust God completely to give us new life after death.

2. **He is not here.** It was right for them to look for Jesus, but they
were looking for Him in the wrong place. They were told that He
would be found in Galilee, where they lived and worked. Jesus is
to be found to-day especially in the homes and places of work of
followers, i.e., where people meet together. It is chiefly in serving
and caring for others that we find and honour Jesus Himself (Matt.
18. 20; 25. 40).

v. 7. Go, tell his disciples and Peter, that he is going before you . . .

This is part of the message from Jesus.

1. **Go, tell:** See Matt. 28. 19. All followers of Jesus have been given
this command to share the news about Him with others. This news
is that He has risen and is alive. (Note that they were too frightened
to obey at first (v. 8), but Christians in Acts 2. 22–24 are beginning
to obey boldly.)

2. **And Peter:** This is a special message for Peter so that he should
not think that he had been rejected by Jesus because he had disowned Him. 1 Cor. 1. 3 tells how Jesus met him; John 21. 15–20
tells how Jesus entrusted him with new work. Peter, like other
Christians since, found that Jesus' love was so great that it could
forgive even the worst sin. (See note on 14. 29.)

3. **Going before:** Jesus never pushed His followers. (See note on
14. 28.) He went first, faced the difficulties, and said "Follow"
(John 14. 3). The message added that He would go north to Galilee
and meet them there. This troubles some readers because Luke
24 and John 20 say it was in Jerusalem that He met them. But it is
likely that He met them both in Galilee and in Jerusalem.

v. 8. They were afraid.

1. They were afraid because they were not expecting to find the tomb empty (Luke 24. 37). Some people have said that Jesus did not really rise: they say that His followers were so sure that they would see Him again that they had dreams, or imagined that they were seeing Him again. But in fact they were not expecting this at all. They saw Him only because He really did rise.

2. These are the last words which we have of the book which Mark wrote. The sentence is not completed. What has happened to the remainder? Perhaps Mark was arrested while writing this sentence (he wrote while Christians were being persecuted); or the last part of the roll may have been torn off after his death.

The story is not completed. It is probable that in the last part of his book he described how Jesus met His disciples in Galilee. But of course no one can ever complete the story of people discovering that Jesus is alive. Every day there are new people and new families making the discovery with joy, and being added to the number of those being saved (Acts 2. 47).

Study Suggestions

Note: All Bible references are to St Mark's Gospel unless otherwise stated. The reference given at the *beginning* of each question shows which section of the Guide it refers to.

1. (1. 1–8) Read also Matt. 3. 1–12; Luke 3. 1–18; John 1. 6–8 and 19–28 about John the Baptist:
   a. What was the chief message in John's preaching?
   b. What was the chief difference between John's preaching and that of Jesus?

2. (1. 9–11) Why did Jesus ask John to baptize Him?

3. (1. 12, 13) a. One student said: "If the devil is a real person then there are two gods, one bad and one good." Do you think Satan is a real person, or only a way of describing the power of evil? Give reasons for your answer.
   b. Another student said: "In the Bible we read of Satan and angels as real people. If they are not real people, then I cannot trust the Bible." What is your opinion?

4. (1. 14, 15) Which of the following statements about "the Kingdom of God" are true, and which are untrue? Give reasons for your answer in each case.
   a. It has come already.
   b. It will not come till all men obey God.
   c. It is not a place: it is God ruling.
   d. We join it when we join the Church.

5. (1. 16–20) The first disciples left their fishing to follow Jesus.
   a. Why did they believe that this was the right thing to do?
   b. In what ways do you, and Christians of today, discover the right thing to do?

6. (1. 21–28) i. Read the following passages and say in each case why people were astonished at Jesus:
   (a) Mark 1. 22   (b) 6. 2, 3   (c) 10. 23   (d) 10. 32
   (e) 11. 18   (f) 12. 17
   ii. Would Christians astonish people more if they were more Christlike? Give reasons for your answer.

7. (1. 21–28) "A man had an evil spirit or 'demon'" (1. 23). Do you think that this is just a way of saying that the man was ill and that the cause of the illness was not shown, or do you think that evil spirits do exist and enter people? Give reasons for your answer.

8. (Additional Note: Miracles) In 1968, a man travelling round the moon in a spacecraft spoke to his wife in the USA. If Mark had heard of this he would have called it a "miracle". What do you think is the difference between this event and the "miracles" which Jesus did?

9. (1. 21–34) Look at the pictures and caption facing p. 22. Two-thirds of all the people in the world live in continual hunger. The other one-third receive 88 per cent of the income of the world.
   i. In the light of this statement and of the pictures themselves, what is your opinion of the caption to the pictures?
   ii. In what ways is your government relieving the needs of the poor: (a) in your own country? (b) in other countries?
   iii. In what ways could the congregation to which you belong join in the fight against great poverty?
   iv. What do the following passages show about the Christian attitude to great poverty?
      (a) Matt. 25. 34–40   (b) Mark 1. 41   (c) Luke 1. 51–53
      (d) 1 Cor. 16. 1–3   (e) James 2. 15–17

10. (1. 35–39) i. Read the following passages and say in each case where Jesus was praying, and, if you can, why He prayed:
      (a) Mark 1. 35   (b) 6. 46   (c) 14. 35   (d) Luke 6. 12, 13
      (e) Luke 23. 46
   ii. What do you think is the greatest single difference between Jesus' prayers and your own prayers?

11. (1. 40–45) When Jesus showed compassion by touching the leper, He was going against the custom of all good Jews. When Christians today show Christlike compassion, they too are likely to go against the customs of their country or Church or family.
   Give two examples from everyday life to show how this happens, or ought to happen.

12. (2. 1–12) "Very many people are sick in body simply because they feel deeply guilty of sin." (p. 38)
   a. What verse, if any, in Mark 2. 1–12 suggests that it was a feeling of guilt which caused the man's paralysis?
   b. To whom do people with this kind of illness usually go; do they go to a qualified doctor? or an ordained minister? or someone else? To whom *should* they go? Give reasons for your answer.

13. (2. 13, 14) a. Why did Levi believe that he ought to give up his job in order to follow Jesus?
    b. Give examples from present day life to show when and why it would be necessary and right for a Christian to give up:
        i. his present job,   ii. drinking alcohol,
        iii. considering his own needs before other people's,
        iv. going to Church every Sunday,   v. marriage.

14. (2. 15–17) Jesus ate with despised people.
    a. In the place where you live, what sorts of people are the least honoured?
    b. Say in each case:
        i. why they receive so little honour, and
        ii. what God could do for them through Christians who are willing to be used by Him.

15. (2. 15–17) Show from the study of the following verses what the "grace of God" (shown to us in Jesus Christ) means:
    (a) Mark 2. 17   (b) Eph. 2. 8–10   (c) Eph. 3. 7   (d) Heb. 12. 15

16. (Additional Note: Pharisees and Scribes) a. In what ways did the Pharisees serve God well?
    b. Give one way in which they were often at fault.
    c. Give an example from everyday life to show how Christians today are often guilty of the same fault.

17. (2. 18–22) Answer the question on p. 45: "Since Christ was a Jew, why do Christians not follow the Jewish religion?"

18. (2. 18–22) "Many people reject new things, even good things, mainly because they do not believe that God is alive and leading them to work in new ways." (p. 47).
    What is your opinion? Give examples from everyday life to explain your answer.

19. (2. 23–28) Look at the picture and caption facing p. 23.
    a. What religious tradition was Jesus referring to when He replied to the Pharisees?
    b. Give an example of a Christian regulation or tradition which hinders the work of the Church today.
    c. Give an example of a tradition of another religion, or a social convention, which seems to you to be harmful.
        Give reasons for your answers to b. and c. and say why the traditions were ever thought to be necessary.

20. (3. 1–6) Look at the picture and caption facing p. 56.
    a. For whose sake did Jesus come into conflict with the authorities, according to Mark 3. 1–6?
    b. Why did Christians come into conflict with the authorities, according to Acts 3. 1–5 and 4. 1–10?
    c. Is it possible for anyone who wants justice for other people to avoid conflict with the authorities? Give reasons for your answer.
    d. How can one protest without malice?
    e. Is it ever right to protest with violence? Give an example.

21. (Additional Note: Sabbath) a. Re-read also 2. 23, 24. Give two reasons why the Jews kept the Sabbath as their special day.
    b. Why did Christians make Sunday their special day?
    c. What other names are there for Sunday, and which do you think is the most suitable name? Give reasons. (See 1 Cor. 16. 2 and Rev. 1. 10.)

22. (3. 1–6) "Jesus was fully man as well as being fully God."
    i. In what way does each of the following verses show that He was man?
       (a) Mark 1. 9   (b) 1. 12, 13   (c) 1. 43   (d) 3. 5   (e) 4. 38
       (f) 6. 3   (g) 8. 12   (h) 10. 14   (i) 10. 21   (j) 13. 32
    ii. What difference to your religion would it make if you disregarded these verses, and thought that Jesus was half man and half God?

23. (3. 7–12) "Everyone should know what Jesus has done through His Church." (p. 56)
    a. What are the two greatest things that Jesus has done through His Church in your neighbourhood? Give some information about each of these things and say when they took place.
    b. What do you think are the two greatest things that Jesus wants to do through His Church in your neighbourhood at the present time? Give reasons for your answer.

24. (3. 13–19a) a. What is the chief task of the Christian Church?
    b. How far is the local congregation of which you are a member engaged in this task?

25. (3. 13–19a) a. In what ways is the list of names of the twelve disciples given by Mark different from the list given by Luke?
    b. What would you reply to someone who said that he could not trust the Gospels because they do not always agree?

26. (3. 19b–21) a. "People were saying, He is out of his mind" (3. 21). Why did people say this about Jesus?
    b. "People would say the same today if they could see Him at work in the world." Do you think this is true? Give reasons for your answer.

27. (3. 22–30) i. In what ways do the following verses show that the work of Jesus was to overcome something or someone harmful? Say who or what He was overcoming in each case:
    (a) Mark 1. 25   (b) 3. 5   (c) 6. 13   (d) 7. 35   (e) 11. 15
    (f) 11. 29   (g) 14. 36
    ii. In your experience, what are the two .greatest "enemies" against which a Christian worker has to fight today?

28. (4. 1–9) a. Why did Charles Kingsley refuse to pray publicly for the good health of the people in his town (p. 67)?
    b. What is your opinion of his action?

29. (Additional Note: Parables) Each parable which Jesus told "contains one chief piece of teaching" (p. 68). What is the chief teaching of each of the following parables?
    (a) Matt. 25. 1–13   (b) Mark 4. 21–25   (c) Luke 15. 8–10

30. (4. 10–12) After reading Mark 4. 11, a student said, "Christians are no better than those outside the Church, nor are they wiser."
    a. Do you agree? Give reasons for your answer.
    b. What is the difference between those who are members of the Church and those who are not?

31. (4. 13–20, 26–29) a. In what way is the chief message of the parable in Mark 4. 1–9a like the chief message of the parable in 4. 26–29?
    b. Give an example of some person or group of people to whom these two parables could bring new life today.

287

32. (4. 33, 34) "The methods that were good in our grandfathers' day or in another country may not be the best ones for us to use." (p. 77)
    Do you think you would agree with this statement if you were: (a) a farmer? (b) a father? (c) a minister in charge of a Christian congregation? Give examples to illustrate your answers.

33. (4. 35–41) a. Why do you think Mark chose to record the story of the wind ceasing on the lake?
    b. Do you think that Jesus' words "Be quiet" caused the wind to cease? Give reasons for your answer.

34. (4. 35–41) Look at the picture and caption facing p. 57, and read the following passages about people who were afraid:
    (a) Matt. 25. 25   (b) Mark 4. 40   (c) 6. 20   (d) 9. 32
    (e) 11. 32   (f) Acts 9. 26
    Say in each case: (i) what the people were afraid of, and (ii) what their fear prevented them from doing.

35. (4. 35–41) Many nations today are damaging themselves. They are so afraid of other countries that they spend huge amounts of money on bombs rather than on the health of their own people.
    a. Of what three things are you and your friends most afraid at this time?
    b. Describe in each case what damage this fear does to yourself.

36. (5. 1–20) "If we have never wanted to escape from God, is it because we have never met God Himself?" (p. 83)
    What is your opinion?

37. (5. 1–20) Read also Mark 1. 23–26; 1. 32–34; 3. 11, 12; 7. 25–30; 9. 17–27.
    a. How have people explained "madness" in the past?
    b. How do people explain it today?
    c. How did Jesus treat those who were thought to be "mad"?

38. (5. 1–20) "We sometimes think that people are made better by being told to obey God. But really it is the stories of what God has done and is still doing that make men love Him and obey Him." (p. 84)
    a. Why is this so?
    b. Consider two sermons you have heard recently, and say how far each of them emphasized what God has done and is doing.

288

39. (5. 21–24) Jesus helped Jairus, who was a member of a group that was against Him.
    a. What is the connection between this act of Jesus and Rom. 12. 21 and 1 Pet. 3. 3, 9?
    b. Why is this kind of action so difficult?
    c. Give an example from everyday life of someone doing this.

40. (5. 25–34) i. What were the things that Jesus "could not do", according to the following passages?
    (a) Mark 5. 30   (b) 6. 5   (c) 7. 24   (d) 9. 16   (e) 13. 32
    ii. What would you reply to someone who said, "If there were things that Jesus could not do, then I cannot believe that He is God"?

41. (5. 35–43) "People weeping and mourning loudly" (5. 38). When someone dies, certain customs are observed by the mourners, but these customs change. What mourning customs, if any, do you think should be changed in your country at the present time? Give reasons for your answer.

42. (5. 35–43) "Little girl, get up" (5. 41).
    a. In what ways has the attitude of grown-up people to children in your country changed during the last fifty years?
    b. In what ways is the new attitude more Christian, and in what ways is it less Christian?

43. (5. 35–43) "Give her something to eat" (5. 43).
    a. How many of the stories in Mark 1–5 (i) describe Jesus' meeting people's bodily needs; (ii) describe His meeting their spiritual needs; (iii) describe both? (See the Contents pages, v and vi, for list of stories, and give chapter and verse references to support your answer.)
    b. What does your answer to a. above show concerning the task of Christ's Church today?

44. (Additional Note: Faith) Look at the pictures and caption facing p. 104.
    a In what ways was the faith of Heyerdahl and his friends (i) like, and (ii) unlike, a Christian's faith in God?
    b. What is the difference between "having faith" and:
       i. gambling?
       ii. holding certain ideas?
       iii. keeping rules?
       Explain your answers with examples from everyday life.

45. (6. 1–6) Jesus was a carpenter. Yet in many countries carpenters, masons, motor mechanics, are given less honour than those who work in offices.
    a. Why is this?
    b. What action, if any, could be taken to correct this wrong attitude?

46. (6. 1–6) a. Why, in your opinion, was Jesus rejected by the people of Nazareth?
    b. Give two reasons why any leader of a club or political party or Church congregation may be rejected today by those whom he leads.
    c. What would be the best thing for the leader to do in each of the cases you have given in answering b. above?

47. (6. 7–13) Read also Luke 10. 1–16.
    a. What is the difference between what Jesus told the Twelve and what He told the Seventy: (i) to do? (ii) to say? (iii) to expect?
    b. Who in the Church today should be carrying out what Jesus told the Twelve to do and say and expect?

48. (6. 7–13) "He forbad them to take anything for the journey except a staff" (6. 8b).
    a. Why did Jesus forbid this?
    b. Is a Christian leader today more useful if he owns as few possessions as possible, or is unmarried, or desires no regular payment? Or is he more useful if he lives like other people? Give reasons for your answer.

49. (6. 17–29) Read also Acts 5. 3 and Gal. 2. 14. "John rebuked Herod" (6. 18).
    a. Give two reasons why it was difficult for John to do this.
    b. Give two examples from the New Testament and one example from present day life of someone rightly rebuking another person.
    c. What makes it a difficult thing to do?

50. (6. 30–34) "Rest a little" (6. 31).
    i. What do the following verses tell us of the way in which Jesus treated His own body?
    (a) Matt. 26. 12   (b) Mark 4. 38   (c) Mark 11. 12
    (d) Luke 4. 2   (e) John 4. 7

ii. Why is the right treatment of our own bodies important?

iii. What makes it difficult?

51. (6. 35–44) In the caption to the picture facing p. 105 it is said that the task of feeding the world's population is not too great for God to perform. It is also said that the task of providing food will be done through human beings.

    a. Through which human beings did Jesus feed the crowd of five thousand?

    b. Mention two other very great problems facing the world today, and say through whom and by what means you think God might solve them.

52. (6. 35–44) a. In what ways was the Feeding of the Five Thousand like the Lord's Supper recorded in Mark 14. 22–25?

    b. In what ways was it different?

53. (6. 35–44) "Looking up to heaven" (6. 41).

    a. Why did Mark (and others) use "picture language" which suggests that God lives in the sky?

    b. Give two examples to show how people in the Church today use the same kind of language.

    c. What are the dangers, if any, of our doing this?

54. (6. 45–52) a. What are your own answers to the questions on p. 108. i.e.:

      i. Did Jesus, being truly man, really walk on the water? If so, how did He?

      ii. Was it necessary for Him to do such a miracle?

      iii. Why did He wish to pass them by (v. 48)?

    b. If someone told you that he could not answer any of these questions, would you call him wise? or wicked? or lazy? Give reasons for your answer.

55. (7. 1–13) a. What did Jesus mean when He used the word "hypocrisy" or "double-dealing"?

    b. What do you think is the connection between hypocrisy and the picture facing p. 114?

    c. In what ways were the following people "hypocritical"?

      i. The people mentioned in Isaiah 29. 13.

      ii. The Pharisees mentioned in Mark 7. 6.

      iii. The men sent to Jesus by the Jewish Council according to Mark 12. 13–17.

56. (7. 14–23) It is the spirit of the written law (in the Old Testament) that we are to see and obey, not the "letter" (p. 117). Read the following passages and say in what ways (if any), and why, Christians today should obey each command.
(a) Exod. 20. 10 (b) Lev. 11. 4–8 (c) Lev. 12. 3
(d) Num. 29. 8 (e) Deut. 14. 22–26

57. (7. 24–30) "For that word the evil spirit has gone out" (7. 29).
a. Do you think that the words of the woman changed Jesus' mind?
b. If so, what was there in her words that produced the change?
c. Is praying for other people asking God to change His mind?
d. If not, what is it?

58. (7. 24–30) Look at the picture and caption facing p. 115.
a. What was the attitude of Jesus (who was a Jew) to other races or nations or tribes? (Matt. 15. 24; Mark 5. 20; Luke 7. 2–9; John 12. 46 may help you to answer.)
b. Is it possible for a nation or tribe to be proud of its own special achievements without living in distrust of other nations and tribes? Give reasons for your answer.

59. (7. 31–37) Jesus healed a deaf man. Find out:
a. what are the causes of deafness;
b. what is being done in your country to help deaf people;
c. how long this work has been going on;
d. who started it;   e. why they started it.

60. (8. 11–13) Why did Jesus refuse to give signs?

61. (8. 14–21) "Do you not remember?" (8. 18)
i. What had the disciples forgotten?
ii. What, according to each of the following passages, was being remembered or forgotten?
(a) Deut. 8. 2 (b) John 16. 4 (c) 1 Cor. 11. 24
(d) Gal. 2. 10 (e) Heb. 10. 32
iii. In your experience, what parts of Church services are especially concerned with "remembering"?

62. (8. 22–26) When someone works to heal or cure "it is God who heals" (p. 129).
    i. Read the following passages and say in each case whom God used to do His work, and what the work was:
       (a) Acts 3. 2–6 (b) Acts 9. 17 (c) Acts 14. 8–15
       (d) Acts 19. 11
    ii. What is the difference between the healing described in Acts 9. 17 and using "magic" in order to be healed?
    iii. Give two examples of people whom you know who are in need of healing, and say in each case who are the people through whom you think God can heal them.

63. (8. 27–30) Jesus said, "Who do the people say I am?"
    i. What was the opinion of the people mentioned in the following verses of St John's Gospel?
       (a) 7. 12a (b) 7. 12b (c) 7. 40 (d) 7. 41a
    ii. If you know people who have heard of Jesus but who are not members of the Church, find out how they would answer the question, "Who is Jesus?".
    iii. Why is it an important question?

64. (8. 27–30) a. According to the following verses, Jesus is reminding the disciples of one thing. What is it?
       Mark 6. 31; 6. 37; 8. 29a; 13. 9; 13. 23; 13. 33
    b. Give an example from everyday life to show the importance of this reminder.

65. (8. 27–30) "You are the Christ" (8. 29b).
    a. Compare this translation of the Greek title "*Christos*" with the translation of it given in:
       (i) another English version; (ii) any other language you know.
    b. What did Peter mean when he used this title to describe Jesus?
    c. Do you think the title is a sufficient description of Jesus? If not, suggest two ways in which you would want to correct or add to it.

66. (8. 31–33) a. What was "necessary", according to Mark 8. 31 and 9. 31?
    b. Why was it necessary?
    c. What did the disciples think about it?
    d. Why did the disciples think that?

293

67. (Additional Note: The Son of Man) "Son of Man" is a name which Jesus used for Himself. What special meaning does this name have in each of the following verses?
(a) Mark 9. 31 (b) Luke 5. 24 (c) Matt. 26. 64

68. (8. 34–9. 1) Look at the picture facing p. 142.
a. What is the player at the left of the picture losing, and what does he hope to gain?
b. Give examples of:
i. someone mentioned in the New Testament,
ii. someone known to yourself,
who "lost his life in order to save it". Explain your answers.

69. (9. 2–8) In the story of the Transfiguration the disciples were instructed to listen to Jesus rather than to Elijah and Moses (9. 7).
a. What did Elijah and Moses each stand for?
b. What does this instruction tell Christians about their use of the Old Testament?
c. Give an example from everyday life to show why it is a necessary instruction today.

70. (9. 2–8) The writers of the Gospels gave special meanings to many of the ordinary words they used. What special meanings did they give to:
a. the number "twelve" (3. 14a)   b. heaven (6. 41)
c. deafness (7. 32)   d. a cloud (9. 7)
e. cup (10. 38)   f. waters (10. 38)

71. (9. 9–13) "Elijah has come already" (9. 13).
Some people believe that Jesus meant that the soul of Elijah was born again into the world when John the Baptizer was born. What is your opinion, and why?

72. (9. 14–29) a. What do we learn about the feelings of Jesus from the following verses?
(a) Mark 3. 5 (b) 4. 40 (c) 7. 18 (d) 8. 12 (e) 9. 19 (f) 10. 14 (g) Luke 12. 50
b. Give an example from everyday life to show how verses like these can encourage a Christian leader today.

294

73. (9. 30–32) Look at the picture and caption facing p. 143.
    i. Why was Jesus hated, arrested, and killed by the authorities?
    ii. "Every good leader must expect to be hated." What is your opinion?
    iii. What help can a Christian who is suffering persecution get from the following passages?
    (a) Psalm 119. 67   (b) Mark 8. 34   (c) John 15. 18
    (d) Rev. 2. 10

74. (9. 33–37) "If anyone wishes to be first, he shall be servant" (9. 35).
    a. Why did Jesus say this?
    b. The word "servant" is a translation of the Greek word *diakonos*. Compare this with the translation of it given in: (i) another English version; (ii) any other language you know.
    c. Can a leader also be a *diakonos*? Give an example to illustrate your answer.

75. (9. 38–41) The disciples tried to stop a healer who was working "in Jesus' name" (9. 38).
    a. Why did they do this?
    b. What guidance did Jesus give concerning the attitude of one group of Christians towards another group of Christians?
    c. Give an example of Christians opposing, or separating from, other Christians for the wrong reason.

76. (9. 42–50) "If the salt has lost its saltness" (9. 50a).
    a. Give two examples to show how Christians can be "salt" in their neighbourhood.
    b. Give two reasons why Christians often "lose their saltness".
    c. How could they get back their "saltness"?

77. (10. 1–12) A man was considering whether to ask a girl to marry him, and consulted a friend: "What are the questions I should ask her in order to see if we could make a Christian marriage together?"
    a. If you were the friend, what questions would you suggest?
    b. In what way (if at all) would Mark 10. 1–12 help?

78. (10. 1–12) Look at the picture and caption on p. 176.
    a. Answer the question "Is marriage necessary . . . ?", giving reasons for your answer.
    b. In some countries many couples get married in Church, although they have no serious intention of keeping their marriage vows. They may separate, and even abandon their children, as soon as they get tired of each other.

    In other countries many couples live together all their lives and bring up their children with love and faithfulness without ever getting married. They would be ashamed to have a Church wedding without expensive new clothes and a big party for all their friends, but they are too poor to afford these things.

    Which of these two kinds of life do you think is nearest to the teaching of Jesus about marriage? Give reasons for your answer.

79. (10. 1–12) Jesus expected the man and woman of a marriage equally to be faithful to one another.
    a. How did this differ from the law as recorded in Deut. 24. 1–4?
    b. Do most people in your country today expect one standard of behaviour from the man and a different standard from the woman? If so, in what ways?
    c. What is your own opinion on the subject?

80. (10. 13–16) "Receive the kingdom of God as a child receives" (10. 15).
    a. Suggest two ways in which a Christian should be like a child.
    b. Suggest two ways in which you think a Christian should be unlike a child.

81. (10. 17–22) i. Jesus used many different phrases to describe people accepting the great gift He was offering, e.g. "gaining everlasting life" (10. 17). From the following verses list five other phrases which He used to describe this acceptance: (a) 9. 47 (b) 10. 21 (c) 10. 24 (d) 10. 26 (e) 10. 30
    ii. In which of these verses does it seem that people can accept this gift now, and in which does it seem that people will have it in the future?

296

82. (10. 23–27) What would you reply to someone who said: "I can see that Mark 10. 23 is an important verse for people like St Francis, who was born rich and sold everything he had, but I can't see that it is important for others."?

83. (10. 28–31) According to Mark 10. 30 Jesus promised rewards to His followers. But Christians often use a prayer in which they say, "Teach us to labour and not to ask for any reward save the joy of knowing that we do thy will".
    a. Do you think people are right to use this prayer? Give reasons for your answer.
    b. In what ways might God reward someone who (i) went without sleep all night in order to nurse a sick neighbour, or (ii) chose to work for 30 years in a village in a famine area on very small pay?

84. (10. 35–40) i. Compare the kind of prayer recorded in Mark 10. 35 and 10. 37 with the prayer recorded in each of the following verses:
    (a) Mark 5. 23   (b) 14. 36b   (c) Luke 17. 5
    ii. What would you reply to someone who said, "It would be better not to pray at all than to pray the kind of prayer recorded in Mark 10. 35, 37."?

85. (Additional Note: The Blindness of the Disciples). Each of the following passages records a mistake made by one or other of the disciples:
    (a) 4. 38–40   (b) 8. 31, 32   (c) 9. 33–35   (d) 9. 38, 39
    (e) 14. 37–41
    i. What were those mistakes?
    ii. Why did Mark choose to record these passages?
    iii. "As we read these stories we feel quite sure that Mark's Gospel is a true story." (p. 174)
    Explain and comment on this statement.

86. (10. 41–45) a. The Greek word *doulos* in 10. 44 is translated "slave". Compare this with the translation of it given in:
    (i) another English version; (ii) any other language you know.
    b. In what ways is every Christian a slave of God, and in what ways is he *not* a slave of God? Give examples from everyday life.

297

87. (10. 41–45) A reader of Mark 10. 45 said, "That is what Jesus did. But the members of His Church today are more interested in meeting each other in a church building than in serving their fellow human beings in the world."
    a. Do you agree? Give examples to support your answer.
    b. What two things could enable the congregation which you know best to avoid the error that the reader described?

88. (10. 46–52) The Greek work *sozo* in 10. 52 is translated "save".
    a. Compare this with the translation of it given in:
       (i) another English version; (ii) any other language you know.
    b. What other words are used in the various English versions to translate *sozo* in Mark 5. 23; 5. 28; 5. 34; 10. 26; Luke 19. 10; and 1 Tim. 2. 4?
    c. What do you learn from this word study about the meaning of the word "save" in the verse "I have come to *save* the world" (John 12. 47).

89. (11. 1–11) Many of the people who shouted "Victory" or "Hosanna" (11. 9) wanted Jesus to help them to get political freedom.
    a. From whom did they want Him to free them?
    b. Is it right for a group of Christians today to ask God to help them to gain political freedom, e.g. in a country where no opposition to the Government is allowed? Give reasons for your answer.

90. (11. 1–11) The words "He who comes" (11. 9) remind us that Jesus came and comes in various ways. What kind of "coming" did the writer of each of the following verses have in mind?
    (a) John 12. 15   (b) John 14. 18   (c) 1 Cor. 4. 5
    (d) 1 Tim. 1. 15   (e) 2 John 7

91. (11. 15–19) When Jesus drove out people who were selling in the Temple courtyard He was protesting because they were treating two groups of people unjustly.
    a. Who were these other groups?
    b. How successful was the protest which Jesus made?
    c. How useful is protest if it is not successful at the time?

298

92. (11. 15–19) The head of an Employment Exchange was recently convicted of keeping back information about jobs until applicants had paid him a large sum of money.
    a. Give two examples of injustice and corruption of this kind which are common in your experience.
    b. "Jesus wanted to do away with injustices" (p. 185). In what ways, if any, can (i) an individual Christian, and (ii) the Church as a whole, help to do away with such injustices?

93. (11. 20–26) a. Why do you think that people find it hard to accept forgiveness from God?
    b. Why do people find it hard to forgive other people?
    c. Why is it hard to pray when we are not forgiving other people?
    Give examples from everyday life to illustrate your answers.

94. (11. 27–33) Look at the picture and caption facing p. 177.
    a. Draw up a list of the chief ways in which other people claim to speak to you and your friends with authority, e.g. through the radio, Church, advertisements, cinema, etc.
    b. Which *two* of these ways influence your life most, and why?
    c. If, as a Christian, you believe that their influence is not good, what can you do about it?

95. (11. 27–33) "There is no verse in the Bible which forbids slavery." (p. 192)
    a. Where did Christians like William Wilberforce get their authority for saying that slavery was against God's will? How did they know?

    b. Give another example (from life as it is lived today) to show how a group of Christians can discover the will of God. (E.g. is it by searching the Bible? Is it by listening to God in prayer? Is it by discussing the question together?)

96. (11. 27–33) i. Read the following passages and say in each case who was being asked a question by Jesus, what Jesus wanted that person to do, and what answer that person gave:
    (a) Mark 2. 19   (b) 3. 4   (c) 3. 33   (d) 8. 29   (e) 10. 18
    (f) 11. 30   (g) Luke 10. 36

299

ii. Give two reasons why Jesus so often asked His hearers questions.

iii. What can a teacher or preacher learn from this study of Jesus' questions?

97. (12. 1–12) i. Which part of the Parable of the Wicked Farmers reminds us of the truth that God's purposes for mankind cannot be overcome?

    ii. In what ways is the same truth proclaimed in the following verses?

    (a) Jer. 23. 3   (b) Acts 13. 46

    iii. In what situation in the present life of your nation or Church or family would you find it helpful to remember this truth?

98. (12. 13–17) a. How does v. 17 affect a Christian's attitude to paying taxes?

    b. When, if ever, might a Christian have to refuse to obey the State? Give examples.

99. (12. 18–27) Look at the picture and caption facing p. 196.

    a. What are the traditional beliefs about life after death held by non-Christian people known to you?

    b. What is the greatest single difference between those beliefs and the Christian belief?

100. (12. 28–34) Some Christians were discussing this passage. One said: "I compare this passage with Matt. 25. 40, and I think I show my love to God by working as a nurse in hospital and caring for His people there." Another said, "This passage shows that love for God comes first and loving other people is second in importance." What is your opinion about each of these remarks?

101. (12. 35–37) i. Why did Jesus use the name "Messiah" or "Christ" for Himself?

    ii. What other names did people use for Jesus, according to the following verses?

    (a) Mark 3. 11 (b) 4. 38 (c) 6. 3 (d) 7. 28 (e) 10. 48 (f) 14. 67

    iii. What name do you yourself most often use for Jesus, and why?

102. (12. 38–40) a. In what ways did the religious leaders go wrong, according to Jesus?
  b. What do you think are the two most serious temptations which religious leaders face today?
  c. Are these temptations of all leaders, or especially of religious leaders? Give an example from everyday life.

103. (12. 38–40) Read also Matt. 23. Is the attitude of Jesus to the Pharisees as recorded in these two passages an attitude of love? Give reasons for your answer.

104. (12. 41–44) A man who had just been baptized asked a friend for guidance as to how he should contribute money to the Church. If you were that friend what guidance could you offer him from each of the following passages?
  (a) Jesus' words about the widow's offering (12. 43, 44)
  (b) Matt. 6. 1–4   (c) 1 Cor. 16. 2   (d) 2 Cor. 8. 5

105. (13) Look at the picture and caption facing p. 197, and read 1 Thess. 4. 11 with 2 Thess. 2. 1–3.
  a. What mistake were Paul's readers making?
  b. What did he tell them to do?
  c. Which passages in Mark 13 (e.g. v. 7) could help the following people, and what help could they give?
    i. Someone who was so afraid of possible future wars that he could not live properly,
    ii. A student who was working so hard for peace among all nations that he failed in his examinations,
    iii. A Christian leader who neglected his own children while leading other people to receive eternal life.

106. (13) "The good news must be preached to all the heathen" (13. 10).
  The Orissa (India) Freedom of Religion Bill (1967) said that: "No person shall attempt to convert any person from one religious faith to another." It adds: "Conversion involves an act of undermining another's faith."
  If you were a Christian living in Orissa:
  a. What would your feelings be when you heard of this Bill?
  b. To what extent (if at all) could you obey Jesus' words?

107. (14. 1, 2) Jewish religious leaders looked for a way to "catch Jesus by treachery".
    a. Why could they not "catch" Him openly?
    b. Is there open opposition to the Church or the Gospel where you live; or is the opposition hidden and often unnoticed? Give examples.

108. (14. 3–9) "Why was the oil wasted" (14. 4).
    a. Why did the people in Simon's house say this, and what did Jesus say?
    b. Consider the following ways of "spending", and say in each case whether you think the spending is "waste" or "a beautiful thing" (v. 6):
        i. A congregation buying an expensive musical instrument for use in their Church,
        ii. A young doctor dying of cholera beoause he chose to look after people who were suffering from that disease,
        iii. A girl making herself a fine wedding dress,
        iv. Parents giving their daughter advanced education,
        v. A teacher refusing promotion in order to stay in a village where he is needed.
    Give reasons for your answers.

109. (14. 10, 11) Do you think Judas betrayed Jesus because of greed? anger? cowardice? pride? or for some other reason? Give reasons for your answer.

110. (14. 12–16) "They used to sacrifice the passover lamb."
    a. What event did Jews remember at the Feast of the Passover? (See Exodus 12. 1–3, 11–14, 24–27.)
    b. Name two important ceremonies in the Passover Feast for which preparations had to be made.
    c. In what ways was the self-offering of Jesus in the Lord's Supper and at His death like the Passover?

111. (14. 17–21) What would you reply in each case to people who said:
    a. "Judas cannot be blamed for betraying Jesus, because according to Mark 14. 21 he had no choice in the matter."
    b. "Judas cannot be blamed because it was through his action that Jesus died on the Cross for our sins."

112. (14. 22–25) a. The service which some Christians call "Holy Communion" is called "Eucharist", "Lord's Supper", "Mass", "Breaking of Bread" by other Christians. Which do you think is the best name for it, and why?
   b. At this service the minister performs actions which Jesus Himself performed. What are these actions?
   c. What did Jesus do at the Lord's Supper which no one else can do?

113. (14. 22–25) Look at the picture and caption facing p. 242.
   a. Since Jesus has made it possible for men to be free from sin, does that mean that Christians never sin?
   b. If it does not mean this, from what, do you think, does Jesus set people free? Give examples.
   c. In your experience, what prevents people from accepting the freedom which Jesus offers?

114. (14. 26–31) What is the difference between the promises to serve God faithfully which Christians sometimes make in public worship and Peter's words in Mark 14. 29?

115. (14. 32–42) a. What four phrases in this passage show that Jesus suffered greatly in the garden of Gethsemane?
   b. Why did He suffer?
   c. Which of these sufferings of Jesus are also experienced by a faithful Christian leader today? Give examples to illustrate your answer.

116. (14. 32–42) i. What was Jesus tempted to do according to: (a) Mark 14. 35, 36a (b) Matt. 4. 3, 6, 9
   ii. Which of these temptations are also experienced by faithful Christian leaders today? Give examples.

117. (14. 43–52) a. Jesus probably rebuked the disciple who drew his sword to show that a good thing (freeing Jesus) could not be obtained by bad methods (cutting off the slave's ear). Give two examples from everyday life in which people try to obtain good things by bad methods.
   b. Some people say that Matt. 26. 52 shows that Christians should never fight in order to kill. What is your opinion?

118. (14. 53–65) a. If you were Caiaphas and were writing down the reasons why Jesus must die, what would you write?

b. What groups of people today regard the Christian faith as harmful, in your experience? What reasons would they give for their attitude?

119. (14. 53–65) a. Describe how Jesus behaved when He was unjustly accused.

b. Why is unjust accusation so painful?

c. Give an example from everyday life of someone being unjustly accused, and say how you think he should behave.

d. What makes it possible to behave in a Christian way in this situation?

120. (14. 66–73) Which of the following statements do you think are "true", and which do you think are "untrue"? Give reasons for your answer in each case.

a. Peter wept because his pride had been hurt, not in penitence.

b. Mark recorded this incident in order to show his disapproval of Peter.

c. Peter should be praised, not criticized, for his action. The other disciples did not even try to stay near Jesus.

121. (15. 1–15) a. In the events described in this passage, who were afraid?

b. Say in each case what they were afraid of.

122. (15. 16–20 and 21–41) a. What orders had been given to the soldiers, according to 15. 15–27?

b. Find out from a Christian soldier or a policeman in your neighbourhood, if there are any, what he finds most difficult in his work.

c. What, if anything, could the Church do to help him overcome these difficulties?

123. (15. 21–41) Look at the picture and caption facing p. 243.

a. In what ways was the action of the Buddhist monk like the death of Jesus?

b. In what ways was it *un*like the death of Jesus?

124. (15. 21–41) "My God, my God, why hast thou forsaken me?" (15. 34)

The following are interpretations of what Jesus was feeling

304

when He said this. Which of them are true and which are
untrue? Give reasons for your answer in each case.
a. He no longer believed that there was any God.
b. He believed that God no longer wanted to help Him.
c. He was in pain and nothing He said had any meaning.
d. He felt separated from God because He had made Himself
one with the sins of the world.
e. He felt separated from God because He was fully human
and human beings in pain often feel this.

125. (Additional Note: The Death of Jesus) What does a study of
the Crucifixion of Jesus tell us:
a. about God?   b. about human beings?

126. (15. 42–47) Read also Matt. 27. 60. According to these passages, Joseph of Arimathea offered a grave into which the
body of Jesus could be placed.
a. Read Mark 3. 9; 4. 1; 11. 7; 14. 14 and say in each case what
things people offered to Jesus for His use.
b. Give three examples of what Christians can offer for Jesus
to use today.

127. (16. 1–8) i. Compare the accounts of the Resurrection of
Jesus given in the following passages, and say in each case
what differences you see between the two accounts:
(a) Mark 16. 1 with Matt. 28. 1
(b) Mark 16. 3, 4 with Matt. 28. 2
(c) Mark 16. 5 with Luke 24. 4
(d) Mark 16. 7 with Luke 24. 6
(e) Mark 16. 8 with Matt. 28. 8
ii. What would you reply to someone who said that he could
not believe that Jesus rose again because the Gospel
accounts of His Resurrection do not agree?

Key to Study Suggestions

1. a. See p. 7, last 6 lines and p. 8, note on v. 4.
   b. See p. 9, note on v. 8.

2. See p. 11, note on v. 9.

4. a. True: see p. 19, lines 4–6.
   b. Untrue: see p. 19, lines 7–10.
   c. True: see p. 18, lines 24–28.
   d. Untrue: see p. 114, lines 9–18.

5. a. See p. 21, note on v. 18.

6. i. (a) See p. 24, note 1 on v. 22.
      (b) See p. 94, note 3 on v. 3.
      (c) See p. 166, note 1 on v. 23.
      (d) See p. 171, note 2.
      (e) See p. 185, line 18.
      (f) See p. 197, last 3 lines.

9. iv. (a) To give to human beings in need is to give to God.
       (b) We need to show the compassion of Jesus.
       (c) Those who are rich now must not think that God desires them to remain so.
       (d) It needs regular and planned giving of money.
       (e) To bless a poor person with words is not enough.

10. i. (a) In a lonely place.
       (b) On a hillside.
       (c) On the ground in the Garden of Gethsemane.
       (d) On a hillside.
       (e) On the Cross.

12. a. v. 5.

13. a. See p. 40, note on v. 14.

15. (a) God (in Jesus Christ) is concerned to help rather than condemn weak and sinful people.
    (b) God gives salvation as a gift and because He loves us, not because we have earned it.
    (c) God gives it so that the believer can do His work.
    (d) A Christian must be ready to receive it.

16. a. See p. 43, note 1, first para.
    b. See p. 43, note 1, a, b, and c.

17. See, for example, p. 47, para 1.

20. a. The man with the wasted hand; all human beings in need.
    b. Because they cured a sick man in the name of the Risen Jesus (whom the authorities had killed).

21. a. See p. 53, para 1 of the Additional Note.
    b. See p. 54, para 4.

22. i. (a) He was baptized.
        (b) He was tempted.
        (c) He spoke sternly.
        (d) He was angry and pained.
        (e) He went to sleep.
        (f) He was a carpenter.
        (g) He sighed deeply.
        (h) He was indignant.
        (i) He loved a man.
        (j) He said there were things He did not know.

24. a., See p. 58, note on v. 14b.

25. See p. 58, note 2 on v. 14a.

26. a. See p. 61, note 2b.

27. i. (a) In healing: He overcame the evil spirit.
        (b) In healing: He overcame the paralysis of the hand.
        (c) In healing (through His disciples): He overcame illness.
        (d) In healing: He overcame deafness.
        (e) In driving out people who were selling: He overcame those who cheated defenceless people.
        (f) In argument: He overcame those who wanted to trap Him.
        (g) In prayer: He overcame temptation.

28. a. See p. 67, note 1 on v. 8.

29. (a) Be ready. Be ready for each situation in which you have to take a decision and will be judged by God.
    (b) For example: A Christian shares the things which are most precious to him.
    (c) It is God's way to look for people whose lives have gone wrong, and to care for them, and Christians must have the same attitude.

30. They are different, for example, in the Person whom they serve.

31. a. See p. 66, note b and p. 74, note 1 at foot of page.

33. a. See p. 77, last line and p. 78, lines 1 and 2.
    b. See p. 79, note on v. 39.

34. (a) (i) Being rebuked by the owner.
        (ii) Trading with the money.
    (b) (i) Being drowned.   (ii) Being at peace.
    (c) (i) Being accused.   (ii) Killing John.
    (d) (i) Being rebuked.   (ii) Asking Jesus what He
                                           meant.
    (e) (i) Being criticized by the people.
        (ii) Saying that John was not sent by God.
    (f) (i) Being harmed by Saul.
        (ii) Having fellowship with Saul.

37. a. See, for instance, p. 81, note on v. 4.

39. a. The passages from Romans and 1 Peter refer to blessing
        and helping enemies.

40. i. (a) See p. 87, note 3 on v. 30.
        (b) See p. 94, note on v. 5.
        (c) See p. 118, note on v. 24.
        (d) See p. 147, note on v. 16.
        (e) See p. 222, last 7 lines.
    ii. See p. 222, last line and p. 223, lines 1–9.

43. People's interpretations will vary, but one interpretation is as
    follows:
    (i) None.
    (ii) 1. 14, 15; 1. 16–20; 1. 35–39; 2. 13, 14; 2. 15–17; 2. 18–22;
         3. 13–19a; 3. 19b–21; 4. 1–34.
    (iii) All the other stories.

44. a. (i) See p. 92, 2, a, c, d, and e.
        (ii) See p. 92, 2b.
    b. i. See p. 92, 2c.
        ii. See p. 92, 2b.
        iii. See p. 92, 2a.

45. Based on p. 93, last 3 lines and p. 94, lines 1–8.

47. a. (i) According to Mark the twelve disciples had "authority
            over evil spirits"; according to Luke the Seventy were
            told to "heal" and also to prepare for Jesus (v. 1b).

308

The Twelve could wear sandals, the Seventy must not wear sandals.

The Twelve must not take money or food or spare shirt; the Seventy must not take a "purse".

The Seventy must not greet people on the road.

   (ii) Luke reports what Jesus told the Seventy to say (see Luke 10. 5, 9, 11).

  (iii) The warning to the Seventy: "Some people will reject you", is stronger than the warning to the Twelve (see vv. 3, 6b, 10, 11).

48. Based on p. 97, note on v. 8b.

49. b. Peter rebuked Ananias. Paul rebuked Peter.

50. i. (a) He paid attention to it.
      (b) He gave it sleep.
      (c) He gave it food.
      (d) He withheld food from it.
      (e) He gave it drink.

51. a. See p. 106, note on v. 37.

52. See p. 105, last 10 lines and p. 106, lines 1–7.

53. See p. 107, note 3.

55. a. See p. 113, note on v. 6a.
     c. i. See p. 113, note on v. 6b.
        ii. See p. 113, lines 12–18.
       iii. See p. 198, note on v. 14.

56. (a) See p. 54, para 4.
     (b) See Acts 10. 11–15 and p. 116, note on v. 19.
     (c) See Acts 15. 1 and 5–11.
     (d) See Heb. 9. 11–14.
     (e) See for example, 1 Cor. 16. 2; 2 Cor. 8. 3–11; 9. 7.

57. Based on p. 120, last 7 lines and p. 121, lines 1–3.

58. a. For example:
      Matt. 15: He was concerned for all races but at that time was reaching other nations through the Jews.
      Mark 5: In practice He showed that He cared about non-Jews.
      John 12: He was for "the world".

60. See p. 125, note on v. 12.

61. Based on p. 128, note on v. 18.
    i. See Mark 6. 35–44 and p. 127, note on v. 16.
    ii. (a) That God brought the Israelites through the wilderness.
        (b) What Jesus said.
        (c) Jesus.
        (d) Poor people.
        (e) The days when Jewish Christians had survived perse-
            cution.

62. i. (a) Peter and John: to cure a lame man.
       (b) Ananias: to cure Saul of his blindness.
       (c) Paul: to cure a lame man.
       (d) Paul: to work miracles.
    ii. See p. 123, lines 1–5. Saul believed that Jesus had sent
        Ananias to heal him. Someone who uses magic believes that
        by using the right words or performing special actions he
        can cause an unseen power to heal him.

63. i. (a) A good man.   (c) A deceiver.
       (b) A prophet.   (d) The Christ (the Messiah).
    iii. See p. 131, note on v. 29a.

64. See p. 103, note 2 on v. 31; p. 106, note 2 on v. 37; p. 131,
    note 2 on v. 29a; p. 217, note 1 on v. 9; p. 223, note 1 on v. 33.

65. b. See p. 132, note 1 on v. 29b.

66. a. and b.   See p. 135, note 1 on v. 31.
    c. and d.   See p. 136, note on v. 32.

67. (a) See p. 137, para 2 of Additional Note.
    (b) See para 1 of Additional Note.
    (c) See para 3 of Additional Note.

68. a.   Losing the ball; winning the match.

69. a.   See p. 142, last 3 lines and p. 143, note on v. 4.
    b.   See p. 144, note on v. 8.

70. a.   See p. 58, note 3 on v. 14a.
    b.   See p. 107, note 3 on v. 41a.
    c.   See p. 121, last 2 lines.
    d.   See p. 144, note 1 on v. 7.
    e. and f.   See p. 172, note on v. 38.

71. Based on p. 146, note on v. 13.

72. Based on p. 148, note on v. 19.

73.   i.   See p. 254, note on v. 53.
      iii. For example:
            (a) There are some things we never learn except as a result of suffering.
            (b) See p. 139, "Take up his cross".
            (c) A persecuted Christian is following in Jesus' footsteps.
            (d) Persecution cannot be escaped, but it is worth risking it in order to obtain the sort of life God offers.

74.   a.   See p. 151, note on v. 35.

75.   a.   See p. 154, note on v. 38.
      b.   See p. 153, Introduction.

79.   a.   According to Deut. 24. 1–4, a man was free to send his wife away for certain reasons, but the wife was not free in the same way.

80.   a.   See p. 162, note 2 on v. 15.

81.   i.   (a) Enter the Kingdom of God.
            (b) Have treasure in heaven.
            (c) Enter the Kingdom of Heaven.
            (d) Be saved.
            (e) Receive everlasting life.
      ii. Probably in all these passages it is taught that the gift can be accepted both now and in the future. Or we might say:
            (a) now   (b) now in and the future
            (c) now   (d) now and in the future
            (e) in the future.

82.   Based on p. 167, note 2 on v. 23.

83.   Based on Notes on p. 169.

84.   i.   (a) This is also a prayer of asking. But in it Jairus was praying for his daughter, not for himself.
            (b) In this prayer Jesus did not say "Do this for me", but "What thou wilt . . .".
            (c) This was a prayer of asking, but asking for something much more worth having than "the important seats" (Mark 10. 37).

85.   See Additional Note on p. 173.
      i.   (a) See p. 79, lines 1, 2 and last line.
            (b) See p. 136, note on v. 32.

(c) See p. 150, last 2 lines and p. 151, lines 1–4 and note
    on v. 34.
(d) See p. 154, note on v. 38.
(e) See p. 249, note 3 on v. 38.
  ii. See p. 173, para 1 of Additional Note.
 iii. See p. 174, note c.

86. b. See p. 175, note 2 on v. 44.

88. b. Made well; made whole; saved; cured; find salvation; etc.

89. See p. 181, note on v. 9.

90. Based on p. 182, note 3, "Him that comes".
    (a) See note 3b.
    (b) See note 3c (and probably d. and e. also)
    (c) See note 3e (d) and (e) See note 3a.

91. a. a and b. See p. 186, note 4 on v. 15 and note on v. 17.
      c. His work of protesting still continues through His
      Church.

93. Based on p. 189, note on v. 25.
    c. See p. 189, last 2 lines and p. 190, lines 1, 2.

95. Based on p. 191, note on v. 28.

96. Based on p. 192, notes 3 and 4 on v. 30.
    i. (a) John's disciples and Pharisees. See p. 45, note 1 on
         v. 19. No answer is recorded.
     (b) Pharisees. See p. 51, note 1 on v. 4. No answer is
        recorded.
     (c) The crowd. He wanted them to think out the meaning
        of v. 35. No answer is recorded.
     (d) See p. 131, note 1 on v. 29a. See p. 132, note 1 on v. 29b.
     (e) "A man". See p. 163, last 2 lines and p. 164, lines 1–7.
        Mark 10. 20 contains the only answer recorded.
     (f) See Mark 11. 27. See p. 192, note on v. 30. They
        answered, "We do not know".
     (g) See Luke 10.25. Jesus wanted him to think out the
        meaning of "being a neighbour". His answer, "The
        man that showed kindness".

97. i. See p. 196, para 4.
    ii. (a) Even when the People of God have been scattered, God
        saves a "remnant".
     (b) When the Jews would not listen, the Gentiles listened.

98. See p. 199, paras 2 and 4.

99. Based on p. 202, notes 1, 2, and 3 on v. 25.

100. Based on p. 204, "Jesus' answer".

101. i. See p. 207, lines 18-end.
     ii. (a) Son of God   (b) Master
         (c) The Carpenter, the Son of Mary, the Brother of James
         (d) Sir   (e) Son of David
         (f) The Nazarene

102. a. See p. 210, Introduction.

103. Compare Ephesians 4. 15.

104. (a) See p. 213, lines 4–8.
     (b) Give without wanting praise from other people.
     (c) Give regularly. Give from what has been saved.
     (d) Giving money is to be a sign of the giving of ourselves.

105. a. Neglecting their present responsibilities because they were thinking too much about the end of life on earth.
     b. See 1 Thess. 4. 11.

107. Based on p. 226, note on v. 1b.

108. a. See p. 228.

109. Based on p. 230.

110. a. That God set His people free from Egypt.
     b. See p. 233, note on v. 12b.
     c. See p. 232, note 3b and p. 238, last 11 lines.

111. a. See p. 236, note on v. 21. b. See p. 237, note 3.

112. b. He "takes bread", "says the blessing", "breaks the bread", and "gives it" to the people.
     c. See p. 242, Summary of Teaching.

113. a. No.

114. See p. 244, note on v. 29.

115. a. See p. 246, note on v. 34.
     b. See p. 247, lines 3–19.

116. i. (a) To leave Jerusalem and His enemies and so avoid suffering and death.
        (b) See p. 14, note 1 on v. 13.

117. b. Based on p. 251, note 3 on v. 47.

118. a. Based on p. 254, note on v. 53.

120. a. See p. 259, paras a and b.
 b. See p. 259, para c.
 c. See p. 259, para d.

121. See, for example, p. 254, note 2 on v. 53 and p. 263, note on v. 15.

122. a. See Mark 15. 15, 22, 24, 27.

123. a. For example, he offered himself to die on behalf of other people.
 b. See Summary on p. 242.

124. Based on p. 272, note on v. 34.
 a. and b. Untrue: see note 3b.
 c. Untrue: see note 1b.
 d. True: see note 2a.
 e. True: see note 1b.

125. a. See p. 275, note 2.
 b. See p. 275, note 3.

126. a. A small boat; a boat; young ass; a room.

127. i. (a) *Mark:* Three women.   *Matt:* Two women.
 (b) *Mark:* They spoke, then saw the stone had been moved.   *Matt:* An earthquake. Then an angel rolled back the stone.
 (c) *Mark:* A young man.   *Luke:* Two men.
 (d) *Mark:* "He will go to Galilee."   *Luke:* "When he was in Galilee, He told you . . ."
 (e) *Mark:* They said nothing.   *Matt:* They ran to tell the disciples.
 ii. See p. 279, lines 5–21.

INDEX

of subjects referred to in the notes and principal proper names

When a fuller treatment than usual has been given to a subject in the notes, the page number is printed in bold type, e.g., **62.** Only those proper names which occur in the Gospel itself have been included in the index.

315

Citizenship, *see* State
Coming of Jesus, 182, 214–224
Commandments, 49, 51, 53, 54, 111, 159, 164 (*see also* Tradition)
Communism, 244
Confession, 8 (*see also* Repentance)
Confidence, *see* Faith
Conscience, 63, 64, 101, 191
Conversion, 8, 130, 162
Courage, 100, 101, 257, 259, 276
Covenant, 238–242
Cross, 139, 269
Crucifixion of Jesus, *see* Death of Jesus
Cup, 240, 247
Cursing, 116, 183, 236, 244, 258
Custom, *see* Tradition

David, 48, 181, 207–209
Deafness and Hearing (physical), 121–124
Deafness and Hearing (spiritual), 67, 68, 121–124, 144
Death, 89, 139, 140, 281 (*see also* Life after death)
Death of Jesus, 135, 145, 146, 150, 170, 171, 176, 194, 221, 225, 229, 238, 239, **266–275**
Decapolis, 84, 121
Decision, 55, 70, 72, 131, 257, 264
Demons, 25, 82, 120
Devil, **15,** 62, 63, 71, 136, 236
Disciples, 20–22, 32, **57–59,** 89, 95–98, 102–104, 171, **173, 174,** 236, 245, 249–252 (*see also* John; Judas; Peter, etc.)
Discipline, *see* Sacrifice
Divorce, 158–161

Elders, 226
Election, *see* Call
Elijah, 6, 99, 131, 142–146
End (of the world), 137, 215–224
Enemies of Jesus, *see* Opposition
Eternal Life, *see* Life
Eucharist, *see* Holy Communion
Evangelism, 21, 59, **73,** 95–97, 102, 103, 157, 187, 218, 281 (*see also* Preaching)
Evil Spirits, *see* Demons

Faith, 3, 17, 36, 37, 75, 79, 86–89, **91–93,** 96, 108, 126, 148, 173, 178, 187–189, 224
False Teachers, 216
Family Life, 22, 64 (*see also* Marriage)
Family of Jesus, 60, 64, 94
Fasting, 45, 46, 149 (*see also* Sacrifice)
Fate, 109, 135, 169, 237, 244, 248, 252 (*see also* Free-will)
Fear and Anxiety, **79, 80,** 83, 87, 98, 109, 126, 171, 216, 218, 252, 254, 258, 264, 282 (*see also* Faith)
Fellowship, 65, 153, 154, 158, 240
Flesh, *see* Body
Following Jesus, 20, 21, 125, 126, **138–141,** 165, 166, 169, 171, 178, 281
Force, *see* Violence
Forgiveness, **36–38,** 63, 189, 190, 206, 239–241, 259, 274
Freedom, 6, 133, 134, 176, 181, 182
Free-will, 94, 95, 126, 141, 168, 173, 237

317